The Education *of a* University President

The Education *of a* University President

Marvin Wachman

FOREWORD BY JAMES W. HILTY

TEMPLE UNIVERSITY PRESS
Philadelphia

Temple University Press
1601 North Broad Street, Philadelphia PA 19122
www.temple.edu/tempress

Copyright © 2005 by Temple University
All rights reserved
Published 2005
Printed in the United States of America

Text design by *Ox and Company*

⊗ The paper used in this publication meets the requirements
of the American National Standard for Information Sciences—
Permanence of Paper for Printed Library Materials, ANSI Z39.48-1992

Library of Congress Cataloging-in-Publication Data

Wachman, Marvin, 1917–
The education of a university president / Marvin Wachman; foreword
by James W. Hilty.
p. cm.
Includes index.
ISBN 1-59213-376-2 (cloth : alk. paper)
1. Wachman, Marvin, 1917– . 2. College presidents—Pennsylvania—
Biography. 3. Lincoln University (Pa.)—Presidents—Biography.
4. Temple University—Presidents—Biography. I. Title.
LC2851.L53W33 2005
378.11`1–dc22
[B]
2004062046

2 4 6 8 9 7 5 3 1

To Addie,
my love, my companion, and
my partner in all ventures,
both private and professional,
for sixty-three years

CONTENTS

I N THIS ILLUMINATING MEMOIR, Marvin Wachman, son of Russian Jewish immigrants, reflects on his six-decade odyssey in American higher education. A quintessential liberal optimist, Wachman apparently never met anyone of irredeemable value or virtue. Nor did he ever encounter a problem that could not be resolved through patience, perseverance, understanding, good humor, and a willingness to put oneself in the other person's shoes, at least long enough to resolve otherwise irreconcilable differences. Marvin never sees people as friend or foe, hero or heretic, facilitator or roadblock along his intended path, and he did not write a memoir to avenge himself on his rivals or second-guess his successors. Rather, he seems perpetually inclined to see the best in all of us. Marvin Wachman's life and career as teacher, scholar, humanist, and lifelong advocate of human rights and equality of opportunity exemplify the better angels of our nature.

Some may choose careers in higher education as an outlet for their creative energies, and some merely as a means of livelihood. By contrast, Marvin sees his role in higher education as part of a lifelong quest to reify ideals ingrained in his youth. Those ideals, by his own definition broadly encompassed within America's liberal tradition, were nurtured in classrooms of a dozen prestigious institutions around the world, tested on the battlefields of Europe, dissected and reexamined in a series of difficult and challenging administrative positions. At the peak of the 1960s Civil Rights Movement, Wachman served with notable distinction as the white president of Lincoln University, the nation's oldest traditionally black university, and he set a steady, prudent, often inspired course in steering Temple University through the series of economic crises besetting higher education in the 1970s.

This first-person narrative tells us much about Wachman's career and his perspectives on ever evolving challenges facing American higher education. What it cannot tell us – because Wachman's modesty prohibits more than passing reference to accolades – is how great was his impact on the people he met and influenced and the institutions he has led in a long teaching and administrative career. "A teacher affects eternity," Henry Adams wrote, and surely in Wachman's case, "he can never tell where his influence stops."

Marvin Wachman's chosen title – *The Education of a University President* – immediately brings to mind *The Education of Henry Adams* (1907), in which Henry Brooks Adams (1838–1918), intellectual scion of the famous political family, offered sage observations on the human condition. But Marvin Wachman is not the preachy, pedantic type, eager to offer wordy philosophical proscriptions. Rather, his memoir is filled with common-sense observations, and one must often read between the lines to find the deeper essence of the lesson gained from each experience, as Wachman humbly invites readers to draw their own conclusions.

The organizing theme of Wachman's memoir is his continual effort to learn in an ever changing world, to become educated to its nuances and shifting boundaries, transforming social trends and political reverberations, all with respect to the challenges posed to American higher education and, therefore, also to him personally. Two of Henry Adams's postulates resonate throughout Wachman's memoir: "All experience is an arch, to build upon" and "Knowledge of human nature is the beginning and end of political education."

From his childhood in Milwaukee and growing to maturity during the Great Depression while overcoming the often rampant anti-Semitism of the era, Marvin advanced himself using his knowledge of human nature and keen political intuition. He leveraged prodigious skills on the tennis court and a congenial personality to open otherwise closed doors. Combining manifest social skills with an abiding intellectual curiosity, a strong work ethic, and a determined will to succeed, Wachman honed innate leadership talents in a succession of challenging situations of increasing responsibility.

Wachman received his undergraduate degree from Northwestern University and completed graduate work at the University of Illinois, defending his Ph.D. dissertation (on the Socialist Party in Milwaukee) the weekend before his induction into the U.S. Army in August 1942. Ultimately experiencing combat in France, Marvin Wachman may have been the only platoon sergeant in the U.S. Army during World War II who held a Ph.D. When the war ended, he taught at a GI College in Biarritz, France, before accepting appointment in the History Department at Colgate University, where he rose quickly to the rank of full professor. Wachman went on to pioneer the establishment of American studies as a separate discipline, first in the United States, and then in European universities through his directorship of the Salzburg (Austria) Seminar.

In 1961, two luminaries of African American history, Thurgood Marshall and Ralph Bunche, personally persuaded Wachman to assume the presidency of Lincoln University in Pennsylvania. After an eventful eight and one half years filled with myriad accomplishments, during which the Civil Rights Movement shifted emphasis away from integration and became more militant, Wachman selflessly decided that Lincoln appropriately required an African American president, so he resigned to accept the position of vice president for academic affairs at Temple University. Some measure of Wachman's influence at Lincoln can be gleaned from his final commencement when he found himself embarrassed by a surfeit of speakers. When Supreme Court Chief Justice Earl Warren, Carl Stokes of Cleveland (the first black mayor of a large American city), and the Reverend Jesse Jackson all agreed to speak, Marvin seamlessly incorporated these three dignitaries into a deftly managed and memorable farewell commencement.

Arriving at Temple in January 1970, Marvin was greeted immediately by student sit-ins protesting university expansion plans and confronted that summer by the Black Panthers, who held their national convention on Temple's campus. That fall, I joined Temple's History Department, and in the years since I have worked with Marvin in various capacities, as a faculty member and in several administrative positions, including acting dean of the graduate school. Like many others, I came to appreciate Marvin's abiding commitments to academic excellence, to the responsibilities of the urban university as a vehicle for social change, and to Temple's mission and all associated with it.

On July 1, 1973, Marvin Wachman succeeded Paul R. Anderson, becoming Temple's sixth president. His appointment won the unanimous endorsement of the nominating committee and the overwhelming support of administrators, faculty, alumni, and students. "All constituencies approve choice," read the *Temple Times*, an administration newspaper. He was anointed "Marvelous Marv" by the Temple student newspaper, and the Temple marching band, in what must have been a first for that or any era, saluted the president-elect by spelling out "Marv" during a football halftime performance.

The complex roles of a university president, University of California Chancellor Clark Kerr once observed, include those of "leader, educator, wielder of power, . . . officeholder, caretaker, inheritor, consensus seeker, persuader, bottleneck. But he is mostly a mediator." Indeed, most of Marvin Wachman's time at Temple appears to have been taken up with mediating one crisis or another.

A joke circulating among university administrators tells of a president who awakens one night from a nightmare in a cold sweat, trembling and ranting. His concerned wife asks, "What's the matter?" He answers, "I just dreamt that we had *two* hospitals and *two* football teams." Most of Marvin Wachman's

presidency was consumed by one financial crisis after another, the most serious centering on the accumulated debt of Temple University Hospital, which
threatened the survival of the university itself. A creative political solution, en-
gineered with the assistance of Board of Trustees Chairman F. Eugene Dixon
Jr., insured the hospital's survival. Wachman's presidency also saw the return of Temple to big-time, Division 1-A football and several winning seasons
and national rankings under Coach Wayne Hardin, although many remained
skeptical of the commitment and costs involved.

To modernize the message of Founder Russell Conwell, who stressed the
importance of providing access to higher education for all deserving persons,
Wachman promoted Temple as "The People's University" and encouraged the
further diversification of the student body, faculty, and academic programs.
Marvin's many experiences abroad, including stints at the University of
Maryland in Europe and the Salzburg Seminar and his service as State Department specialist in African affairs, led him especially to value international education programs. Under Wachman's personal direction, Temple strengthened
its program in Rome and launched new programs in Paris, Dublin, London,
Ghana, Greece, Israel, Nigeria, China, and Japan.

At home Wachman presided over a burst of capital construction that
brought five new Commonwealth-funded buildings to the Main Campus.
In addition, he directed expansion of the Ambler campus and construction
of two buildings facilitated by gifts from F. Eugene Dixon Jr.; opened a new
Center City campus (TUCC); secured funding for construction of a new Temple
University Hospital and a new dental clinical facility; and negotiated a contract
to operate the Woodhaven Center, providing education and training for the
developmentally disabled.

Wachman also fostered improved relations with the immediate community in Temple's neighborhoods, formalized administrative procedures concerning alumni affairs, and, in 1981, persuaded the Board of Trustees to right
a lingering wrong by reinstating Barrows Dunham, former chair of the Philosophy Department, who was fired in 1953 for refusing to answer questions
before the U.S. House Committee on Un-American Activities concerning past
associations with the Communist Party. Dunham's reinstatement helped alleviate the stigma of McCarthyism's most notorious and painful imprint on
Temple.

Wachman's memoir relates his candid, forthright versions of other less
palatable developments that occurred toward the end of his Temple tenure,
including stressful negotiations with the Temple faculty union, which was
formed in 1973. As rancorous as those first negotiations appeared at the

time, they paled in comparison to the two faculty strikes that occurred after Wachman left office.

When a sharp decrease in enrollments hit the university between 1978 and 1981, and as costs vastly exceeded net revenues, Wachman faced his most agonizing decision. Unable to stanch the flow of red ink and unwilling to dump the problem on his successor, Wachman moved to retrench fifty-eight faculty members in schools and colleges affected by the enrollment decline, eventually rescinding all but four of the notices to tenured faculty.

The once highly popular president faced unbridled faculty wrath. Liberal arts faculty condemned Wachman's "arrogant disregard for established academic procedures" and his "display of unreason." More than two decades hence, the painful memories of those final days echo in Wachman's explanations, but so, too, does an insistent note of pride in forestalling a looming financial catastrophe and in leaving Temple financially better off than when he assumed office.

A then mandatory retirement policy required Wachman to step down from the presidency at age sixty-five. On June 30, 1982, he was succeeded by Peter J. Liacouras, dean of the law school, and Marvin became university chancellor, a largely honorary office. Like those of former U.S. President Jimmy Carter, Marvin Wachman's "retirement" years have been filled with an impressive array of accomplishments. The stamina and athletic conditioning that served him so well as a champion tennis player allowed Marvin to undertake an amazing range of challenging tasks, including team-teaching a Temple course in American studies, assuming the presidency of the Foreign Policy Research Institute and the acting presidencies of Philadelphia University and, later, Albright College. He also survived a politically charged stint as acting executive director of the Pennsylvania Higher Education Assistance Agency. Only when heart problems struck in recent years did he begin to slow down.

Steadfast at Marvin's side throughout, Adeline (Addie) Schpok Wachman perfectly complemented her husband. Fused by common origins, shared values, a penchant for teaching and service, the Wachmans' joy of being together radiated forth when entering a room or greeting old or new friends. Their powerful partnership deeply affected the people and institutions they touched. Wherever they served at whatever post, Addie and Marvin made their home a social and academic haven. A gifted teacher and theater enthusiast, Addie became confidante and adviser to countless students, faculty, administrators, and trustees along the way. For five decades, Addie served as ambassador-at-large (without portfolio) for her husband at countless receptions, formal and informal gatherings, graciously assisting Marvin's advance literally around the globe.

In their lifetimes, the Wachmans met many national and international leaders, including presidents Moise Tshombe of Zaire, Kwame Nkrumah of Ghana, and Nnamdi Azikiwe of Nigeria; prime ministers Edward Heath of Great Britain and Malcolm Fraser of Australia; and Chinese Premier Deng Xiaoping, to name a few who appear in the memoir.

All things considered, it has been a remarkable journey for the former Milwaukee newsboy. The story of that journey, as revealed in the following pages, serves several purposes. His personal testament, a self-effacing examination of his successful rise through academe, offers guidance and hope for those who may find themselves hindered by birth or circumstance from gaining access to higher education or to opportunities for social or economic advancement. Marvin's indelible optimism and quiet confidence yield a story mostly about what is possible and attainable, not about the impossible or the unattainable. In this age of relentless self-promotion and ruthless competition, Wachman's inner-directedness, natural modesty, and gracious manner are refreshing reminders of the timeless values and many sacrifices of America's greatest generation.

Marvin Wachman's memoir also reaffirms his devotion to the higher purposes of the university. "A university," British Prime Minister Benjamin Disraeli once said, "should be a place of light, of liberty, and of learning." Throughout his long, illustrious career, Marvin Wachman brought more light and diversity into each university he served, held firm to his liberal beliefs concerning the university's obligation to promote liberty and social justice, and maintained the high standards of scholarship and learning that have made American universities preeminent. Finally, and most important, Wachman has demonstrated through his own example that all of us, university presidents included, must never stop learning.

James W. Hilty
Professor of History, Temple University

H ARRY GOLDEN, the late publisher of the *Carolina Israelite*, titled one of his books *Only in America*. His title fits my story. I was born to immigrant parents from Eastern Europe who had little formal education, yet I graduated from college and became first a professor and then president of two unique and distinguished American universities. While teaching and serving as an administrator, I had the good fortune to live and work in Western Europe and to spend time in Eastern Europe, Africa, and parts of Asia, including Japan, mainland China, and Taiwan. I owe all these rewarding opportunities to the happy accident of having been born and educated in the United States.

I have often felt frustrated by America's seeming inability to live up to its lofty ideals – for example, in delivering civil rights and fostering equality of opportunity for all citizens. Also, at times, I have had serious reservations about our foreign policy. But compared to the alternatives (past as well as present), this is a progressive country. Scratch beneath the surface of those foreign critics who scold Americans as arrogant, self-centered, conceited, and chauvinistic and you will often find envy, jealousy, and a yearning to visit the United States or live among us.

For more than eighty-five years I have dwelt in a world in which change was a constant. Born during World War I, I grew up and attended college during the Great Depression of the 1930s, fought in World War II, lived through the Korean and Vietnam wars, democracy's Cold War with Soviet communism, two Persian Gulf wars, and three different types of revolutions: in civil rights, sex, and communications. I taught in and managed several colleges and universities from the 1940s to the turn of the twenty-first century. At one of these – Lincoln University in the 1960s – I found myself leading a historically black college at the peak of the U.S. Civil Rights Movement. At Temple University, in the 1970s and early '80s, I managed a very large urban university during the ups and downs of enrollments, crises in finances, and rocky race relations. Through all these events I often felt that I was receiving a greater education than my students were.

My ability to survive and even flourish through these chaotic times can be attributed, I believe, to the intellectual anchors acquired during my early years at home and then in high school and college: such liberal concepts as secularism, relativism, multiculturalism, open-mindedness, and a belief in human progress. My concept of secularism does not preclude – indeed, it embraces – the notion of the sacredness of human beings and the critical importance of integrity among humans and their institutions. Only when these ideas are reflected within a body of laws can individuals function freely. My relativism is based on the role of reason – that is, the notion that no one owns a monopoly on truth or justice (including, of course, liberal relativists). My sense of multiculturalism grows out of the same notion: We must respect and accept other racial, ethnic, and religious groups – for our own benefit as well as theirs.

All of these principles, to my mind, fall under the rubric of "Liberalism." Yet there was a time when I resisted as too confining formal classification as a conservative or liberal. Only during the so-called Reagan Revolution of the 1980s, when liberalism came under widespread attack, did I begin openly identifying myself as a liberal. It struck me that the kind of liberalism I stood for was the philosophy upon which the United States was founded and continued to exist, and those of us who subscribe to that philosophy should be proud to assert it.

The educational system in which I have spent my adult life has, I believe, played a major role in fostering the unique dynamism of American society and government. That dynamism stems from the conviction that we can always make our democracy more effective and productive for those who live under its umbrella. It has been my privilege to play a small role in this unending process through most of the twentieth century. I offer my experiences and insights here for the benefit of those who will continue the work long after my contemporaries and I are gone.

The Apprentice

T HE ONLY EXCEPTIONAL THING about my family background is how unexceptional it was. My parents belonged to that huge wave of desperate Russian Jewish immigrants who, in the late nineteenth century, turned to America as a refuge from anti-Semitism, pogroms, and compulsory service in the tsar's army. These poor, trembling, parochial *shtetl* dwellers summoned up a supply of courage they didn't know they possessed and committed themselves to the terrifying prospect of an ocean voyage to a strange and distant land whose language was unknown to them. Their numbers were so great that, in the process of being transformed by America over the next few generations, they and their descendants transformed America as well, mostly for the better. Immigration to America was the best thing that ever happened to these families – and, I like to think, one of the best things that happened to America, too. My family was merely one of hundreds of thousands that made a difference in some small way. We were not unique, but America was, and what America did to us, and vice versa, is what makes each individual story so fascinating.

When I began writing this memoir, I searched for specific data in family documents and found some information about my parents. However, I had never been certain of their dates of birth and arrival in the United States, since they were both long gone, and my older sisters and brother had given me differing accounts of those landmark events. Finally, in August 1993, my wife, Addie, and I visited the National Archives in Washington, D.C., and found the facts we needed in the 1900 Census Report.

My father, Alex Wachman, was born in Riga, Latvia, in 1869 and migrated to the United States at age eighteen in 1887; my mother, Ida Epstein, was born in 1874 in Kletsk, a *shtetl* near Minsk, Russia (now Belarus), and arrived in the United States at age sixteen in 1891. Prior to their arrival, both Alex and Ida had received letters from friends who wrote about wonderful opportunities for young people in this relatively new country. Ida's mother had died, and when her father remarried she decided to lead her own life. Arriving in New York, Alex almost immediately continued on to join acquaintances and find his fortune in the Midwest. Ida worked briefly in New York sweatshops, rolling cigarettes; then she, too, traveled by train to Wisconsin, where several young people from her Russian village had settled. These two young immigrants met by chance in Eagle River, Wisconsin. They were married in Ironwood, a small town in the Upper Peninsula of Michigan near the Wisconsin border, in 1893 or 1894.

Alex was then an itinerant vendor, or "peddler," working out of Ironwood or the neighboring town of Hurley, Wisconsin. In his quest for a better life, Alex moved the family, in 1906, to a much larger city – Milwaukee – where he operated a second-hand store. Subsequently, he and a partner acquired a working-class restaurant in downtown Milwaukee. There he labored twelve hours a day, seven days a week, supervising waiters, waiting on tables, and keeping the books.

Like most immigrants of their day, Alex and Ida were largely self-educated. In Latvia, Alex had learned to speak Latvian, Russian, German, and Yiddish, and by the time I was growing up in the 1920s he was speaking English, as well – without any discernible accent. He received little formal education before immigrating to the United States. Ida – "Ma" to her children – did manage to receive a bit more education in Russia but still not much. Once in this country, she taught herself to speak and read English well enough to become an avid reader of newspapers and other publications, whenever she was able to take time from the grueling regimen of caring for her children, cooking, baking, sewing, and keeping her house and her family's clothes clean.

I was the last child born to Alex and Ida, on March 24, 1917. My mother was forty-three at the time, and my sisters (Minnie, Anna, Lillian, and Helen) sometimes referred to me as an afterthought or a mistake. Despite this teasing, I grew up cheerful, confident, and appreciative of my membership in this large family.

Our flat consisted of seven small rooms and a single bathroom, which eight of us shared. My brother Harold and I slept together in a narrow double bed. It may seem an oppressive arrangement by today's standards, but we measured our lives by a different yardstick. Our parents – surely the first relativists I encountered in my life – constantly stressed how lucky we were to be living in the United States rather than in Latvia or Russia.

The Brown Street Elementary School (called Grammar School in the 1920s and '30s) was a solid, conservative institution, where children did their homework and teachers insisted that we redo assignments until every mistake was corrected. In addition to academic courses, the school offered boys what was called "manual training" – how to make breadboards, tables, and other presumably useful wooden objects. (Girls, conversely, received cooking instruction.) Between the ages of nine and fourteen, I became a voracious reader, particularly of biography, history, and short stories. I read all of Mark Twain, P. G. Wodehouse, and many other authors, and spent much of my spare time at our neighborhood library, browsing through its books and magazines.

At about the age of ten, I began earning small amounts of money by shining shoes in our basement, selling magazines, and, at age twelve (the minimum legal age for that activity), selling newspapers on a daily paper route near our home. From each customer I received 12 cents a week – 18 cents if the customer took the Sunday paper as well. By the time I was sixteen I had accumulated $89.83 in the Park Savings Bank, most of which vanished in 1933 when the bank failed during the Great Depression. Like most of my contemporaries, I emerged from that experience very conservative about taking financial risks.

Although my parents weren't zealously observant, our family belonged to a Conservative Jewish synagogue, and I studied Hebrew and Torah there several days a week, after school. At the same time, since we were the only Jewish family in our neighborhood, I often participated in sports and other programs at the Roman Catholic school next door – my first exposure to the virtues of what is now called "multiculturalism." In addition, I belonged to a Young Pioneers Club, a watered-down version of the Boy Scouts, that met regularly at the Methodist church in our neighborhood.

Pa and Ma took their religion quite seriously, even though Pa was too busy managing his restaurant to attend synagogue services regularly. Ma kept separate (kosher) dishes and silverware for meat and nonmeat meals. Still, she said to me on one occasion, "You really don't have to be kosher to be Jewish, as long as you live by the fine principles of Judaism." That comment revealed the broad religious beliefs of our family, which stayed with me throughout my entire life.

Pa suffered with diabetes, and by the time I was sixteen years old, he had been ill and in great pain for months from a gangrenous foot. He was eventually hospitalized but refused to allow the doctors to amputate. At the age of sixty-four, with my mother, my sister Lillian, and I sitting by his bedside in the hospital, Pa died. His death was a deeply felt loss for all of us, and it was only our religious beliefs, and the closeness we shared as a family, that enabled us to begin the adjustment to Pa's absence from our household.

After a period of formal bereavement, I returned to my high school classes. I attended Milwaukee's Washington High, a large, traditional high school that was very similar to the one described by James B. Conant in his 1950s book *The American High School Today*. All students were enrolled in a curriculum that included American and European history, civics (now called political science), literature, geography, science, mathematics, and a foreign language. There were also courses in the arts, but they were not emphasized. Speech courses, which included debate, were quite valuable in teaching students how to organize an oral presentation, and how to think on our feet.

It was while delivering newspapers that I discovered the Washington Tennis Club off one edge of my peddling route. It consisted of only two clay courts and a practice backboard surrounded by alleyways and modest single- and two-family homes. I had been practicing hitting tennis balls against a garage door near our house but wanted to perform on regular tennis courts. I persuaded the club's caretaker to let me play on his courts in return for helping him sprinkle the courts at night, roll them in the morning, and paint white lines on the courts each day. I also learned how to string tennis rackets by using ice-pick–like devices called awls to keep the strings taut in the frame (this was before stringing machines).

Largely as a result of playing at the club, I became a fairly skilled tennis player. By age fifteen, I had won several tournaments, including the Western Boys' Tournament at St. John's Military Academy in Delafield, Wisconsin. In the spring of 1934, my athletic career at Washington High School reached its peak when I won the state high school tennis championship. In 1935, I reached the quarter-finals of the National Junior Tennis Championships (for those eighteen and under) at the Culver Military Academy in Indiana. I lost in a very close match to Bobby Riggs, who later became the Wimbledon champion. As a result, I earned a high national ranking in the junior category. Those victories did wonders for my self-confidence; they also led to my being recruited by Northwestern University.

I came to realize that tennis wasn't merely a rewarding physical outlet but an entrée to other fields that had no direct connection to athletics. It was at the Los Angeles Tennis Club in the mid-'30s that I met the movie star Errol Flynn, who came there one afternoon looking for a game and subsequently played with me several times. It was also through tennis that I met Arthur Nielsen, chief executive of the A. C. Nielsen Company, the nation's largest polling company at that time. Because he was a tennis buff, he invited me, as a college student at Northwestern University, to play with him or his son on his private court near the campus, and he subsequently offered me a job at a company that was not otherwise known for hiring Jews.

My tennis ability led to matches with such champion players as Don Budge and Alice Marble. Alice, who was recognized as the best women's tennis player in the world in the '30s, came to the Chicago area to play some exhibitions during my freshman year at Northwestern. She liked to play with men to get good practice. Coach Paul Bennett was approached by Alice's coach, Eleanor "Teach" Tennant, and asked to provide a young, male player who would play a practice match against Alice one day and a mixed doubles exhibition event with her the next. These events were to take place on the new courts of the North Shore Tennis Club in a northern suburb of Chicago. Paul selected me.

Alice came to the Northwestern University Tennis Shack to pick me up in a large black Packard automobile with red wheels. Accompanying her was Ms. Tennant and a professional tennis promoter, Jack Harris. Jack sat in the front seat of the limousine with the driver, and I was asked to sit in the back seat between the two ladies. Their perfume almost overwhelmed me. By the time we reached the Tennis Club to play our practice match, the combination of the perfume scent and the trepidation I felt at having to oppose such a celebrity player had made me quite nervous.

After we warmed up and started playing, I felt more at ease. However, Miss Marble soon began playing as if this were a tournament match. She hit drop shots on the very slow red clay (*en tous cas*) court. The court was so new and soft that, when I raced forward to reach the drop shots, I slid and cinders came up through the clay surface. At that point, I was no longer overwhelmed but getting angry. Miss Marble had won three games very quickly by using the drop shot and then passing me or lobbing over my head for the points.

I had heard that women run much better from side to side than they do forward and backward, so I thought I would give her some of her own medicine. I began drop shotting and lobbing and won the next six games, winning the set by a score of six games to three. Alice then decided she would just practice hitting balls back and forth with me in front of the crowd so she could get ready for the real match the next day against Eugenie Sampson Kamrath, a popular player who hailed from Chicago.

The next day, Alice played Eugenie in a two set exhibition match, and Alice and I played against Eugenie and her husband, Karl, a fine player from Texas, in a mixed doubles match. It was customary for a man to play the backhand court and poach as much as possible in order to cover more than half the court, since women were considered to be slower. I did this a few times in the match, and Alice, who volleyed better at the net than I did, came up to me with anger in her eyes and said, "Marvin, the next time you poach on me I will wrap my racket around your head!" I promptly ceased poaching, and we won the match quite handily.

That episode taught me never to underestimate women athletes. It also led to something of a friendship with Alice Marble. Over the next several years, whenever I was playing in a tennis tournament in the New York City area, she invited me to the West Side Tennis Club in Forest Hills to practice with her on the grass courts – a real treat for a nineteen- or twenty-year-old.

Had it not been for tennis, I probably would have attended Marquette University in Milwaukee, where my brother went to law school, or the University of Wisconsin, both of which were less expensive than Northwestern. Although there were no tennis scholarships at Northwestern in the 1930s, and I was not a brilliant student, my high school grades were high enough that the coach could help me get a tuition scholarship for my freshman year (tuition was then $300, a sizeable sum in the 1930s). He also helped me get a job for my room and board, waiting on tables in a university dining room, and hired me to string tennis rackets at the university's Tennis Shack. In the depths of the Great Depression, such an arrangement was too good to turn down. Many of my acquaintances in Milwaukee had to go directly into the workforce as bookkeepers, shoe salesmen, or laborers during the continuing Depression.

In offering me the dining-room job, the director of dormitories, J. Leslie Rollins (known to everyone as "Whitey"), stressed how lucky I was to be at Northwestern. "There is a general understanding," he added, "that the enrollment of any one religious group at the university should not be greater than its percentage in the general population." Although I was offended by his reference to my Jewish background, I bit my lip and did not respond, knowing that I needed the job. It was certainly not the last time in my career that I subordinated my pride to some larger goal. In this case, as in most similar situations, I'm glad that I held my tongue. Eventually I came to realize that Rollins was sincerely interested in the growth and development of young people of whatever background; in his remarks about Northwestern's informal quota system, he was simply talking to me candidly, as one adult to another. In later years, Rollins and I became good friends, and after he went to Harvard University as an assistant dean of Harvard Business School, I had a number of contacts with him, particularly after I became a college president.

By the time I entered Northwestern, my mother had sold the family home and moved in with my oldest sister, Minnie. So Lindgren House, a men's dormitory, became my home for five years, through the completion of my bachelor's and master's degrees. In my junior year I became the dorm's president. While living in Lindgren House, I was able to win a Big Ten divisional title and a Western Regional Collegiate Championship and to get to the semifinals (final four) of the National Intercollegiate Tennis Tournament, the climax to my college tennis career.

Near the end of my junior year, our house resident assistant – a graduate student charged with supervising the undergrads – was asked to leave school for both academic and personal reasons (he had a drinking problem). Although resident assistants were always graduate students or instructors – usually with master's degrees in hand and working on Ph.D.s – Whitey Rollins recruited me for the job. "Even though you're an undergraduate and it will violate our normal practice," he said, "you know all the men, you have been working with them, and you're very active as a leader here." This was to become a recurring theme in my career: An administrative or supervisory job would open up, I would be asked to fill it, and I – flattered by the offer – invariably accepted.

My skills as a counselor were severely tested one spring evening. A group of mischievous students unhooked the fire hose and turned on the water while I was out; when I returned to Lindgren House around midnight, water was running out the front door. I had a hunch who the culprits were, and who was probably the leader, so the first thing I did was bang on the door of Bob Blandford, a big, red-headed junior from Grand Rapids, Michigan.

"Bob," I said, "get your ass out of bed and round up the rest of the guys who worked with you on this thing and clean this place up." I knocked on doors, routed everyone out of bed, and had them all mopping floors and drying carpeting with fans until the sun came up.

I learned a valuable lesson about dealing with college students that night: If you treated them firmly but fairly, and they knew they had gone off the deep end, you could usually convince them to do the right thing and make amends. Student pranks were de rigueur, but if you were constantly alert to booby traps, like finding a bucket of water over the door to your room, you could survive them with good humor. Besides, this was tame stuff compared to the civil rights demonstrations and antiwar protests of the 1960s. But then, as we shall see, even those incidents tended to roll off my back like water. For whatever reason, I was blessed with the sort of temperament that sees value in even the angriest confrontation.

My parents, like many immigrants of their generation, hoped their sons would become doctors, lawyers, or successful businessmen. By the time I entered Northwestern, three of my sisters had married professional men, and my own brother had finished law school. But my passion was history. I wasn't terribly interested in making a fortune; I just wanted to live a fairly comfortable and interesting life. Teaching history struck me as the ideal career path.

For my master's thesis, "The Chicago Race Riot of 1919," I spent a good deal of time on Chicago's South Side, combing through the files of the Negro newspaper the *Chicago Defender*. My thesis provided a historical account of the movement of Southern blacks to Chicago and other Northern cities before and during the First World War. This movement resulted in a series of race riots, and my thesis, while focusing on the Chicago riot, discussed other riots for the purpose of comparison.

Professor William Byron of the Sociology Department, a member of my thesis committee, resented the fact that a history student was writing about what he felt were sociological issues. He argued with my adviser, Professor Tracy Strevey, that I should have chosen another thesis topic. But Strevey defended my approach, arguing that it was necessary to cross academic disciplines in order to tell a full story. (Byron doubtless also objected to the injection of my own integrationist viewpoints into the thesis.)

Although I had no way of knowing it at the time, this entire research and writing experience would greatly increase my growing interest in race relations and culminate, a generation later, in my appointment as the white president of the historically black Lincoln University. (Unfortunately, this rigorous master's thesis experience, which provided much of the foundation of my subsequent professional life, was denied to later generations of graduate students, since many universities downgraded the M.A. thesis into little more than a perfunctory exercise on the way to a Ph.D.)

In the summer of 1940, Professor Strevey invited me to continue studying at Northwestern for my Ph.D. in history. But once again, tennis entered the picture. Howard Braun, the head tennis coach at the University of Illinois, invited me to move to Champaign and assist him with the tennis team while I worked on my Ph.D. there. (I had come to know Howard when Northwestern played against his teams.) Illinois, Howard suggested, had a much larger history department than Northwestern's, and I would be able to study under a new and larger group of professors. Even my Northwestern professors, to whom I felt an emotional attachment, agreed that it would be better for my academic development to change scenery and work in the Illinois graduate program. In effect, they put the welfare of their student ahead of their institutional loyalty, a demonstration of their academic integrity for which I remain grateful to this day.

Howard Braun arranged meetings for me with several professors as well as with the chairman of Illinois's History Department, who offered me an assistantship. Between that teaching post, a job stringing rackets at a local sporting goods store, and a job as an adviser at Tau Delta Phi (a Jewish fraternity house), I was able to support myself while I finished my Ph.D. work.

"I came to Northwestern with $25 in my pocket," I remember thinking as I loaded my rickety 1927 Model-A Ford for the move to Champaign, "and I'm leaving five years later with two college degrees, a little money in the bank, and a car." I had acquired something else, as well: the confidence that I could adjust quickly to a new life in a new place.

The Ph.D. program in history at Illinois required courses in four fields of history, as well as one full-year course in a related field. Thinking that I should build upon my study at Northwestern, I chose American, modern European, English, and Latin American history. World War II had begun the previous year, and so I was eager to study the ramifications of the military invasions and territorial acquisitions of Germany, Italy, Japan, and the Soviet Union. As a result, I chose international law as my course in a related field. After taking the lecture courses and seminars, doctoral students had to take oral and written examinations (called "prelims") in each field, as well as read tests in two foreign languages (my choices were French and German). The final requirement was a book-length dissertation and a published synopsis of it.

Today such an extensive program is rare. Fewer courses are required of doctoral students, and study in fields outside the major is not considered essential. While two foreign languages were required before World War II, subsequently only one, or sometimes none, became necessary. To be sure, one foreign language is required today to earn a Ph.D. in the study of a foreign country. But the increased use of computers and the Internet and their ability to translate seemingly everything has often eliminated the second language requirement. However, if we truly live in a shrinking world, that strikes me as an even stronger reason for *all* educated people to know at least one widely used language other than their own, and for doctoral candidates to know two.

When I arrived at Illinois in the fall of 1940, Hitler had conquered Western Europe and was preparing to attack Great Britain. Most male students (and their girlfriends) didn't want their lives disrupted by service in the armed forces, and by 1941 antiwar demonstrations had become common at Illinois and other universities. Even after Germany's invasion of Russia in the summer of 1941, most students continued to hope for a settlement that would keep America out of the war. I sympathized with the British and strongly supported President Roosevelt's Lend–Lease Program of aid to Britain, but I was still somewhat torn on the subject of U.S. involvement in the war.

Against this backdrop, my work as a graduate assistant to the distinguished European history scholar Albert H. Lybyer was no mere academic exercise but a front-row seat at the great unfolding events of the day. Lybyer was a baldish, stooped, and serious man who resembled the stereotypical ivory tower professor; in fact, he had served as a U.S. adviser at the Versailles peace conference following World War I and had written a landmark study on the "opening up" of the Middle East (which concluded that the Middle East had never been closed).

Dr. Lybyer belonged to the William Allen White Committee, which long before Pearl Harbor had advocated U.S. military intervention in the war against Hitler's Germany. He began many of his lectures by discussing the war and comparing contemporary events to World War I or other previous conflicts. As German bombs rained down on London during the Battle of Britain, for example, Lybyer emphasized the threat to the United States should Germany overwhelm Great Britain. "The British are defending us as well as themselves," he would say, "and we must help them."

This position put him at odds with isolationist history professors at Illinois, like Theodore Pease and Frederick Dietz. When these three professors occupied the same room, you could feel the chill in the air. Lybyer defended the Treaty of Versailles, while Pease and Dietz denounced it as an act of vengeance that had inadvertently provoked Hitler's rise to power.

Pease was a large, portly man known for his unusual policy of placing the young women in his classes in the first two rows, apparently so he could peer at their legs. (It was also rumored that he gave them better grades than male students.) Dietz, by contrast, was fair-minded, straightforward, and very well organized (perhaps too well organized; he often lectured from yellowed notes he had used many times before). He was the author of an outstanding English history text and a sensitive, supportive teacher. "If you work hard in graduate school and produce some publications early in your career," he once astutely advised me, "you will lay the basis for success in the rest of your professional life."

At the same time that I was exposed to these historians' heated debates about the European conflict, I was also attending the international law lectures of Professor Valentine Jobst. A lawyer, political scientist, and dyed-in-the-wool skeptic, Jobst scoffed at the very notion of effective international law. He periodically reminded us that most national leaders were hypocrites. World peace could readily be achieved, he noted, if nations merely abided by the principles and laws that they had already agreed upon. This simplistic notion appealed to skeptics who blamed World War I on blunders by European leaders and feared that the United States would stumble into World War II in much the same way. Whether he was right or wrong matters less than the feeling I derived, wherever I turned in my doctoral work, that the work I was doing truly mattered in the world.

The best lecturer I had at Illinois was Raymond Stearns, professor of European history. He kept his classes awake with his lively delivery, his voice rising to a crescendo whenever he described an important action or event. He always maintained good eye contact with students, so we didn't dare let our minds wander. Stearns epitomized the large and admirable segment of American professors, at that time, who believed their duty as lecturers was to bring their subject to life. This model has declined over the last half century as academicians have emphasized "student-centered" learning – that is, focusing more on the students and less on the subject. The instructor's central role has been further undermined in recent years by the popularity of on-line teaching programs and e-mail communication. These technological advances have made higher education accessible to far greater numbers of students and stimulated a diverse variety of teaching styles. But the downside of this bargain, I am afraid, is the decline of the truly fine live classroom lecturers to whom I was exposed.

In the early fall of 1940, while still getting settled at Illinois, I met a young lady named Adeline Lillian Schpok. She had received her bachelor's degree from the university that spring and was teaching and directing plays at the junior high school while doing graduate work. Like me, Addie Schpok had worked at various jobs to pay for her education, serving as a secretary in the university's health services department as well as in the office of a chemistry professor. She also had led several student organizations. The two of us were introduced at what I later realized was a matchmaking dinner at the home of Joseph Katz, the university's ROTC commander, who had known my family in Milwaukee. Given my full agenda at that time, a serious romantic involvement was the last thing on my mind. But toward the end of the evening, when I got up to leave, Addie jumped up and asked if I would give her a lift home – all of four or five blocks. As I escorted her upstairs to her mother's second floor apartment and casually proposed that we get together sometime, she quickly suggested that I'd probably need her phone number. Years later she confessed to me that, despite the fact that she was going steady with another man, she awakened her mother, Mary Schpok, that night and whispered excitedly in her ear, "Mom, I think I've met the man I'd like to marry."

It's often been observed that, while in theory men are supposed to initiate romantic relationships, in practice it's usually the woman who finds a way to get the ball rolling. My first encounter with Addie was no exception. We were married a year and a half later, and she has remained by my side ever since, for more than sixty years.

For my doctoral thesis, I thought Milwaukee's socialist history would make an interesting topic. Daniel W. Hoan, Milwaukee's socialist mayor from 1916 to 1940, had just been defeated for re-election, and it appeared to me that a unique political era in American history – the control of a major city by a party that rejected capitalism – had ended. No organized history of this experience had yet been written. Like many of my contemporaries whose families were devastated by the Great Depression, I was skeptical about the blessings of capitalism and impressed by the effectiveness of two socialist administrations in Milwaukee. All I needed was to find a history professor willing to serve as my sponsor. Then as now, the taint of socialism was not recommended for advancing one's career, especially at a state institution. Fortunately, a suitable professor was on hand at Illinois. Frederick Shannon – a nephew of Eugene V. Debs, the perennial socialist candidate for president – already had a personal interest in my subject and readily agreed to be my sponsor.

Barely had I resolved the question of a sponsor to direct my work when a global crisis seized control of my life and the life of the nation. Japan's attack on Pearl Harbor on December 7, 1941, ended all debate on isolation versus intervention at Illinois – and virtually everywhere else. Two weeks later, I joined many other Illinois students in registering for the draft at an armory in Champaign. My physical exam indicated that I was definitely fit for induction into the army.

In the hope of landing an officer's commission, I decided to enlist rather than enter via the draft. During a visit to Los Angeles, I filled out applications for Officers' Candidate School (OCS) at all five branches of the armed forces. Unfortunately, the OCS physical revealed that, for military purposes, I was color-blind (I couldn't visualize numbers formed by dots of certain colors) and thus ineligible. There was nothing for me to do but return to Champaign, resume work on my thesis, await the call from my draft board – and marry Addie. We were married in Chicago on April 12, 1942. It was a small religious ceremony, attended by the few family members and friends who could get wartime transportation. Our plan was to move to Milwaukee for the summer so I could work full time on my dissertation and, I hoped, finish it before being drafted.

Immediately after the conclusion of our spring semester responsibilities, Addie and I drove to Milwaukee in my mother-in-law's car. In the city, we found a one-room apartment with a Murphy Hide-a-Bed that looked like it was part of the wall but could be pulled down on large hinges into the living room at bedtime. It was in that tiny space that we began housekeeping on our own and enjoyed a new kind of privacy and independence. Our days in Milwaukee were very full, and there was little time for recreation. We did, however, manage to spend some time in the nearby park overlooking Lake Michigan, and occasionally we visited the zoo or went rowing in the lagoon in Washington Park in my old boyhood neighborhood, giving us romantic respites from the daily tedium of writing and typing (and retyping) my thesis.

Early in our stay in Milwaukee, I was informed by my draft board that I was in category 1A on the selective service list, meaning that I could be called up for military service at any time. If I hoped to finish my thesis before leaving for the army, there was no time to lose. I quickly discovered the practical benefits of marriage, especially to a spouse as capable, energetic, and supportive as Addie was. Having lost her father at a very early age and having been raised during the Depression, Addie was accustomed to depending on herself and working hard to attain her goals.

My daily routine in Milwaukee consisted of boarding a bus each morning for center city and its libraries and archives, including the Milwaukee County Historical Society, the Milwaukee Public Library, city government offices, and various newspaper morgues. At these sites I recorded information as fast as I could, by hand. This was before photocopiers, microfilm, and word processors. After I accumulated enough material for a chapter, I would write a draft, turn it over to Addie, and, after dinner and dishes, she would type it for me on an L. C. Smith manual typewriter at the kitchen table. She often worked until 3 A.M. despite having to report to the law firm the same morning for her part-time job as secretary. There was no way I could have completed the thesis before leaving for the army without Addie's patient deciphering of my barely legible handwriting and her tenacity in typing draft after draft of each chapter.

In addition to exploring documentary sources, I interviewed a number of leading Milwaukee socialist figures. One was Emil Seidel, the first of several socialist mayors, who had first taken office in 1910. This elderly, slight, and unassuming former mayor welcomed me into the living room of his small frame home, served me coffee, and spoke for several hours about the Socialist Party's origins in Milwaukee. What came through above all was his pride in the moderate, honest, efficient government that he felt the party had delivered on behalf of the working class.

Frederick F. Heath, a member of the elected Milwaukee Board of Supervisors since 1910, was still on the board in 1942. He had belonged to the Fabian Society and became the original "Yankee" member of Milwaukee's Socialist Party in 1896, when the party's membership was almost entirely German-born and German-speaking. After his arrival, he told me, party meetings were conducted in English rather than German. Frank Zeidler – secretary of Milwaukee's Socialist Party, brother of the sitting Republican mayor, Carl Zeidler, and a future mayor himself (from 1948 to 1960) – was also helpful with information and suggestions.

These interviews revealed something to me above and beyond what I learned about Milwaukee socialism – namely, that prominent public figures are often more accessible than young people suspect. Most are proud of their accomplishments, hungry for appreciation, and frequently more than happy to share their insights with anyone who expresses an interest in their life and work – especially if the interested party is a young man or woman likely to record their achievements for future generations. In the case of retired public figures who miss the spotlight, gaining an interview is often just a matter of picking up the phone or writing a letter.

Professor Selig Perlman, a short, balding, distinguished economist at the University of Wisconsin, was a German immigrant who had written his bachelor's degree thesis on socialism in Milwaukee; since the only extant copy of it was in his office in Madison, I traveled there to review it with him. In the course of our conversation, Perlman tried to convince me to change the focus of my doctorate from history to economics.

"Marvin," I remember his saying, "it will be much easier to get a job in government or industry with a Ph.D. in economics during and after the war than with one in history. It will give you more flexibility than just aiming for an academic position." He was right, of course. But at that late stage of my work, I was in no mood to revise my thesis in a new direction. More important, I had no interest in working for government or industry. I had set my sights on becoming a professor, and Perlman had not dissuaded me.

As chapters of my dissertation were completed, I sent them to Fred Shannon, my thesis adviser. He reviewed them and responded with criticisms or comments. All this communication was conducted by mail, not by phone; there were no fax machines, nor were there personal computers with e-mail possibilities. After receiving his comments, I would revise the chapters, Addie would retype them, and I would send them back for Shannon's approval. That way, we hoped to avoid the danger of my thesis being rejected by the Dissertation Committee. Professor Shannon was a stickler for form, grammar, and, especially, for footnotes and bibliography. I had a tendency to wax overly enthusiastic about events or individuals, and, like many other doctoral students, I sometimes felt stifled by Shannon's insistence on documentation for every generalization and conclusion. But of course Shannon was quite right to shoot down my rhetorical flights, even though he often shared my feelings. He never placed his socialist leanings above his obligations as a professional historian. The resulting dissertation may have been dry to my mind, but it was factual and unimpeachable. Besides, my draft number had come up. Now my job was to finish the dissertation and take my examination on it before being inducted into the army sometime that summer.

I took my final examination on Friday, August 14, 1942. Although I was defending my thesis before a distinguished group of professors at Illinois, Professor Shannon's rigorous methods had already sewn up so many holes in my thesis that there were few openings for questions or argument about my conclusions. What's more, I had read so much about Marxism and socialism – and, of more consequence, had bolstered my reading with personal interviews in Milwaukee – that no one in that room could have known as much about socialism in Milwaukee as I did. As a result, I was able to discuss my thesis with my much older and wiser academic judges with some authority.

Fifteen minutes after completing my defense, I was called back into the room for congratulations: I had completed all requirements for a Ph.D. On that note, Addie and I picked up our belongings and drove to Chicago, where we checked into a hotel near the Loop for what we feared might be our last weekend together. Our mood was both joyful and sad – happy that my doctoral work was finally completed but truly concerned that we might not see each other again for a long time.

After our bittersweet weekend together, I was inducted into the U.S. Army on August 17, 1942. I reported to Fort Sheridan, Illinois, an old military base on the windy shore of Lake Michigan, north of Chicago. In the first week of physical and mental exams, I was interviewed by a tall, good-looking GI psychologist who seemed incredulous about my academic credentials. "You actually passed the orals on your dissertation and received your Ph.D. just a few days ago?" he gasped. "That's amazing. I've got to figure out how to 'label' you for army classification purposes." He confided that he had only recently received his M.A., although he appeared to be closer to age thirty or thirty-five than to my own twenty-five. Later, I learned that when an interviewer was in doubt about what classification to give an over- or under-qualified recruit, he simply labeled him "basic." That was the label given to me, despite the suitability of other classifications for recruits with my background. I couldn't help suspecting that he was jealous.

Preliminary training at Fort Sheridan lasted less than two weeks, and then I was assigned to basic training at an antiaircraft unit at Camp Wallace, Texas. Like most recruits entering the army in 1942, I had no prior military experience and no familiarity with guns or other weapons of war. Army discipline represented a great change from thesis writing, oral examinations, and adjusting to married life, but since all my fellow recruits were in the same boat, it rarely occurred to me to feel sorry for myself. In fact, the training and physical conditioning suited me very well, and I enjoyed being exposed to GIs from many parts of the country and a broad range of ethnic and religious backgrounds. We had a number of Cajuns in our unit, as well as some Polish Americans who could neither read nor write English. But we had no blacks. In 1942, the U.S. Army, like most of American society, remained racially segregated. A separate black unit was housed in a different part of the camp.

My incurable optimism was sustained at Camp Wallace by news that the University of Illinois Press was considering publication of my dissertation as a book in its series Illinois Studies in the Social Sciences. (Due to wartime delays, it didn't appear until 1945.)

Some time after basic training, I was promoted to corporal and asked to assist a lieutenant in organizing a literacy school for trainees. Our objective was to equip illiterate recruits with a fourth-grade literacy level so they would be able to read and comprehend simple commands and work their way through various army manuals. Quite soon – everything seemed to happen quickly in the army, except when one was standing in line for pay, chow, or an appointment to see an officer – I was named assistant principal of the literacy school.

Unfortunately, even though the books and materials the army supplied for the school were adequate, many of the soldiers couldn't learn to read and write in the limited time available. Those who passed literacy competence tests moved into regular units; those who failed were discharged from the army with what was called a Section 8 termination – not quite as bad as a dishonorable discharge, but certainly no source of pride.

Since I'd adjusted to military life and demonstrated an ability to give as well as obey orders, I was offered a position on the camp's permanent staff – "the Cadre," as it was called. This was considered a plum appointment, and it meant staying at the camp indefinitely, perhaps until the end of the war. I seriously considered accepting it, especially since Addie had joined me and we shared a rented room in Galveston. But then I learned about the Army Specialized Training Program (ASTP). That program had been created to provide training in languages and foreign area studies for use in military intelligence and, as our troops advanced, in the occupation of enemy territory. The army was opening units at several universities around the country. The ASTP seemed to relate much better to my chosen profession – it would put me back on a college campus, rather than an army base – and offered me a greater opportunity to contribute to the war effort. I applied and, in the summer of 1943, passed the Army General Classification Test with room to spare.

I reported for duty at the University of Missouri in Columbia early in September 1943. There, unlike at Camp Wallace, I found myself among college types, mostly quite young, with a fair sprinkling of older college grads and language specialists thrown in. We were billeted in dormitories and fraternity houses just as if we were civilian college students (although Addie eventually joined me in a furnished apartment), and we were expected to spend most of our time attending classes and completing homework assignments. Aside from strenuous physical education courses required by the army, our lives were blissfully free of the military regimen.

We GIs took Russian, German, and Italian "area studies" – the better to comprehend those three critical societies – and all of us were assigned to intensive work on one European language. Our instructors were not soldiers but learned professors at the University of Missouri. Since the army high command hoped to occupy Germany soon, about fifteen soldiers (including me) were assigned to study German. This first-class education should have paid off handsomely for use in Europe. But as the war dragged on during the fall and winter of 1943, the ASTP ran into political resistance. Newspaper columnists and radio commentators publicly wondered why healthy young soldiers were taking academic courses while their contemporaries were dying in the Pacific, North Africa, or Italy. Before we could even complete our courses, the ASTP at Missouri was suddenly closed down.

Those of us in ASTP who had done well and almost finished our language and subject-matter classes were transferred to the infantry. Ironically, others, who had flunked out earlier, had been reassigned to intelligence units or other plush services. Despite their failure, the army correctly perceived these men to be brighter than average and assigned them accordingly. By the time we survivors – who presumably had demonstrated even greater intellect and persistence than the failures – were reassigned, such considerations had to be subordinated to the political needs of the moment. So instead of being allowed to contribute my knowledge to the postwar reconstruction of Europe, I became gun chief of a platoon in the Cannon Company of the 66th Infantry Division, based at Camp Rucker, Alabama.

On November 13, 1944, the 66th Infantry Division began its voyage across the Atlantic Ocean, packed like sardines aboard the *George Washington*, a decaying German luxury liner that had been captured at the end of World War I. "It's hard for a single individual like me to understand," I wrote to Addie during the crossing, "how a guy can be expendable one minute, and not expendable the next. I guess the only explanation to fall back on is . . . that the exigencies of war preclude the possibility of fair play to everyone, and of everyone finding his proper niche in the army." However, I added, "You know I'll do the best I can in whatever they give me to do, and also be ready to take whatever position or job I'm given, or whatever opportunity comes my way."

This line pretty much summed up the philosophy that guided my life and the lives of many others of my Depression generation. And in retrospect, it was a pragmatic philosophy that served us well – for, as I discovered in the army, life's irrationalities had a way of canceling each other out. In England, as we prepared to go into combat in Belgium around Christmas 1944, a call went out for volunteers to serve as assistant truck and jeep drivers to the debarkation point at Southampton for the trip across the English Channel. Since I had the requisite license, I volunteered. And because I was driving troops to the debarkation point, I was not aboard the troop ship *Leopoldville* when it was sunk in the channel by a German submarine torpedo with a loss to the 66th Infantry Division of over eight hundred dead and hundreds more injured. Consequently, instead of fighting the Battle of the Bulge in Belgium – which cost 40,000 American lives, the most brutal battle in U.S. military history – our division spent the final four months of the European conflict in Brittany, bottling up the remaining pockets of German resistance.

We spent 133 days at the front lines of the St. Nazaire/Lorient pockets, where 50,000 German troops were protecting seventeen submarine pens and probing for weaknesses in our lines of defense. At the beginning of our Brittany campaign, the Germans thought they could break through and join their comrades. After American and British troops pushed back the Germans in their last big offense in the Battle of the Bulge, the German troops in Brittany wanted to make certain that they were able to hold their positions until the end of the war. Our job, beginning with a depleted division, was to patrol the short distance between the two front lines, direct fire at moving targets, and round up German prisoners.

Some of us were killed there – most jarringly, for me, a bright young university graduate from Indiana who was shot while on the same type of reconnaissance mission that I regularly went out on. But what sustained me during that difficult time were the truly democratic bull sessions we platoon members conducted in the hidden huts we built during our stay in Brittany, especially when no lights were permitted because of the danger of air raids. We discussed domestic and foreign politics, economics, ways of life and ways of earning a living, philosophies of life, and what we planned to do immediately, and in the more distant future, after we got home. All opinions, from conservative to liberal to radical, were represented. Our meetings were run like debates or seminars – that is, we permitted only one man at a time to have the floor and made every effort to limit discussions to a fairly narrow subject.

Sometimes late at night we played poker; we also lent each other money so that those who were going into town could buy gifts for their sweethearts back home. Each of us contributed to the platoon's welfare in his own way. One GI, a barber in northern New Jersey before the war, gave us haircuts at cut-rate prices. I recall no member of my platoon ever trying to take advantage of another one; each of us seemed to understand instinctively that our lives and welfare depended upon our mutual support and assistance. Looking back to those months in France, I realize how much I enjoyed the company of my army buddies and how they reaffirmed my faith in democratic ideals.

After Germany surrendered in May 1945, our division moved into Germany as part of the occupation of that defeated nation. But after a short time we were reassigned to a newly established base in France at Arles, near Marseilles. There I continued as a sergeant in the Cannon Company of the 66th Division but also was given the title of instructor in information and educational materials. In addition, I frequently served as an interpreter for German prisoners. Some of my duties as instructor required me to lecture to large groups of GIs on the progress of the war against Japan, the general situation in the Far East, peace negotiations, and U.S. domestic affairs. I served as the leader of a group (including four other soldiers – three of whom were former teachers) that was assigned to discuss postwar "readjustment and redeployment" with our fellow GIs. This was satisfying work – the closest thing to a large classroom experience since my student days at Illinois. It enabled me to use my background in history as a filter for whatever I learned from available publications, like *Stars and Stripes*, English and French newspapers, and the army edition of *Time* magazine.

While at Arles, I learned that the Army Information and Education Office (I&E), headquartered in Paris, was establishing a GI College in Biarritz, on the Bay of Biscay in southwestern France, to prepare soldiers for the transition back to civilian life. It sounded like a perfect fit for me – but having witnessed the foul-ups in army communications, I determined not to trust a written application but instead to apply in person. On a furlough (despite being ill with my second bout of army dysentery), I headed for Paris on a troop train crowded with soldiers overflowing the seats onto the floors. At the I&E headquarters I applied for a teaching post at the new college and learned that most of the instructors would be civilians brought over from the United States. However, I&E was also looking to round out the faculty with a few GIs who possessed the appropriate academic background. In my life I hadn't always been in the right place at the right time, but this time I was.

At Biarritz, hotels, villas, casinos, and office buildings had been transformed almost overnight into facilities for a first-class university. The student body, I found to my delight, consisted of young combat veterans eager to resume their civilian lives and get on with their careers. They were so highly motivated that if an instructor casually referred to a book in class, every copy of that book would be checked out of our library (a converted casino) soon after class was over.

Above all, I was thrilled to find myself teaching alongside a star-studded cast of civilian professors (albeit now in uniform) on leave from prestigious academic institutions in the United States. Among my colleagues were Loring Priest, later author of *Uncle Sam's Stepchildren*, a fine book on the American Indians, who subsequently asked me to stand as best man at his wedding; Bill Halperin, a distinguished professor of European history at the University of Chicago; and Charles R. (Ray) Wilson, chairman of the History Department at Colgate, who subsequently offered me a teaching job there.

Biarritz itself became an intellectual center as the war ended, and so this humble army sergeant/teacher found himself accepted on a more or less equal basis by fine thinkers like the French writer Simone de Beauvoir (wife of the existential philosopher Jean-Paul Sartre); the English writer Herbert Marshall (a protégé of George Bernard Shaw); and Marshall's Polish-born artist wife, Fredda Brilliant. At this critical juncture these three were among the leading advocates of postwar détente between the West and the Soviet Union, notwithstanding the horrors committed by Stalin. As had been the case at Northwestern and Illinois in the days leading up to the war, I once again found myself on the front lines of global intellectual issues. I couldn't have asked for a better transition to my own long-awaited civilian life. The slogan, "Join the Army and See the World" has been ridiculed by many GIs, but not by me. On balance, the army did indeed offer me opportunities that enriched my life and career immeasurably.

(To be sure, some lessons I learned in the military proved inapplicable a generation later during the Vietnam war, when I was a college president coping with antiwar protests. The GIs in my division clearly understood what they were fighting for and what values they were upholding; ultimately that's what kept us together. The GIs in Vietnam enjoyed no such rationale for their mission.)

After teaching at Biarritz for three eight-week terms, I had earned enough "points" – calculated through an army formula that awarded points for time on active duty, overseas duty, and combat experience – to merit a discharge. I left the service on March 13, 1946, at Camp Grant in Rockford, Illinois, and quickly boarded an Illinois Central Railroad coach to Chicago. It was at the Illinois Central's Twelfth Street Station on the southern edge of the Loop that I caught the first glimpse, since 1944, of my sweetheart. I will never forget the sight of her, running the length of the platform toward me. My long apprenticeship was over. Now I was ready to claim the prize I had so long yearned for: a teaching position at a major American university.

The Professor:
Colgate University

A FTER MY DISCHARGE FROM THE ARMY and return to Addie, I began the process of becoming a full-fledged civilian once again. That meant discarding my army khakis for a civilian business suit. Addie's uncle Sam Salinsky of Aberdeen, South Dakota, who owned a women's clothing store, introduced me to the Hart Schaffner & Marx distributor in Chicago, and soon I was being fitted for my first postwar civilian suit at a very reasonable price. Since its quality was far superior to anything I had purchased before (and, in fact, to most of those I acquired for many years thereafter), I wore that suit until it was threadbare.

The suit, which was my first order of business upon returning, was critical to my second order of business. At Biarritz, I had joined the American Veterans Committee (AVC), a liberal alternative to the American Legion. Its founder, the visionary Charles Bolté, wanted returning veterans to play a role in the postwar rebuilding of the United States and in the prevention of another world war; "Americans First, Veterans Second" was his motto for the AVC. Bolté's widely read book *The New Veteran* appealed to the idealistic nature of many Americans after the war. I had been elected as the Biarritz Chapter's representative to the AVC's first national convention, scheduled for late April 1946.

Decked out in my new suit, I took the train to Des Moines, Iowa, for the several days' activities. There, navy veterans like Harold Stassen, the former governor of Minnesota, and Franklin Delano Roosevelt Jr. spoke, along with business, professional, and educational leaders. The speakers and meetings reflected the high optimism and feeling of great opportunity for returning servicemen. AVC delegates like me were not interested in rehashing our war stories; we were looking for specific job opportunities.

Along with writing many letters and making many calls, I contacted various teachers' employment agencies, but few of the available positions appealed to me. Paul Bennett, my former tennis coach at Northwestern, attempted to help me by contacting a steel executive friend in Middletown, Ohio, where there was an opening for a history teacher and tennis coach. I was invited to Middletown and spent two days there with this influential executive. He looked me over, introduced me to prominent local people, including the high school principal and officers of the local country club. Then he asked me to show him my tennis teaching techniques. After two very busy days, I was offered positions teaching history in the high school, coaching its tennis team, and serving as tennis professional at the local country club, at a total annual remuneration of about $3,800 – a reasonable sum in those days. I couldn't help feeling that I was valued more for my tennis prowess than my intellectual skills. Nevertheless, in the absence of any other offer, I was prepared to accept that Middletown job.

Luckily for me, as I was considering my options I received a letter from Charles R. Wilson, the head of Colgate University's History Department, who had been my colleague at Biarritz American University. I had written to Wilson and others whom I had met in Biarritz to tell them that I had returned to Illinois and was seeking a position. Colgate, an all-male school, had an opening, he said, and since he had already heard me lecture and was familiar with my written work, he had been authorized to offer me a position for the coming academic year at a salary of $2,400 – considerably less than what Middletown had offered. (In those days, high schools often paid more than colleges for beginning instructors with advanced degrees. Of course, the Middletown offer was really for twelve months rather than eight or nine, and included teaching tennis all summer.) Nevertheless, I accepted Colgate's offer – the first of several occasions when I took a position with lower financial rewards than I could have attained elsewhere. I was eager to teach at the college level, especially at a respectable institution like Colgate, where excellence in teaching and scholarship were highly valued. Against those considerations, the salary was secondary.

My arrival in Hamilton, New York, in June 1946 to teach summer school began a fifteen-year association with Colgate University. I couldn't have asked for a smoother transition into civilian life. Every one of my students that first summer and fall was a returning veteran – and because I was a returning vet myself, I believe that I had a better rapport with those students than with any others in my career. I taught both European and American history and made many friends among students, faculty, and administrators and generally got off to a good start as a college instructor. When the spring semester began in 1947, I was pleasantly surprised to receive a $600 grant – equivalent to 25 percent of my starting salary – from a Ford Foundation program specifically designed to make college teaching more attractive and competitive for young instructors like me. That reward reinforced my own instinctive notion that one should never choose a job solely for the money: If it's the right job for you, somehow your financial need will take care of itself.

Shortly after my arrival at Colgate, the tennis coach, Perrine Rockafellow – a former National Indoor Doubles champion who seemed to know anybody who had ever received some kind of national ranking – asked me to coach the freshman tennis team in whatever free time I had. I was delighted at this chance to get back into good physical condition. This work took me to matches at West Point, Syracuse, Cornell, and elsewhere; equally important, playing against Colgate's athletes helped me sharpen my own game. As a result, during my years at Colgate I played in summer weekend tournaments throughout upstate New York and New England, winning or reaching the finals of almost all of them.

Tennis also helped me develop a relationship with Colgate's president, Everett Needham Case, who would call me from time to time for a game. Like many tennis players, Ev would forget the tennis etiquette rule that at least every other time one plays with an opponent, he should supply the tennis balls. Invariably, he would be embarrassed that he had left it up to me, an underpaid instructor, to bring the balls. But I never quibbled, because my access to him was worth more than the cost of the balls. Ev Case and his wife, Josephine, a poet and writer, were wonderfully creative and intellectual people who made their home a center for literary and political discussion. Ev also acted and sang in local community Gilbert and Sullivan productions.

My first fall of 1946, and the following autumn as well, the Colgate football team suffered mediocre seasons. A number of alumni, including several trustees, placed the blame on the sudden infusion of supposedly "radical" new faculty members, especially refugees from Europe, who allegedly failed to appreciate the value of a winning sports program. As an outspoken liberal who had written his doctoral thesis on the Socialist Party of Milwaukee, I was one of those newcomers summoned to appear before a committee of the alumni investigating this matter.

In the process I discovered that some of the committee equated "radicalism" with support for the New Deal, FDR, and the incumbent president, Harry Truman. "If they are radical," I suggested, "over half of the country could be described that way." Yet I suffered no repercussions for my remarks. My status as (a) World War II combat veteran and (b) tournament tennis player had placed me beyond reproach, at least on this issue.

In September 1946, Addie and I settled down in a small three-room apartment with dormer windows on the third floor of an old house in Hamilton, near the university. We had no car – affordable new automobiles were in short supply at the end of the war, and used cars were mostly in poor condition – so we walked, hitched rides, or took the infrequently scheduled buses to reach the nearest cities, Utica and Syracuse. Another faculty couple, Bob and Jean Elder, sometimes drove us to Syracuse for dinner in their very small coupe with one seat behind the two front seats: I climbed in and Addie followed me, sitting on my lap for the entire 110 mile round trip to Syracuse. After almost a year on waiting lists, we were able to scrape together enough money from my increased salary, army-pay savings, and Addie's small bank account to purchase a new Dodge. In the rural area around the village of Hamilton a car seemed to be indispensable, and we were most pleased when we were finally able to get one, late in the spring of 1947.

Our life in Hamilton was quickly filled out by Addie's teaching job at Hamilton High School and by many college and community activities. Like most faculty members in our small town, we attended almost all student events – intellectual, musical, and athletic. Housecleaning on Saturdays regularly included my mopping the kitchen floor to help us get out of the house and over to the little football stadium in time for home games, or to Archbold Stadium in Syracuse for games against "big, bad" Syracuse University. We were also active in Democratic Party programs in Hamilton and elsewhere in Madison County.

After my summer teaching experience in 1946, I was assigned to teach mostly American history and "general education courses." Colgate was a pioneer in "general education," a required undergraduate liberal arts core curriculum that included courses in social, natural, and biological sciences, philosophy and religion, and literature. This approach to curriculum was springing up in colleges nationwide. It was a time, for instance, when Columbia developed its Western Civilization program and Harvard offered similar courses. But Colgate carried its program of certain disciplinary and interdisciplinary core courses further than most, mandating them all the way from the freshman through the senior year.

My first general education assignment was a freshman course featuring *Men, Groups, and the Community*, a text written by members of Colgate's School of Social Sciences. In the later 1940s, the "case method" was adapted to whichever of these "core courses" it would apply, and so my social science course became "Problems in Public Affairs." The aptly named Everett Case had promoted this method as an assistant dean at the Harvard Business

School and subsequently did the same at Colgate. So among young instructors at Colgate, the "case method" became known as the "Everett Case method."

In 1949, the Cold War between Western democracy and Soviet communism was heating up, and colleges nationwide were increasingly challenging their students to examine competing national creeds and philosophies. As a result, to round out its core curriculum, Colgate decided to organize a new one-semester core course for seniors called "The American Idea in the Modern World" in order to (as the catalogue described it) "determine the validity and effectiveness of the 'American Way' in the current conflict of ideologies at home and abroad."

Ray Wilson, chairman of the History Department, had been charged with directing this new course. As a brilliant lecturer as well as a political activist who twice ran unsuccessfully for a congressional seat as a Democrat in solidly Republican Madison County, Ray was eminently well suited for this task. But he also had a lot on his plate. In addition to his departmental obligations, he spent a great deal of time each year organizing a summer conference on foreign policy, bringing to the campus leading national and international personalities.

"Marv," he said to me, "you know how busy I am, and I'm not really interested in interdisciplinary courses. Why don't you take over this project for me?" My job was to develop the course from scratch, including syllabus and book of readings. I dropped my upper class course – "American Social and Intellectual Development" – and concentrated on the new course. At many institutions, such a course meant studying communism, fascism, and democracy, as well as competing religious views. Our Colgate committee ratcheted up the discussion, with readings that included examination of American individualism in the changing postwar times – works like David Riesman's *The Lonely Crowd*; C. Wright Mills's *White Collar: The American Middle Classes*; William H. Whyte's *The Organization Man*; and Robert A. Nisbet's *The Quest for Community: A Study in the Ethics of Order and Freedom*.

This course was subsequently expanded into "American Ideals and Institutions," a two-semester junior course – one semester devoted to historical and philosophical views, and the second to an analysis of economic, social and political institutions, as they related to the history and theory of American democracy. Meanwhile, I was also assigned to draft and direct a new senior core course called "America in the World Community," which would cap a required four-semester sequence for undergraduates that began with the study of a specific foreign area's culture and history.

These "American" courses were by their very nature in a constant state of flux, and as director of both the junior and senior courses I had to edit materials, provide introductions to readings, secure permission from publishers to reproduce book chapters and articles, and, most important, assemble a diverse and quality faculty. Perhaps more challenging, I had to solicit cooperation not only from history and political science teachers but also from those in economics, anthropology, and sociology, philosophy and religion, and literature, many of whom had not previously worked together. I found that gathering these professors after classes for drinks or dinner helped morale and cultivated cooperation toward our ultimate goals: writing course descriptions, developing outlines, and attracting funding.

With the aid of Colgate's development office, we submitted a grant proposal to the Carnegie Corporation. After a personal trip to Carnegie's office in New York, I was able to announce that there would be support for six consecutive years at an average of $20,000 per year, a significant sum at that time.

This extra funding enabled us, for example, to spend several weeks in the summer doing nothing but reviewing materials, debating their adequacy for our courses, and deciding which articles or chapters or books would best fit our goals for each course. At these gatherings, a professor would often bring in copies of a particular book that he insisted be part of the course, only to hear the book torn apart by his colleagues as lacking in good scholarship, theoretically flawed, or poorly written. Among ourselves we debated the roots of our values, their legitimacy, and whether and how we, as a nation, lived up to them. The gap between our pronouncements in the Declaration of Independence and the Constitution and our practices, especially in matters of race, occupied a good deal of our time. We struggled to find a balance between applause and criticism for American institutions. Then we turned to a comparative discussion of the values and institutions of other nations.

The reader blessed with hindsight will recognize these experiences as excellent training for my subsequent career as a university administrator. But nothing of the sort occurred to me at the time. I remember thinking only that these were some of the most intellectually stimulating discussions I had experienced – and I still feel that way today, more than half a century later.

It was only natural for some of us involved in these core courses to become active in the newly developed American Studies Association. That organization was launched at the end of World War II by professors engaged in American studies programs and courses at schools such as Amherst, Chicago, Columbia, Dartmouth, Minnesota, Pennsylvania, and Virginia. Some critics felt that such an association was unnecessary or even counterproductive – that no professor could do adequate justice to fields outside his or her own discipline. The charge against both American studies and general education courses was that they were too broad in subject matter. Students, it was felt, should continue to take separate courses and blend the substance of their learning on their own, as best they could.

Those of us in general education contended, by contrast, that integrating the material from various disciplines was necessary to develop a clear picture of our nation's culture and values. If *teachers* couldn't work across departmental or disciplinary boundaries, we argued, how could we expect students to do so?

Our argument must have carried the day, because interdisciplinary general education courses continued to develop, American studies programs sprang up across the country, and the American Studies Association grew. State and local associations were founded, including a strong upstate New York association that I helped organize along with Robert Elias, an English professor at Cornell.

Although I was deeply committed to interdisciplinary American studies, I remained devoted to American history. Many of the materials I found in research and taught in my classes were also put to use in speeches I made at the university and at high schools, Rotary Clubs, and even political clubs. (At the Hamilton Democratic Club, I gave separate addresses on each of the Democratic presidents, from Thomas Jefferson to Harry Truman.)

It was my practice always to be involved in some project related to my teaching or research interests. Hence, I wrote articles on "The Use of Problems as an Approach in Teaching American History," "Chauvinism and American Studies," "Writings on the Theory and Teaching of American Studies," and "Cultural Unity and the European Intellectual's Image of America." Also, I reviewed dozens of books for the *American Historical Review*, the *Mississippi Valley Historical Review* (now called the *Journal of American History*), the *Journal of Higher Education*, and the *Journal of Politics*.

In the mid-'50s, with two of my Colgate colleagues, I outlined and began writing a high school textbook in twentieth-century American history. Several publishers expressed interest in the chapters we had written. Those chapters are still with me, filed away, but the text was never completed because of other, more pressing assignments. I also engaged in a research project on the history of the American town meeting, with an emphasis on New England. That venture involved working at the Library of Congress, the Massachusetts Historical

Society in Boston, and the American Antiquarian Society in Worcester, Massachusetts. In addition, it required visiting a number of small New England towns and delving into their archives and historical collections. That enterprise yielded an abundance of good teaching materials for both history and general education courses.

This research had nonacademic side benefits: After working all day at the Historical Society in Boston, I was able to walk over to Fenway Park and watch Ted Williams hit home runs for the Boston Red Sox. But it also had its hazards: On one of my research jaunts to the American Antiquarian Society, Addie and I ran into the northern end of a hurricane and found ourselves waylaid for several days inside a sturdy hotel building in Worcester. Fortunately, I had brought plenty of notes and copies of documents with me, so I was able to do some writing.

While I was occupied with teaching, writing, giving speeches, and directing core courses, Addie was also very busy. During our first year in Hamilton, she taught a sixth-grade class of forty-two youngsters. Then she taught English literature and directed plays at Hamilton High School, where her pupils included many children of Colgate faculty, including President Case. She also took several courses in speech therapy at Syracuse University and established a small practice of speech correction and speech therapy for sufferers of cleft palate and stuttering.

Since there were no female students at Colgate, young faculty wives were often sought out to take female roles in the university's theater productions. Addie appeared in leading roles in *Arsenic and Old Lace* (performed on the stage of the local movie theater), *Bell, Book and Candle*, *Twelfth Night* and several other Shakespeare works, not to mention the chorus of a Gilbert and Sullivan production.

In the summer of 1952, I was invited to spend the next academic year and summer teaching history to GIs and civilians at army and air force bases in Europe, under the auspices of the University of Maryland's Overseas Program there. This program's mission was similar to that of Biarritz American University when I taught there seven years earlier, so I was well prepared for such a task. But in retrospect my contacts counted as much as my credentials: My appointment resulted directly from the recommendation of Wesley Gewehr, chairman of Maryland's History Department, whom I had met at Biarritz and with whom I had kept in touch at various history conventions. Gewehr also arranged an appointment for Addie to teach English in the overseas program part time. This meant we could travel together and receive many of the perks of military service, like subsidized housing, use of the Post Exchanges (PXs), and tax-free gasoline stations.

Colgate granted me a year's leave, and the army granted me the simulated rank of colonel, which meant I was eligible for fairly high-level services and quarters – quite a promotion for a former combat infantry sergeant.

To prepare for our European teaching assignments, Addie and I traveled to Washington, D.C., in early September 1952 for security clearances and for an extensive regimen of tetanus, typhoid, and smallpox shots. We expected to leave immediately after receiving the authorization and shots, and so we rushed up to Massachusetts to catch a scheduled army airplane. In typical military style, however, we were kept waiting for a week before finally taking off. This was our first airplane flight together, so it offered us special excitement: lunch at Westover, Massachusetts; dinner at St. John's, Newfoundland; and high tea the following day in Ayr, Scotland. Because Keflavik, Iceland, had been zeroed in by the weather, we could not change crews there, so we waited over in Ayr for our crew to get a night's sleep and arrived at the Rhein–Main Air Base near Frankfurt, Germany, two days after leaving Massachusetts.

Before taking on my regular teaching duties, I was sent to Munich to lecture U.S. troops on several subjects. There, at the Oktoberfest – a combined fall festival, circus, and vaudeville show – Addie and I ate chicken on a spit and drank German beer in thirty-two–ounce mugs (the first beer Addie, a native of dry South Dakota, had ever tasted). We sat at long tables alongside our erstwhile enemies the Germans, eating, toasting, and singing German folk songs far into the night.

During our first eight-week term in the Maryland program, we lived in an old hotel in the ancient Roman city of Augsburg, near Munich. Weekend trips took us to beautiful vacation spots like Berchtesgaden (Hitler's favorite) and Garmisch-Partenkirchen. Thanks to my simulated military rank, we were given comfortable accommodations on these trips – which meant at least a private bathroom, a rare privilege in war-torn Europe.

Because of a last-minute opening at the army base in Augsburg, Addie was able to teach English in the city where we lived. I, on the other hand, commuted thirty miles by car, over narrow roads, to one twice-weekly class at Landsberg and sixty-five miles by train to Munich and then by army automobile to another class at Freising. Still, this was time well spent: Both my German and my insight improved as I discussed everything from democracy to Nazism with my German drivers and my train compartment companions.

The GIs Addie and I taught, like those at Biarritz in '46, were highly motivated adults and consequently a pleasure to teach. Although library facilities were limited and the GI students lacked time to complete lengthy papers, they faithfully read their assignments and did all the written work required. They were genuinely thoughtful and inquisitive about such questions as, "How could a Hitler rise to power?" and "Was the Versailles Treaty one of the underlying causes of World War II?"

Just three days before the end of our term in Augsburg, we were able to purchase an Austin A7 – a tiny, four-door car that, as Addie wrote home, "made the Austins which we had seen in the United States look like Cadillacs!" But such a small car, we quickly found, was ideally suited for narrow European roads and exceedingly inexpensive to operate, especially since we could drive forty-five miles on a gallon of tax-free GI gasoline.

The Austin arrived just in time for us to drive to Heidelberg, where I lectured in English on America's role in the postwar world to an enthusiastic audience of University of Heidelberg students at the U.S. Information Service's Amerika Haus für Jederman. Then, on November 30, we took off for my next Maryland Overseas Program assignment, in Trieste. With our heads barely visible above the baggage in the back seat, we drove through Germany and Austria to sunnier southern climes. What a glorious sight it was, like the lifting of a dark gray curtain, leaving the rain-swept, densely fogged Brenner Pass and descending into northern Italy, where we saw rows of yellow corn drying in the bright sunlight.

We lived in the Slavic section of Trieste, called Barcola. Our beautiful new apartment building overlooked the Adriatic Sea, and we strolled along the shore almost daily, as did the Triestini. As Addie wrote, "It was prettier than any picture-post card with its rocky hills etched sharply against the bright blue sky just behind our building, a brilliant azure sea in the foreground, and on clear days, the Italian Alps to our right." In this case, as in so many cases throughout my life, we owed these broadening adventures to the opportunities afforded us by academic life, and our willingness to seize them.

Trieste had been the main port of the old Austro-Hungarian Empire, but the border between Italy and Yugoslavia had not yet been resolved following the end of World War II. So now Trieste was a disputed "free city" that hosted 5,000 American troops, along with 5,000 British troops, and 5,000 Italian police. Because of the border dispute between Italy and Yugoslavia and the rivalry between the Communist Party and all others, Trieste was very active politically. Here I taught American history and American diplomatic history to U.S.

troops. They tended to be older and higher ranking (as high as colonels) than those in my classes in Germany, with more firsthand knowledge of World War II and its antecedents. So teaching them American foreign policy was a challenge: Instead of accepting my pronouncements at face value, they forced me to justify my own analyses and conclusions in discussions that sometimes grew heated.

In one lecture, for example, I took a strong position about the negative effects of the U.S. Senate's refusal to endorse U.S. membership in the League of Nations in 1919–20. Several isolationists in the class took the side of Senators Lodge and Borah, and soon we had a full-fledged argument not only about the League of Nations but about the United Nations, as well.

Several blocks from our apartment in Trieste, we chanced upon a small tennis club. There we met several professors from the University of Trieste who generously invited me to play. After that introduction, I met other Italians who also invited me to play as their guest. Once again, tennis had provided me with an entrée, this time to Italian life and culture.

One of the club members was Guido Devescovi, head of the German Department at the University of Trieste. He took me to the university's new campus, some distance from the center of Trieste, to meet a few of his colleagues. He especially wanted me to meet the chairman of the Political Science Department, a respected Triestini antifascist whose name I have forgotten but whose words I clearly recall. When asked what he taught, he replied, "I teach what I know; what do you teach?" That was not a flippant remark; rather, he was stressing that he taught the truth as he discovered it through his reading, research, and experience and did not deviate from it, regardless of his government's political or ideological stance. I certainly agreed with his approach and have always tried to follow it in my own teaching.

The opposite approach was exemplified by Oscar de Ebner, the very best tennis player in Trieste, with whom I played frequently at the tennis club. He was half Italian and half Austrian, and he believed, for example, that Italy had been much better off under Mussolini. I never *did* succeed in persuading him that Mussolini's alliance with Hitler was the root of all of Italy's wartime and postwar difficulties. The closest he came to conceding my point was his remark that, "If not under Mussolini, you've got to agree that Trieste was better off when it was the main port for the Austro-Hungarian Empire."

Trieste became our launching pad, from which we could travel easily to Venice, to Florence, and to cities in Yugoslavia. Traveling to Yugoslavia was difficult because of the border dispute and the problem with getting visas. But by working patiently through the American Consulate we obtained visas and drove our little *"piccola machina,"* as the Italians called it, across the Yugoslav border. It was necessary to take along cans of gasoline, because filling stations were rare in Yugoslavia. Also, the mostly unpaved, bumpy dirt roads were so bad that every nook and cranny in the Austin was soon filled with dust and sand, as were our hair and clothes. We traveled as far as Zagreb in Croatia and observed for ourselves the dismal effects of a regimented communist country where the state controlled production, the sale of goods, and many aspects of the personal lives of its citizens – a far cry from the moderate, enlightened, efficient brand of socialism I had admired in Milwaukee, where the government controlled only the public utilities. (The only thing Milwaukee-style socialism and Yugoslav socialism had in common was their professed opposition to Soviet communism.)

After completing my assignment in Trieste, we returned to Heidelberg, where we stayed for more than four months while I taught in both Heidelberg and Stuttgart. Heidelberg, with its famous university, research institutes, and beautiful location on the Neckar River in a region of orchards and vineyards, completely captivated us. Twice a week I made a trip to Stuttgart, usually staying overnight in the noisy center of the city, because my class ended too late to find transportation back to Heidelberg. The changes that had taken place in Germany during our five months' absence were phenomenal. The country's rapid economic and political movement toward full sovereignty following the Allied occupation was the subject of widespread commentary, but what most impressed us were the psychological changes. When we strayed from American enclaves and associated with ordinary Germans on a personal basis, we heard students and professors candidly criticizing Germany's past infatuation with Hitler. We could sense their growing confidence that Germany would soon cast off its ignominious Nazi past.

Although we continued to travel in our trusty Austin, at that time no one could drive across East Germany to Berlin because of Soviet restrictions. So in June 1953 we took the approved overnight train, arriving in Berlin shortly after the East Berlin worker riots, when tensions were high. Although we saw signs reading, "Ami [that is, Americans] Go Home," we were received cordially by the Germans we met. We also visited the Free University of Berlin, making contacts that were useful later on. But Berlin's Russian sector was off-limits.

While teaching in Heidelberg, I had the good fortune to receive an invitation to join the Schwarz Gelb (black and yellow) Tennis Club as a nonpaying member. I also played at the U.S. Army's tennis courts. In one army tournament at Stuttgart that summer I defeated the all–European army champion in the finals. Later, in a civilian tournament in the Schwarzwald (Black Forest), I lost to an excellent, hard-hitting German player in the finals. During a time when human relations between Germans and Americans were still a bit stiff and sensitive, tennis proved a real ice-breaker in many of our relationships. It expanded our contacts beyond the usual German groups we met – those who worked with the U.S. military or government.

In all, my year's leave from Colgate was a remarkable experience. It broadened our horizons, generated new trans-Atlantic friendships, and stimulated our interest in returning. Because American travel to Europe was still relatively rare in the wake of World War II, upon our return to Colgate in the fall of 1953 we found ourselves the objects of intense local curiosity in Hamilton, New York. Using our hundreds of 35 millimeter slides, Addie developed a talk on "Women in Europe," comparing the roles of women in various countries we visited with those of women in the United States. I, too, put together several slide-assisted talks on German political issues and the status of Trieste. These went over well in presentations to Rotary Clubs and similar groups, but we encountered serious competition from newly purchased television sets in the homes of our friends.

A lot had changed in the interim. Many of our friends now owned television sets and were spending more time at home with their new electronic companion. The Korean war and the attendant Red scare spearheaded by Wisconsin's U.S. Senator Joe McCarthy were chilling debate and ushering in an age of suspicion. Troubling questions regarding the use of nuclear power and the exploding issue of race relations all provided the basis for impassioned discussions in many different forums, both on campus and in town. Students and faculty alike avidly read and debated ideological tracts like Clinton Rossiter's *Conservatism in America*, Arthur Ekirch's *The Decline of American Liberalism*, Russell Kirk's *A Program for Conservatives*, Alan Valentine's *The Age of Conformity*, and Louis Hartz's *The Liberal Tradition in America*.

In the midst of this ferment I weighed into the debate with a paper titled, "A Re-Assertion of Liberalism," which I presented at a student chapel and again at one of Colgate's weekly Friday afternoon faculty seminars. This talk prompted Professor Leo Rockwell, a senior faculty member and director of the Division of Language and Literature, to write to the *Colgate Maroon* that my title should have been "Liberalism Wachman 1956."

"Marvin Wachman," he wrote caustically, "did the campus a genuine service in his lecture unraveling the tangled skein of 'liberalism.' His historical approach was sound, and his analysis of the constituent attitudes excellent. But in the short time at his disposal, he could not fully develop a definition."[1]

---

[1] *Colgate Maroon*, March 28, 1956.

Professor Rockwell went on to appropriate some of my liberal concepts for conservatism. I in turn responded on the op-ed page of the *Maroon* by thanking him for agreeing "with the basic ideas and attitudes I tried to portray." But in answer to his basically conservative stance, I wrote that "a major element in the liberal position is dynamism, activism, or change – not change for the sake of change, but change because the condition of man always needs to be bettered. If conservatives today agree with the liberal position of twenty-five or one hundred years ago, this does not make them liberals at all, since the liberal has moved ahead to new positions.... Dr. Rockwell and I have been debating 'the truth' for ten years, and I trust we shall keep on doing exactly that."[2]

These liberal–conservative issues were further probed by a succession of guest lecturers whom I brought to campus in my function as director of the core course "American Ideals and Institutions." Overflowing crowds packed our large chapel to hear speakers like Thurgood Marshall (fresh from his success in arguing the *Brown* school segregation case before the U.S. Supreme Court), liberals like the economist John Kenneth Galbraith and the journalist Max Lerner, and conservatives like Clinton Rossiter and Russell Kirk. Those who read this book today – a time when conservative spokesmen like William Bennett and William Kristol routinely attract large audiences on college campuses – may be astonished to learn that in the 1950s it was difficult to entice conservatives to speak to college audiences, because they feared being booed or heckled. Kirk and Rossiter were the exceptions. In retrospect, it also amazes me now that we were able to book these outstanding speakers at minimal cost – as little as $50 or $100 per lecture, plus travel expenses. The only holdout was Kenneth Galbraith, who contended that his talk was worth at least two of anyone else's lectures, and rather than lose him we paid him $400 – twice our customary $200 maximum honorarium. In defense of this craven cave-in, I can attest that Galbraith certainly gave us our money's worth: He not only responded at length to our questions after his Chapel lecture to the student body but engaged a smaller group of students in discussion and debate for several hours afterward in the Student Union.

In the early '50s, I was offered a position with the Central Intelligence Agency (CIA). At that time, the CIA was concerned about the possibility that the French Communist Party might take control of the French government. The agency needed "France-watchers" to keep an eye on the situation. I spoke French, had spent time in France during the war, had studied European history, and was

---

[2] Ibid.

well recommended by one of my former students at Colgate, an army veteran whose father was a high-ranking official in the CIA.

I visited CIA headquarters in Washington and was impressed by the number of historians and political scientists I found working there. Some of them I had already met at the American Veterans Committee Convention in Des Moines in 1946; others I knew from history conventions. The salary offered by the CIA would have doubled my Colgate earnings. But I had serious reservations about accepting any position that would require almost complete secrecy on my part. I had become accustomed to, and very fond of, the academic life, in which few limits are placed on what can be disclosed and discussed. So despite my interest in the work that I would have done, I declined the invitation.

In the spring of 1956, I was promoted to full professor. I had spent the previous ten years climbing through the ranks as instructor, assistant professor, and associate professor. But this final promotion had been expected, and other news we received at the same time seemed much more important: Our adoption application had been approved, and a baby would soon join our family. On April 25, 1956, we picked up Lynn Alison Wachman at the Louise Wise Adoption Agency in New York City and flew home with her. Friends and neighbors trooped in daily to share our happiness. Our pride and joy was only two and a half months old, so we went through the usual rigors of frequent bottle feedings, diaper changes, and being awakened by wailing in the middle of the night.

About a year later, feeling that two children would be better than one for a rounded family, we contacted an adoption agency in Rochester, New York, and soon afterward welcomed Kathleen Marie, our second child, into our home. Kathie (who later changed her familiar name to Katie) was almost three when she came to live with us and had endured several very difficult years of being shuffled from one foster home to another.

With two children, we needed more space than our relatively small apartment offered. One of our friends, a retiring professor, offered to sell us his hundred-year-old home on University Avenue, and, with the aid of a 2 percent GI mortgage, we bought it. We hired a carpenter to renovate the kitchen and level the kitchen floor (which in the course of a century had sunk a full six inches at one end). Addie insisted on painting our new kitchen cabinets herself. I painted the study, and our faculty friends came over to help us paint the rest of the house. And just about the time when we were settled down in our renovated home, I received an opportunity to go overseas once again.

THREE

Exporting the American Idea:
The Salzburg Seminar

I N THE SPRING OF 1958 I RECEIVED an unexpected phone call from Dexter Perkins, a well-known specialist in the history of American foreign policy at the University of Rochester who had moved recently to Cornell. I had met Dr. Perkins while serving as an external examiner for Rochester's honors program. Perkins wore a second hat as president of the Salzburg Seminar in American Studies, a year-round postgraduate institution based in Austria that offered month-long courses to Europeans. Because he knew of my role as a founder of the New York State American Studies Association and as director of the American studies portion of the Colgate core program, he felt I would be a suitable assistant director for the Salzburg Seminar.

Perkins's call came at an opportune time. Only a few days before, I had remarked to Addie, "After twelve years of steady teaching, including summers, I'm getting bored. I'm certainly tired of grading blue books." So shortly after Perkins's call, on a beautiful April day, I drove to Ithaca to visit him. On the surface we were a study in contrasts: I was an athletic forty-year-old tennis player, and he was a paunchy, Dickensian sixty-year-old with a squeaky voice, a shock of white hair, and a hearty appetite (especially for rich desserts). But what sold me on him was his keen intellect and fine sense of humor. Over lunch we hit it off almost immediately, as he engaged me in vigorous debate about American studies, American politics, and U.S. foreign policy. Since I expressed a reluctance to accept the post of assistant director at Salzburg, he confided to me that the program's European director was leaving in the summer, and he was prepared to offer me that position if I could get a two-year leave from Colgate.

The salary was quite modest – $6,000 per year with no fringe benefits other than room and board for my family. But at that juncture in my life, this opportunity to recharge my batteries struck me as an offer I couldn't refuse. "If Colgate won't give me a two-year leave to take this job," I reasoned to Addie, "I'll resign and look for another teaching position when we come back from Europe." Happily, that wasn't necessary. President Case kindly offered the leave of absence (without pay) if I wished to take on this new assignment.

In retrospect, he understood that he couldn't force me to stay, and his best hope of keeping me on the Colgate faculty was to keep me happy. But he added: "I'm afraid you won't return to Colgate." I assured him that I had no intention of leaving Colgate; the European experience, I insisted, would be good for me and my family and would improve my teaching.

The following months were hectic. We completed the redecoration of our house, stored furniture in the attic and basement so that the professor replacing me could move in, and prepared for a new adventure. In July, we took a number of hurried trips and made many frantic long-distance telephone calls in order to obtain final adoption papers for Kathie and to secure passports covering all of us before our July 31 plane departure.

International travel in those propeller-plane days was not for the faint of heart, and certainly not for families. We departed from Syracuse on schedule, loaded down with suitcases, oddly assorted camera bags and briefcases, four coats, exuberant two-year-old Lynn kept in tow by a harness, and Kathie (not yet four), who was my responsibility. After two airplane and one helicopter ride (between New York City airports), the four overloaded Wachmans debarked in Frankfurt. It had been a seventeen-hour trip, including a plane change in New York and a refueling in Newfoundland, where our girls padded through the airport in pajamas, half asleep.

We arrived in Frankfurt just in time to hear a loudspeaker paging us; Ed Downie, a Colgate professor, had learned of our plans and was at the airport to welcome us and take us to lunch. After one more flight, to Munich, we were driven to Salzburg and our new home, which Kathie and Lynn immediately dubbed "Our Castle."

"Castle" was quite appropriate, as our home for the next two years was Schloss Leopoldskron, a baroque palace built in 1736 by the Archbishop of Salzburg, Leopold Firmian, at a picturesque site about a mile from the city center. You've probably seen it: It served as home of the Trapp family in the 1965 Julie Andrews musical, *The Sound of Music*. The Castle, with its four stories and twenty-foot and higher ceilings, overlooked carefully manicured formal English gardens and a small lake covered with water lilies and inhabited by noisy ducks and trumpeter swans. In the distance we could see a magnificent mountain, the Untersberg. Our family occupied a ground-floor apartment with three rooms and a bath, looking out on this storybook setting. The two assistant directors and their families lived on the upper floors, also with choice views.

When we arrived on the scene, the Castle was still recovering from the ravages of World War II. Some of its grandeur had been restored, but its living conditions were spartan; students slept in large, drafty dormitory-like rooms, and heating was often unpredictable. (The Schloss, as well as the neighboring building, the Meierhof, were ultimately purchased by the Salzburg Seminar, and recent visitors will testify to the superior work that has been done in making them comfortable for faculty and students.)

The Salzburg Seminar had been created in 1947 by an Austrian-born Harvard graduate student and two colleagues determined, in their words, "to create at least one small center in which young Europeans from all countries and of all political convictions, could meet for a month in concrete work under favorable living conditions ... and to lay the foundations for a possible permanent center of intellectual discussion in Europe."[1] They had perceived that postwar European students needed books and intellectual stimulation, and that American students could benefit from exchanges with Europeans. Also, the Europeans then were short on food, so Americans bearing provisions could help feed the Europeans' stomachs as well as their minds.

The faculty received no remuneration other than travel expenses; nevertheless, the very first session in 1947 included the anthropologist Margaret Mead; the Nobel Prize–winning economist Wassily Leontief; the Harvard professor of government Benjamin F. Wright, later president of Smith College; and the Harvard English professor F. O. Matthiessen. These names acted as a magnet for the U.S. Supreme Court justices, other Nobel laureates, university presidents, distinguished business and labor leaders, and prize-winning poets and novelists who subsequently taught there.

The first two Seminars were six-week summer sessions. After several years, the Seminar developed into a regular pattern of six four-week sessions per year, from January through mid-April and from June to mid-September.

During my tenure from 1958 to 1960, fifty to sixty fellows (that is, students) from nearly all Western European countries, plus the United States, participated in each session; their ages ranged from twenty-three to forty-five. (Some of the fellows in the higher-education sessions were a good bit older.) Their numbers included lawyers, judges, teachers, government officials, businessmen, artists and writers of all sorts, journalists, and graduate students. All lived in dormitories at the Schloss and ate with faculty and staff in a magnificent marble-floored dining room on the second floor, ten to a round table, replete with crystal chandeliers, ceiling paintings, and Archbishop Leopold Firmian staring down at the participants from his lofty twenty-five-foot painted portrait on one wall.

---

[1] Thomas J. Eliot and Lois J. Eliot, *The Salzburg Seminar* (Ipswich, Mass.: Ipswich Press, 1987), vii.

Some Eastern Europeans participated as fellows in the Seminar's first sessions. But as the Iron Curtain descended across Eastern Europe, the Soviets and their satellites refused to permit their citizens to participate in the Seminars at Salzburg. Yugoslavs attended into the 1950s, but when I arrived as director it was still a struggle to get Yugoslavs of the Seminar's choice rather than official Yugoslav government appointees. Poland was another matter. In 1959, it took me nine months just to get a visa to enter Poland to recruit fellows. This struggle is worth recounting, if only as a reminder of the paranoia of totalitarian states when confronted by simple free inquiry.

On the advice of the Ford Foundation in New York, I began my quest by writing to Dr. Julian Hochfeld, director of the Institute of International Relations, a Polish think tank in Warsaw. After making some inquiries, he informed me that no one in the Polish government wanted to take responsibility for officially authorizing a visa for me. He pragmatically suggested to officials he knew, "Just let them" – meaning Addie and me – "come in," without the specific approval of any government official. Evidently, they had thought that American studies were subversive and that I might be an editor (although my application labeled me an educator.)

Visas in hand, Addie and I flew to Warsaw via Vienna, not knowing how we would be received. Fortunately, Hochfeld had made it possible for me to interview a number of candidates at his institute. With Hochfeld's assistance, the help of an American studies professor at the University of Warsaw, and some suggestions from the U.S. Embassy, I was able to interview at the University of Warsaw. I spoke no Polish, but my French came in handy with some of the senior administrators, including the rector and several professors, who spoke no English. (They understood that English was a requirement for all Salzburg Seminar student candidates.)

I also interviewed some candidates at my hotel and in restaurants and cafés over coffee. These proved the most interesting. In such informal settings, the candidates felt free to talk about American history, literature, and politics. Although the senior people parroted the communist line, the young writers and scholars we met were very pro–West and eager to learn more about Western Europe and the United States.

Of more than a dozen I interviewed, I invited five to attend the Seminar; all accepted and were cleared. However, shortly before their sessions began, I received a cable from the Polish government stating that "for official reasons" they could not come to Salzburg. That was not an unusual occurrence in academic and government circles in Eastern Europe at that time. So you can imagine our surprise when one of the five invited Polish fellows, Henryk

Skolimowski, arrived in March 1960 for our session on "Art, Architecture and Music in America." He said he had been in London, claimed that he hadn't received word that the Polish government had canceled his clearance, and asked us to let him attend.

Of course we welcomed him, since in theory all applications were individual, not governmental or national. He turned out to be an excellent participant, freely contributing an Eastern European point of view to the classroom and informal evening discussions. He later taught at the University of Michigan and the University of Southern California and married an American fellow he had met in our art session. There were always some Poles who knew how to get around the strict regulations – precursors of the Polish Solidarity Movement of the 1980s that led to the downfall of the Soviet bloc in 1989.

Mornings at the Seminar were devoted to lectures, held in the beautiful Venetian Room, followed by twenty-minute discussion periods, which frequently became so heated that they stretched to as long as an hour. This was especially true when it came to subjects like foreign policy or race relations. Since the professors attended each other's lectures and frequently disagreed with their colleagues, the discussion periods were exciting, and exchanges often continued at the lunch and dinner tables.

I attended as many lectures as possible, so that I could participate in discussions and in the give-and-take during meals and in informal evening gatherings. Small seminars were held in the afternoon, and fellows selected the special area in which they wished to participate. Assignments were given regularly, and the Seminar's library of 14,000 volumes, plus periodicals and learned journals, was used extensively. Wives of the director and assistant directors served as our unpaid librarians. Just beyond our library was the beautiful Chinese Room whose walls were decorated with fine murals. It was used as a music and reading room, housing daily newspapers and over one hundred periodicals.

Our first session in August 1958 was titled, "American Literature and Criticism." The faculty included Louise Bogan, poet and critic for the *New Yorker*, and Carl Bridenbaugh, professor of American history at the University of California and former director of the Institute of American History and Culture in Williamsburg, Virginia. Carl was the only Salzburg faculty member whom I knew well; we had both lived at the University of Minnesota Faculty Club while teaching a summer session there in 1950. Other professors were the Columbia University English Professor Robert Gorham Davis, a writer and critic who had been published in the *New Yorker*, *Partisan Review*, *Encounter*, and *New York Times Book Review*; and Irving Howe, professor of English at

Brandeis, who wrote widely on literature and history and later became editor of *Dissent*.

For Addie and me, this was a lively and absorbing introduction to the Seminar. But in our second four-week session, titled "Races and Minorities in America," we really felt at home and participated actively in all programs. This time the faculty included John Hope Franklin, professor and chairman of the History Department at Brooklyn College – the first African American scholar to receive such an appointment. The session was held in the wake of Arkansas Governor Orville Faubus's attempt to prevent racial integration of public schools in Little Rock. Professor Franklin and I appeared together in several programs, one before an entirely Austrian group in which we presented a white and black perspective on race relations in our country. We agreed on all the facts concerning events in Arkansas, but I stressed the positive aspects of developments, given the sad history of race relations in the United States, while John Hope was more pessimistic.

These and other discussions generated a valuable byproduct: From observing them, the European fellows perceived the process of American professors disagreeing with each other and taking a critical stance toward American history and American contemporary society. This willingness to disagree, to be self-critical, and to listen to students' positions on any subject was an eye-opener for the Europeans in every session of the Salzburg Seminar. In Europe, by contrast, professors generally brooked no disagreement with their pronouncements. "We are simply astounded that professors will listen to what we have to say," one fellow from Heidelberg told me. "In the universities I have attended, the professor lectures, the students write down his comments and repeat them in any examination or paper which they are required to write."

Another eye-opener for the European fellows was the informal manner with which the American instructors and their wives mixed with each other and with all of the participants, in contrast to the formal and distant bearing of professors in their native lands. The fellows were amazed and most appreciative that an instructor like James Bryant Conant, former president of Harvard, who had been U.S. High Commissioner for Germany during its occupation and later U.S. ambassador to Germany, would often join them and other members of the faculty in the evening at a local *Gasthaus* for beer, raucous toasts, and a continuation of classroom discussion.

In almost any field one could name, other than the pure sciences, the fellows were future leaders of their countries. I know of no other situation where this kind of interchange could continue for a full four weeks during formal classes and seminars, as well as at meals and other informal gatherings. As you might expect, the close social and intellectual contacts among fellows – while skiing, mountain climbing, or taking weekend trips to Vienna – sometimes led to love, sex, and even marriage. In later years, when the Seminar's sessions were much shorter, that may have changed. But the Salzburg Seminar's basic conceptual structure – as a marvelous intellectual outpost for America in Europe – persists to this day. And it remains a coveted assignment for American professionals in many fields, whether professors or practitioners.

For some Salzburg faculty members, teaching in Europe posed special challenges. All the lectures and discussions were delivered in English, but English was only a second or third language for the great majority of fellows. So it was necessary to avoid colloquialisms. For instance, one instructor spoke of a successful presidential decision by saying, "He hit a home run with that edict," thereby confusing the fellows in his class who knew nothing of American baseball. In addition, it was necessary to enunciate as clearly as possible in order to respect the language adjustment that fellows had to make. In a few cases, I had to call a faculty member aside and explain these matters.

On the other hand, self-deprecating American-style humor was welcomed and relished. Seelye Bixler, president of Colby College, enlivened his classes with anecdotes like the one about the Swedish ambassador to the United States who received an honorary degree at an American college: "The citation was in Latin, and the ambassador carefully replied in excellent Latin, followed by remarks by the president, also in Latin. Then a member of the board of trustees whispered to a colleague, 'It's the first time I've ever heard the president speak Swedish!'" The fellows howled at such stories.

Then there was the question of using informal, American-style lectures, which assumed a basic knowledge of the subject discussed. For instance, Europeans in our economic sessions expressed great interest in U.S. antitrust legislation and antitrust cases. They could not understand the highly adversarial relationship between corporations and the U.S. government, given that large corporations also exacted favorable legislation and regulation from the Congress and the executive branch. When I mentioned this to Leland Hazard, a director of the Pittsburgh Plate Glass Company, he included in his lectures discussions of an antitrust case in which his company filled an entire floor of a hotel with its lawyers, and the Justice Department prosecutors filled another floor of the same hotel with an equal number of lawyers. When Logan Wilson, president of the University of Texas, explained the sensitivities in Texas after the beginnings of desegregation under the 1954 *Brown v. Board of Education* decision, he used examples of cases he had dealt with personally at the University of Texas. Real-life stories of this sort gave the fellows more of the flavor of U.S. legal practices than mere generalizations could have provided.

The openness and frankness of the faculty – specifically, how far they, as American citizens, could go in criticizing American practices and laws in a foreign country – was a constant issue at Salzburg. It was complicated by the erroneous suspicion held by many fellows (especially those from France) that the Salzburg Seminar was run by the U.S. government, possibly by the Central Intelligence Agency. To be sure, the Seminar did maintain friendly relations with the U.S. Information Service (USIS) and its libraries and offices around Europe (where we conducted some of our interviews with potential fellows), as well as with various U.S. embassies and consulates. The USIS, which employs native Europeans as librarians and for many other purposes, was especially helpful in identifying potential fellows to us. In fact, a number of USIS foreign employees attended the Salzburg Seminar as fellows themselves. So many of us on the Salzburg staff and faculty felt pressure to bend over backward to assert our independence.

My own impression is that the faculty members felt much less inhibited at the Salzburg Seminar than they would have felt while addressing an American audience back home in the States. On the other hand, if an instructor went too far in criticizing the United States, he or she could appear to the Europeans as unpatriotic – or, at least, as unappreciative of America's unique benefits. I believe that the Salzburg faculty walked this tightrope skillfully – discussing America's past and present faults as well as what our country was doing to correct them. As the sessions progressed, even the most skeptical fellows realized that the Seminar and its faculty were independent of any government influence. (In later years, the Salzburg Seminar has received financial assistance from the U.S. government – without giving up its independence, so far as I know.)

The city of Salzburg itself, Mozart's birthplace, provided a rich resource for our faculty and fellows alike, from the famous Salzburg Festival in the summer to concerts and musical presentations the rest of the year at the Mozarteum as well as at the eighteenth-century Mirabelle Castle, where one could listen to baroque music performed on the harpsichord and other antique instruments. There were the world-famous Salzburg Marionettes and the medieval play *Everyman* (*Jederman*) performed in the Cathedral (Dom) courtyard in the summer to throngs of tourists. At the Schloss, we danced polkas and waltzes played by Toby Rieser and his wonderful Salzburg folk music group. Students from the Oberlin College Music Conservatory, studying at the Mozarteum, often came to the Schloss to perform for us. And of course, there was the important (to me, at least) Salzburg Tennis Club, located across the Salzach River in a well-kept park, which fellows and faculty could use whenever they had free time. As in Trieste and Heidelberg in 1953, tennis was a great door-opener for me. The U.S. ambassador to Austria, Llewellyn Thompson, among many others, invited me to his home for dinner and tennis on his private court whenever I visited Vienna on Seminar business.

Our small daughters, Lynn and Kathie, attended a spotless model public kindergarten only a mile from the Schloss, where the principal, called Tante Anna, was marvelous with the children. Each day our *Kindermädchen*, Helga Fuchs, propped the girls in seats in front and in back of her on her bicycle and cycled them to school. There they were kept busy all day, learning Austrian songs, doing household chores, and buying and selling items in a make-believe grocery store. Before we knew it, they were thoroughly bilingual, and Lynn soon became the *Dolmetcher* (interpreter) whenever any English-speaking child visited their kindergarten. When Lynn received candy and stars in her notebook as a reward for performing this service, Kathie, who had declined the honor previously, decided that she, too, would like to be an interpreter.

Life at the Schloss was not always idyllic, of course: Living and working in such close quarters day and night inevitably produced tensions. A series of petty differences between assistant director Bill Cowan and Irma Kuchler, a long-time staff secretary, came to a head in December 1959 when Cowan exploded and demanded that Irma be fired or he would leave. Since everyone else worked well with Irma and supported her, and since Bill would not budge from his position, I accepted his resignation. But that was really the only serious staff conflict the Seminar experienced on my watch.

I feared it might be difficult to find a replacement for Bill on short notice, given the low pay scale and particularly since I was, at the time, about to leave for Scandinavia to recruit new fellows. Fortunately, however, the Seminar enjoyed a network of contacts with Americans working in Europe. Through the good efforts of Franz Wendt, director-general of the Nordic Council in Copenhagen, I managed to reach Norman Holly, an American who was then doing doctoral research in Denmark on the council, an intergovernmental agency for Scandinavian countries. Holly and I met for dinner at Wendt's home on my way to Helsinki. A week later, as I was en route back to Salzburg, he and his wife, Ruth, met me again during an early morning layover at the Copenhagen airport, where we sipped mushroom soup (the only food available at 5 A.M.) and got to know each other a little better. Like many Americans abroad, the Hollys were an adventurous couple, ready and eager to accept new challenges.

Returning to Salzburg, I serendipitously found that another of our assistant directors, Lou Garinger, had known Holly when both of them were graduate students at Harvard. After a bit more investigation, I phoned Holly on December 22 and offered him Cowan's vacant position. Holly, his wife, and their three-month-old son Tad (born in Copenhagen) arrived in Salzburg the day after Christmas.

Sometimes we administrators were called on to defuse the tensions that inevitably arise when people from diverse nationalities and cultures are thrown together. Some of our Italian and Finnish women fellows came close to blows about whether to close or open windows in the large, drafty dormitory-like bedroom during winter sessions. The Italians were certain they would contract pneumonia with open windows, while the Finns thought they would suffocate without fresh air.

But these conflicts weren't as difficult as you might expect. The Finnish ladies defused the conflict by performing a hilarious Saturday night skit about the "window issue" for the fellows, trotting about the stage in nightgowns and slippers. And while we fully expected friction between our Irish fellows and their English counterparts, our fears were unfounded: On neutral turf, removed from the poisoned atmosphere of their respective homelands, they got along quite well and rationally discussed the religious, political, and social issues dividing their peoples. "You know," I was told by John Kane, an ultra-nationalist Irish fellow who was a colonel in the Irish Army, "I never expected that living together in this old castle and debating issues with those Limeys would make me say that the English were O.K."

Not surprisingly, our German fellows tended to be defensive about their country's role in the war and the Holocaust. (The skinheads and other neo-reactionary groups that arose in the late twentieth century were then unknown in Europe.) Sometimes Addie and I felt like psychiatrists when young Germans visited our apartment late at night and, over a drink of weinbrand or slivovitz (brandies), talked about their difficulty in reconciling the fine traits of their parents with the same parents' membership in the generation that permitted Hitler to take over. "How could my father and mother sit by and allow all those terrible things to happen?" one young woman asked.

During my two-year sojourn in Salzburg I returned twice to the United States to raise funds and recruit faculty members. During the second trip – to Philadelphia, in 1960 – I contacted my old friends Kirk and Evelyn Petshek, who had been with me at Biarritz American University at the end of World War II, and also at Colgate. Kirk was now the economist for the City of

Philadelphia, and Evelyn was the assistant to Walter M. Phillips, executive director of the Delaware River Basin Advisory Committee. Phillips was a liberal patrician in the best sense of the phrase: a lifelong Philadelphian descended from signers of the Declaration of Independence and the ideologist of Philadelphia's post–World War II reform movement. He was also serving as chairman of the board of trustees at Lincoln University, a small black college an hour's drive from Philadelphia. Evelyn told me that Phillips had been looking for a new president for Lincoln. He had already approached Richard Wade, a history professor at the University of Rochester and an old tennis buddy of mine. Wade knew all about my credentials as a history professor and administrator at the Salzburg Seminar, as well as about my passionate interest in race relations. Wade, Evelyn said, had declined the offer but had recommended me for the position.

On my short visit to Philadelphia, I met with Phillips, who also arranged meetings with several other Lincoln University trustees and a get-acquainted trip to Lincoln's campus. Despite his laid-back, self-effacing personality, Phillips was the most persistent person I have known in my professional career. I was at first skeptical about my suitability for the job, but I was also excited by the challenge of doubling the enrollment and integrating (in reverse) a traditionally black institution. At the end of my visit, Phillips offered me the presidency, which included a substantial increase in my Colgate salary as well as a rent-free home on campus. But I turned down this generous offer, saying that I couldn't make such a decision while I was on leave from Colgate – an unpaid leave, to be sure, but I had made a commitment to return.

During our second year at Salzburg, two other universities sounded me out on my interest in a presidency and deanship, respectively. But since both schools were unwilling to wait until I returned from Salzburg, I didn't even consider them. I had not sought these positions, and after a year and a half away from teaching I was looking forward to resuming my career at Colgate, not to mention returning to the house we had worked so hard to renovate but had barely occupied.

Then, in the early summer of 1960, I had a visit at Salzburg from Walter Phillips's wife, Mary, and their son Frank. It seemed obvious that they had two purposes: to further look me over and to encourage my continued interest in the Lincoln University presidency. Phillips himself had sent me considerable material about Lincoln, and I had made inquiries of my own. Lincoln, I learned, had been founded in 1854 by John Miller Dickey, a "colonizationist" Presbyterian minister from nearby Oxford, Pennsylvania. Dickey did not belong to the Abolitionist Society. He loved his Negro neighbors but despaired of the possibility of achieving the complete abolition of slavery in the South or the equal treatment of blacks in his lifetime and beyond. Rather, he worked for compassion and to create educational opportunities for Negroes.

Rebuffed in his attempts to enroll prospective Negro students at his alma mater (Princeton) and other white colleges, Dickey created a college-level institution for Negroes, one of whose main aims was to train Negroes for service in Liberia. The college, originally known as Ashmun Collegiate Institute for Youth and Men of Color (for Reverend Jehudi Ashmun, agent of the American Colonization Society in Liberia), was renamed in 1866 in honor of the recently assassinated president who had emancipated blacks from slavery. Though modest in size – about four hundred full- and part-time students – Lincoln appeared to be central to the most important American challenges. Its roster of distinguished alumni – including Thurgood Marshall, then a U.S. Appeals Court judge and later the first black justice on the Supreme Court; the poet and playwright Langston Hughes; Kwame Nkrumah, the first president of Ghana after its independence; and Nigeria's first president, Nnamdi Azikiwe – testified to its impact on American and international life.

In many ways, Lincoln was a good fit and an ideal challenge for someone like me. But the issue of my race weighed upon me. Although Lincoln's acting president and his predecessor were white, the previous regularly elected president, Horace Mann Bond, had served as Lincoln's first African American president from 1945 to 1957. By 1960, blacks were increasingly taking over leadership of their own institutions. Replacing an illustrious black role model like Horace Bond with yet another white president struck me as a step backward.

In any case, when we Wachmans returned to Colgate University in September 1960, after twenty-five months in Europe, the last thing on our minds was another change. As we pulled into the driveway, it was a thrill to have friends run over to greet us and neighborhood children troop in with our coats, hats, and luggage, helping to unload our Volkswagen. At the end of two hours, even our furniture had been moved down from the attic and put into place by wonderful friends. Then we began the slow unpacking of trunks and gradual resettling. We were happy to be home and fully expected to settle down permanently in our house in Hamilton.

But barely a month later, Walter Phillips asked me to meet with him as well as with several Lincoln trustees and alumni in New York City. The board members waiting for me constituted a who's who of America's black elite. They included Thurgood Marshall; United Nations Undersecretary Ralph Bunche; and Dr. George Cannon, secretary of the NAACP Legal Defense Fund.

I was also introduced to Wayne Fredericks, a Ford Foundation executive who soon after served in the State Department under President Kennedy, and other important white board members.

Phillips took me to meet Marshall and Bunche in Bunche's office. Since I had hosted Marshall as a speaker at Colgate and had met and talked with Bunche when he visited the Salzburg Seminar, they were not strangers to me. Still, it was a heady experience for a young college professor to discuss his professional future with such awesome men.

"I have some serious reservations about being a white President at the oldest Negro college in the country," I told them.

"Look," Marshall replied, "we have conducted a national search for a new president, irrespective of race. You can be certain we've considered that issue very carefully; your race will not be an impediment as president of Lincoln University." Bunche echoed the sentiment. "We are entering a new era of race relations in this country, and Lincoln will be part of that era," he insisted. "You will be accepted and respected as president."

Other Lincoln trustees, faculty members, and black leaders were encouraging me to accept the position. Only one of them – Thomas L. Farmer, a white Washington attorney and Lincoln trustee – planted a seed of doubt in my mind. While he hoped I would accept the Lincoln post, he wondered aloud about my ability to switch from an elite, predominantly white campus (Colgate) and a sophisticated international institution (Salzburg Seminar) to an all-black, grass-roots setting. Moving to Lincoln, he made me realize, would substantially change my professional and social life. But that wasn't enough to deter me. If I took the job and it didn't work out, I told myself, I could always go back to teaching – which had been my first love in any case.

After the New York visit, Phillips persuaded Addie and me to fly to Philadelphia and drive down to Lincoln with him. He wanted Addie to see the campus, the home in which we would live, and the community of which we would become a part. Thus, early in December 1960, we found ourselves, still somewhat reluctantly, visiting that small college in southeastern Pennsylvania.

Although we were much impressed, we continued to waver. I enjoyed my teaching at Colgate, and we loved our home and our friends in Hamilton. What's more, precisely at that time Colgate's dean of the faculty announced his retirement, and President Case offered me his position. One by one, faculty friends dropped in, urging us to remain at Colgate. Some argued that Lincoln's presidency would be an impossible situation to take on at a very difficult time and that I would secure a much better future for myself if I remained at Colgate.

One of them was Jim Storing, a political science professor (and later dean of the faculty), with whom I'd been working on a textbook. "Stay here and let's grow old together," were his words to me.

On the other hand, one of my closest Colgate colleagues said, "Gosh, Marv, if you're going to leave teaching to be the dean at Colgate, you might as well take this position as president." Others remarked what a great opportunity Lincoln would offer me to do something about solving the race problem rather than just talking or teaching about it. And so my faculty friends framed my dilemma: I could choose security and familiarity at Colgate, or I could plunge into the front lines of a national issue at Lincoln. But I could not do both.

Ultimately, of course, I took my own counsel. As far as American race relations were concerned, I told myself, "It's time to put up or shut up." Phillips, sensing that I was leaning Lincoln's way, flew up to Hamilton in sub-zero weather one Sunday in January 1961 to persuade us to accept. Later that month, we did. And in retrospect, it was Phillips's persistence that tipped the scales in Lincoln's favor.

As I left Colgate for Lincoln, I had only a vague idea of what I was getting into. I did not realize that for some years in the 1960s I would be the only white president of a black college. Nor was I aware that I would be the only Jewish president of a non–Jewish American college or university. And I was taking office at the very moment when black patience, after a century of second-class treatment, had finally run out. America's great Civil Rights Movement was under way, and I would be in the thick of it – just as I had hoped.

Confronting the Race Problem:
Lincoln University

S UNDAY, JUNE 6, 1961, WAS A HOT and humid day in southeastern Pennsylvania. Rain was coming down in the morning and the big issue of the day at Lincoln University was whether to hold that afternoon's commencement exercises outdoors or indoors. To be on the safe side in case it showered again, a committee opted to squeeze several thousand people into the college's cramped, old, wooden, un–air-conditioned gymnasium.

The commencement speaker was Martin Luther King Jr., the charismatic young preacher and civil rights leader who had launched the modern Civil Rights Movement by leading the Montgomery bus boycott in 1955. I was impressed that Lincoln's acting president – the school's librarian, Donald Yelton – and his colleagues had been able to secure Dr. King as commencement speaker, since his national reputation was growing tremendously and he was much in demand. Dr. King was immaculately dressed, polite and friendly to everyone, including me. As the incoming white president of America's oldest black college, I felt apprehensive about subjecting such a prominent figure to less-than-perfect conditions.

But King thrived on precisely such opportunities to transform squalor into splendor. His stirring address that afternoon, titled "The American Dream," delivered in a stentorian voice, brought a message of hope, non-violence, and freedom, and overcame the stifling heat and the audience's discomfort.

"It is not enough to struggle for the new society," King told the audience. "We must make the psychological adjustment required to live in that new society. This is true of white people, and it is true of Negro people. Psychological adjustment will save white people from going into the new age with old vestiges of prejudice and attitudes of white supremacy. It will save the Negro from seeking to substitute one tyranny for another. . . . God is not interested merely in the freedom of black men and brown men and yellow men. God is interested in the freedom of the whole human race and in the creation of a society where all men can live together as brothers, where every man will respect the dignity and the worth of human personality."[1]

Those 1961 commencement exercises and the King speech reinforced my feeling that I had made the right decision in coming to Lincoln. (Addie and I were so impressed by King's address that later that year we sent a transcript of it to all alumni and friends of Lincoln University as our initial Christmas and holiday greeting.) I had arrived on Lincoln's rural campus with deeply held views about the malevolent nature of racial segregation and discrimination. I had no doubt that the United States was on its way to an era of cooperation between blacks and whites in which non-white minorities would finally be incorporated into the nation's mainstream. Lincoln and Morehouse College in Atlanta were the nation's best-known black male colleges. In the nineteenth and first half of the twentieth centuries, their alumni accounted for more African American physicians than all the other institutions in the United States. Their traditional curricula, heavy in classics and the sciences, offered good training for professional schools in medicine, law, dentistry, social work, and education. So I imagined that, as Lincoln's president, I could contribute in some small way to the resolution of what the sociologist Gunnar Myrdal, as far back as 1944, had called "An American Dilemma."

The difficulty of this task was abruptly brought home to me during our very first week at Lincoln, in July 1961. Addie and I were invited to the home of Professor H. Alfred Farrell, head of the English Department and a Lincoln alumnus, to meet his wife and three children over dinner. Our daughters, Kathie and Lynn, were then seven and five. They had met very few black people in their young lives at Hamilton and Salzburg, had never made a comment about skin color, and seemed to be fitting into the evening party very well. But suddenly, while we were sipping coffee with our dessert, five-year-old Lynn started skipping around the table, tapping the back of each chair while singing, "Eeeny meeny miney mo, catch a —— by the toe." Was that critical word "tiger," as Addie had taught her, or "nigger," as some white schoolchildren recited it? Addie and I couldn't be sure; we were too busy raising the level of our own voices in a desperate attempt to drown Lynn out. It was an awkward moment for all four of the adults in that room – and a microcosm of the sort of challenges I was about to face.

---

[1] A full transcription of the commencement address "The American Dream," delivered by Martin Luther King Jr. on June 6, 1961, appeared in a special enclosure in holiday greetings to Lincoln alumni and friends in December 1961. It was then published in full again upon King's death in *Lincoln University Bulletin*, Spring 1968.

Lynn at least had a valid excuse for her insensitive behavior: She was only five years old. But in our first weeks at Lincoln I was dismayed to discover my own ignorance of the nuances of remarks and gestures that might offend black sensitivities. Whenever my office door was closed, for example, my secretary, Grace J. Frankowsky, who was black and the wife of a Lincoln math professor, always knocked before entering. On several such occasions I responded, "Yes ma'am," in my Midwestern Milwaukee twang. One morning I was startled to find on my desk her strongly worded complaint that I was using a Southern accent, which she said was "very humiliating" to her. I immediately discussed my salutations with Mrs. Frankowsky to make certain I didn't offend her or anyone else in the future.

Notwithstanding Lincoln's illustrious past, by 1960 a completely segregated black college north of the Mason-Dixon Line was considered an anachronism by integrationists, particularly following the *Brown* Supreme Court decision of 1954. Some critics questioned the need for a black college, arguing that Lincoln should go out of business or be absorbed by Pennsylvania State University. And since Lincoln had appointed two acting presidents during the previous four years, there was considerable doubt among those critics that the institution could survive.

Chairman Walter Phillips and I, as well as most of Lincoln's trustees, wanted to bring in white students, Hispanics, and other minorities in order to grow the university and better prepare our black students for life in a multiracial world. Admitting women students was important for the same reason. Historically, Lincoln had been completely male, except for several daughters of faculty in recent years. But should Lincoln integrate racially and become coeducational at the same time?

Trustee George Leader, the former governor of Pennsylvania, argued that "the best education brings both sexes together, and the only way to get a larger and academically better student body is to enroll young women in reasonable numbers." But another board member, who seemed to be very progressive about the racial integration issue, felt adamantly that coeducation was going too far, and he subsequently resigned over that issue. Eventually, the trustees left this decision up to the new president.

I personally felt strongly that Lincoln should enroll a larger student body and begin to bring in non-black students and women, while carefully monitoring the effects of such changes on the students and the university. My view was that Lincoln should remain predominantly black but open to all, with a sensible mix of men and women.

My first confrontation with the new age of student protest occurred in the early spring of our first year at Lincoln. Early one morning in March 1962 I arrived at my office to find that a mimeographed sheet had been circulated around the campus, exhorting students to demonstrate their disapproval of an alleged discriminatory hiring policy "in the administration." The sheet referred specifically to the dismissal, "on less than 24 hours notice for dubious reasons," of a Negro clerical worker in the president's office, "and her replacement by an inexperienced young white woman."

Actually, the dismissed employee was a part-time probational worker who could not take dictation in any form, was unable to do filing, and had been given considerable notice and time to find another position. In early February she had discussed her work with Mrs. Frankowsky, apologized that she had not been more helpful, and expressed no surprise that she could not be kept on. The flyer was the result of pent-up feelings among some students regarding hiring policies of the business office (the business manager, Austin Scott, was an efficient black graduate of the University of Chicago, but some students called the Administration Building "Uncle Austin's Cabin"). It might also have represented an oblique protest to the hiring of a white man as Lincoln's president.

Since the protest sheet had been mimeographed on Student Government Association (SGA) stationery, I called to my office the SGA's president, Amnon Ashe, to discuss its statements and to ask him why he hadn't checked the facts before distributing the leaflet. At first, Ashe wanted to take credit for the entire document. But after I raised some questions about its accuracy, he maintained that it had been produced by a committee and he hadn't been able to stop it.

"You are not personally to blame," he told me, "but I haven't seen enough change on the campus thus far to satisfy me." He would have preferred a Negro president, he added, and specifically mentioned the Reverend James H. Robinson, class of 1935, who was then director of Operation Crossroads Africa, a private organization similar to the Peace Corps.

Later that morning, at my invitation, a student "committee of four," including Ashe, came to my office for further discussion. They were careful to absolve me from the charge of discrimination. "You are bearing the brunt of a great deal that has happened over a long period of time," remarked Calvin Morris, who later became a distinguished minister, activist, and scholar.

It became apparent to me that these students were engaged in something of an internal power struggle and were trying to show who was aggressive and who was not. Two of the students, in fact, had been rivals for the presidency of the student National Association for the Advancement of Colored People

(NAACP) organization, and the defeated candidate was claiming that the election had been rigged and the results should be thrown out. The factual errors in the distributed leaflet were glossed over and the general question of long-time grievances was emphasized. The students were frustrated with Lincoln's enrollment decline, with four years of acting presidents, and with the dilapidated condition of campus buildings. The students helpfully suggested that the university contact the Urban League and the Federal Employment Practices Commission offices in nearby Chester and Philadelphia in order to broaden the pool of clerical employees, since most of the qualified people living around Lincoln happened to be white. But their general tone suggested that some kind of student revolt was brewing.

We talked for about an hour and a half, by which time about 150 students were demonstrating outside, many of them with signs protesting college policies. I instinctively felt that in a small college, where rumors spread quickly, it was critical to correct false statements promptly and to demonstrate that the university would not tolerate discrimination of any kind. So around 11:45 A.M. I spontaneously joined the committee and went outside to speak to the demonstrators. Standing on a wooden bench in the middle of the ring of students – the better to make eye contact with them – I told them, "You have every right to pass out pamphlets and leaflets, and to try to seek answers to difficult questions in the area of race relations as well as others. I have only two reservations about the leaflet: first, that it contains so many errors and was not first checked as to facts, and second, that no regular grievance procedure was followed and no one had contacted me at all before sending out the leaflet."

For the next half hour or so I answered many questions and tried to clarify the nondiscrimination policies that existed in the hiring of all employees at the university – that is, we couldn't discriminate in favor of black job applicants any more than we could discriminate against them. And I reiterated what I had said to students on many other occasions: "If you wish to have a program about some issue, you should organize, pick out a date, come to me, and we will get the appropriate officials to discuss the matter publicly or privately with you." I suggested a meeting of the entire student body within two days in order to clarify "student and administrative questions of interest to both groups."

After the rally was over, I continued my dialogue with individual students, walking over to the chapel with some, then to the dormitories and the refectory with others. Most of them seemed sobered by my response to the incident, and many said they felt resentful at having been "taken in" by the leaflet's false statements about "dismissal without cause."

Nevertheless, the next day the student newspaper, the *Lincolnian*, printed an inflammatory article that leveled similar charges against the administration all over again. I immediately called a meeting of student leaders for the next morning – a Friday – in my office, as well as a meeting for all students and faculty on Friday evening. The evening gathering drew almost the entire campus to our chapel, a building that also served as the school's auditorium. There, deep-seated complaints were given a chance to air, and the discussion continued afterward in small, impromptu gatherings all over campus: in the Guest House, in the dining hall, and in dormitories.

The end result, I think, was widespread recognition by administrators and students alike that from this point on, at least, our institution would not resist criticism but, instead, would open itself fully to any discussion of campus issues.

This episode was deemed serious enough that a distinguished alumnus and trustee, Reverend E. Luther Cunningham, chairman of Philadelphia's Civil Service Commission, had appeared before the Friday evening University Assembly to field students' questions and comments. In the process he further persuaded students of the administration's sincere interest in their concerns. This was one of several times during the 1960s when I found it very helpful to involve a member of the Board of Trustees in settling an outbreak of student unrest. In this way, the trustees demonstrated that they were human beings concerned about student opinion. And the black trustees enjoyed a credibility with the students that I lacked, in part because of my skin color and in part because I was so new to the campus.

This experience taught me not to make too many changes too quickly in an institution with a long and honorable history until I was thoroughly accepted and had made crystal clear the direction in which I was taking the university. At the dawn of the civil rights revolution, I was receiving a practical education in black politics that few other whites had acquired. The personal approach to student protest is more difficult at a large university, of course, but it is a lesson I tried to carry with me after I moved on from Lincoln to the much larger Temple University.

Another incident that first year made an indelible impression on me. The town of Oxford stood about three miles from campus and only four miles from the Maryland border and the Mason-Dixon Line, which historically divided America's North and South. In the very center of town, at a busy corner near most of the town's businesses and banks, stood the Oxford Hotel. This hotel offered the most convenient lodging for visitors to Lincoln, but its owner was notoriously racist. Although he claimed he did not discriminate, Negroes couldn't get rooms in his hotel. (Kwame Nkrumah, a Lincoln student in the late 1930s who became president of Ghana in 1960, later recalled entering the Oxford Hotel through the back door, since no blacks could enter through the front.)

Given that background, some Lincoln students and teachers decided to test the owner's practices while I was away from campus. First, a student tried to register for a room and was told that the hotel was completely booked. Minutes later, a young white instructor, Richard Winchester (the first faculty member I had hired), registered and was given a room. When Dick returned to the organizing group with his room key – the necessary evidence – they cheered and immediately launched a demonstration outside the hotel. Local businessmen were by no means eager to give in to the student protest, but they were even less eager to have their businesses disrupted. Under pressure from these merchants, the owner backed down and agreed to open his hotel to blacks.

When I returned to Lincoln and learned this good news, I congratulated Dick Winchester during a faculty meeting. He gave me a sheepish smile in response, apparently because he hadn't consulted me in advance. "I was afraid you'd disagree with me," he explained years later, "and I was very relieved and gratified by your comments. After all, I was a brand-new, young faculty member without tenure."

Shortly after this episode, State Senator John H. Ware III – an Oxford civic leader and Lincoln trustee who I am certain was the major influence on the hotel owner – approached me about joining the local Rotary Club, which held its meetings at the Oxford Hotel. John was a generous and sensitive human being who believed in action rather than giving speeches about equality and justice (as his quiet influence in settling the Oxford Hotel affair attested). Oxford's Rotary Club, like the hotel, was then an all-white affair. So I told John I couldn't join the Rotary Club unless it accepted one or two Negroes at the same time. For starters, I helpfully suggested Austin Scott, Lincoln's vice president for business and finance, and Leroy D. Johnson, dean of the faculty.

The club approved my recommendation; the three of us became members simultaneously; and the Oxford Club continued to meet in the Oxford Hotel. In this manner the hotel opened not only its rooms but its dining facilities, as well, to Negroes. Both Austin Scott and Leroy Johnson, incidentally, eventually became presidents of the Oxford Rotary Club, as did other blacks from Lincoln later on.

But my earliest responsibilities as Lincoln's president in 1961–62 had little to do with solving America's race problem. They were focused on a more mundane matter. At the time I took over, Lincoln had received a "show cause" order from the Middle States Commission on Higher Education. This meant that the university bore the burden of showing why it was worthy of accreditation. The commission was critical of the condition of Lincoln's facilities, its financial instability, its academic offerings (especially in very small departments like teacher education), and its lack of a permanent president since 1957. The commission also criticized Lincoln's ambitious plans to expand course work in African studies, given the university's small enrollment and its need to strengthen existing departments. The "show cause" decree was one step away from complete loss of accreditation, which would have severely hampered our ability to attract students.

My arrival had solved the presidential shortage, of course. And by the time I arrived, some campus buildings were already under renovation, and I pushed for more, as well as for the construction of a new science building and a student center. But my most urgent task, I felt, was to bolster the academic program by bringing in capable faculty. Brimming with confidence and energy, and lacking enough experience to know better, I plunged eagerly into the task. I was so busy that first year – recruiting faculty, raising funds, and trying to increase enrollment by visiting high schools and churches, meeting with alumni, and giving speeches – that I had no time to worry. Occasionally I would wake up at night thinking, "What if the commission withdraws our accreditation? That would be a disaster." But I couldn't even admit that possibility. "We'll just have to work much harder to get it back!" I replied to myself.

We made substantial progress on almost all fronts that year. As a result, at the beginning of the 1962 fall semester the commission restored our full accreditation, and everyone at Lincoln breathed a sigh of relief.

After a full ten months on the job, I was officially inaugurated as president on Founder's Day, April 29, 1962. It is interesting that colleges and universities usually delay the inauguration of a new chief executive for some time – anywhere between three months to a year. Someone quipped that the reason for the delay is to make sure that the new president survives at least a year. This is one of those jokes that cut close to the truth. At Delaware Valley College in Doylestown, Pennsylvania, one president-elect changed his mind and withdrew even after his inaugural invitations had been prepared. Duquesne University once announced James Gallagher's appointment as president before Gallagher had agreed to a contract; he, too, withdrew even before taking the job. And as I write this, all academia is abuzz over the Boston University trustees' vote of "no confidence" in president-elect Daniel S. Goldin just a week before he was to take office. (Boston University bought out his five-year contract for $1.8 million.)

Having committed myself to remain at Lincoln for at least three to five years, I had no intention of resigning before or after any inauguration, regardless of difficulties or crises with which I had to deal. But I did agree that a formal inauguration was a good idea in order to show the outside world that Lincoln was indeed alive and kicking.

My inauguration took place on a glorious spring Sunday, so prematurely warm that I had to dig out a summer suit for the occasion. One hundred and nineteen delegates of universities, colleges, and educational societies participated in the inaugural activities. Many were college presidents, and more than a few were my former colleagues and friends from Colgate and other institutions. Our reunions that weekend inevitably rekindled memories of long-ago mileposts in my career. Three of my sisters and my brother came from California for the events, nostalgically recalling our life together in Milwaukee and my undergraduate college experience. So the ceremony was more than a public relations gesture for Lincoln; it also served to remind me of how far I had come and to reinforce my determination to make good in this new role.

The keynote speaker at the formal inauguration was my old mentor, tennis partner, and friend President Everett Needham Case of Colgate. He generously recalled his struggle with Walter Phillips for my services. "From the fierce competition that ensued," he told the audience, "Lincoln University has emerged as victor, and the president of Colgate is here today to acknowledge defeat with as much grace as he can muster."

William Hallock Johnson, Lincoln's president emeritus and, at age ninety-six, Princeton University's oldest living alumnus, compared my inauguration to one at his alma mater when Woodrow Wilson adopted the motto, "Princeton in the Nation's Service." He advised me to use as the Lincoln motto, "Lincoln in the service of the world."

My inaugural address tackled head-on the issue of racial integration at Lincoln. The decision to open Lincoln's doors to all races, I said, was "a deliberate and considered decision and it took a great deal of courage." Lincoln would take its cue, I said, not from "the preconceived notions of the past in regard to questions of class, status, and race," but from the *Brown v. Board of Education* decision of 1954 and from Martin Luther King's position that integration, not separation, was the key to achieving the American dream.

"I only hope," I concluded, "that all of us who have the opportunity to teach and to hold posts in administration here will have the fortitude and the wisdom to guide this great small college along the path dictated by its tradition and the current needs of humanity."

The speakers at the inaugural luncheon afterward were noteworthy – to my mind, at least – for their ability to spotlight characteristics of mine other than my race. Amnon V. Ashe, the student government leader who had led the campus protest early in March, compared my inauguration to that of John F. Kennedy the previous year as evidence that youth was taking over in America. Leroy D. Johnson, dean of the college, commented on the faculty's pleasure in having their president come "from the ranks of the teaching profession" – in contrast, he implied, with the Presbyterian ministers who had led Lincoln through most of its history. "We have for ten months observed you at work in the daily performance of your task," he said. "We have observed you at play, building morale on the tennis and basketball courts, and we have witnessed not only your own wholesome impact on the campus and surrounding community but that of Mrs. Wachman and your children, as well."

Even a college president needs this sort of moral support now and then. But, of course, shortly after these ceremonies I was brought back to earth by preparations for my first Lincoln commencement program. As a student and professor, I had not been enamored of the commencement ritual; I underestimated its emotional significance for many students and their families. Now, as a college president, I viewed commencements more the way parents view them: as the culmination of an important period in the lives of young people, and as evidence of what a university is trying to accomplish.

For the 1962 commencement speaker I sought out David Riesman, the distinguished Harvard social sciences professor and well-known author of *The Lonely Crowd*, his influential study of post–World War II American society. I had used Riesman's books and articles in the courses I taught, and we had corresponded during my teaching years. When I called him, he agreed to come if he could spend two days with the graduating students in order to learn their interests and their plans for the future. Addie and I were happy to host Riesman in our home on the campus and join in his discussions with students before commencement day. His address was no canned speech but a thoughtful reflection based on these discussions with Lincoln students. He spoke of "the American missionary enterprise of the past century," of which "Lincoln University is an outgrowth," in its broader context of spiritual as well as technical assistance to downtrodden people. But he also warned against the "unintended consequences of trying to do good abroad or at home." (The logical heir to this missionary tradition cited by Riesman – President Kennedy's newly created Peace Corps – actually interested very few Lincoln graduates.)

Riesman also spent a good deal of time discussing what he called the "uniquely American" concept of freedom: "It is the freedom of personal relations: the freedom of women and children . . . , the freedom to talk back to the professor . . . , the freedom to talk back to the boss; the kind of informality, sincerity and candor which seem to me characteristic of the best young Americans today."

In the summer of 1962, Addie and I were invited to participate in a two-week Harvard University seminar for new college presidents. Because I represented a small institution with meager resources, I attended at no cost to me or to Lincoln. We drove to Cambridge, Massachusetts; lived in facilities at the Harvard School of Business; and participated most actively in a program that almost exclusively used the "case method" as the basis for all discussion.

For the first time, the Harvard Seminar included several "veteran" presidents so that we freshmen presidents could benefit from their insights. We learned later that some of the older presidents didn't always practice what they preached. For instance, one of our cases dealt with an actual situation in which the editor of a student newspaper had been extremely critical and aggressive and, in the mind of the college president, absolutely obnoxious. William Tolley, chancellor of Syracuse University, explained to all of us that one should never let a student journalist get under his skin because that would be entirely counterproductive. Lo and behold, that fall headlines in the Syracuse newspaper reported that this same Bill Tolley had chased his student editor down the street with his cane because of comments the youth had written about him. Belatedly, Tolley bequeathed us a practical lesson: Matching theory and practice is often easier said than done.

The case studies (actual cases with the names of the institutions and individuals disguised) were most helpful in assisting a new college president like me to deal with all the complex academic, financial, governance, and student issues I would face over the following thirty years. None of the cases, however, covered the kind of racial situations to which I had already been exposed at Lincoln and with which I would have to deal again at Temple University. In that respect, I suppose, I was something of a pioneer. But within a few short years other college presidents would face similar racial challenges.

On my arrival at Lincoln in 1961, it seemed to me that students and faculty engaged in relatively little open debate about public policy issues. Coming from Colgate, where students and faculty argued constantly about domestic and international questions, I encouraged lectures, seminars, and debates on these matters as a vital part of students' education and civic training. I hadn't realized that in the 1920s and '30s, Lincoln produced excellent debating teams that had competed successfully against Oxford, Harvard, and other institutions. Lincoln even had a slang term – "rabbler" – to refer to a type of student who could get up anywhere, particularly on one of the large stones in front of Cresson Hall, and argue any point. Thurgood Marshall had been notorious among his fellow students for practicing his oratory on those stones and starring on the debating team. Perhaps World War II and the subsequent emphasis on action, through sit-ins and demonstrations, rendered debating irrelevant. In any case, by the '60s the notion of argument and discussion had become timely again, and Lincoln had a rich tradition on which to draw.

Over a few weeks during the winter months of 1961–62, I invited several speakers to the campus, and suggested others to various groups for their invitation. Alumnus Franklin Williams, special assistant to the director of the Peace Corps and adviser to the United Nations, spoke on new opportunities for Negroes; another speaker addressed educational matters in Russia; still another, issues in Berlin. John Ferguson, a Lincoln trustee and director of the Institute of Public Administration at Penn State, spoke on "An Alternative to Dirty Politics," and Lawrence Reddick, a Coppin State University historian who had been to India with Martin Luther King Jr., discussed nonviolent resistance and boycotts. In addition, alumnus Clarence Mitchell Jr., director of the NAACP's Washington office, spoke on the debates in Washington on foreign and domestic issues.

At the height of the Cuban missile crisis in the fall of 1962, the leaders of the Student Government Association organized a public debate in the University Chapel on the appropriateness of America's response. Philip Eyrich, a young political science instructor, and Henry Cornwell, a senior professor of psychology, agreed to defend President Kennedy's policies; Maxwell Primack, an assistant professor of philosophy, and Richard Winchester, the history instructor who "integrated" the Oxford Hotel, represented opposition to the government's policies. The chapel was packed, and an especially large contingent from the surrounding villages attended. The debate, conducted in an even-handed and focused manner, was one of the best I have ever heard.

At the close of the meeting, Addie and I were talking with the four debaters and their wives at the front of the chapel auditorium when Dr. David Rothman, a physician from Oxford, stormed down the aisle from the back of the chapel with his wife and several others. They elbowed their way into our circle and, waving their fingers at me, insisted that I fire Winchester and Primack for failing to defend the president of the United States at a time of national crisis. "Lincoln is supported with our tax dollars," they said, "and should not have people like that teaching our students!"

As the exchange grew heated, I invited all those still arguing – some fifteen to twenty people – to our house next door to continue the discussion. Addie and I adjourned to the kitchen to get some refreshments for our guests and give the debaters a chance to engage in small talk and cool down. When we returned with wine and cheese, I spoke informally to the group on the role of a university in a free society, stating very forcefully that a university must encourage free speech and debate on subjects such as our relations with the Soviet Union and Cuba, and that academic freedom meant that professors could debate issues without fear of retribution as long as they taught their classes without injecting personal political views or irrelevancies into them.

The physician and other townspeople calmed down. Well after midnight, after further talk and consumption of wine and cheese, the meeting ended on a friendly note with no bloodshed. The Rothmans – good people and active liberal Democrats in a conservative Republican town – reluctantly allowed that while Primack and Winchester were young and misled, it was all right if they kept their jobs at Lincoln. I had spoken from my heart, and quite spontaneously, and was surprised later when faculty members expressed gratitude to me for my role in this affair. "Marv, that was one of your finest moments as president," Dick Winchester said later.

To be sure, these types of discussions and relationships were uniquely possible at a small college like Lincoln, where the president lived right in the middle of the campus. But the larger lesson I learned from these experiences can be applied to a campus of any size: Conflict and confrontation should be welcomed, not lamented, because they provide the "teachable moments" that are the very essence of education at its best.

A similar moment occurred one fine morning in the mid-1960s. Addie and I awoke to find the campus – even the trees in front of our home – plastered with flyers proclaiming, "LINCOLN, NO – DOUGLASS, YES!" Many students felt the university should be named for Frederick Douglass, a black hero of the antislavery movement, rather than for the white Abe Lincoln. That afternoon on her way home from school, my ten-year-old daughter Lynn, who happened to be studying Abraham Lincoln at the time, ripped the flyers off every tree and pole she could find. Suddenly she was surrounded by students and confronted by the angry student leader, Tony Monteiro. When he rebuked her threateningly, Lynn shouted, "You can call it Metamorphosis or Nebuchadnezzar University, but it will still be Lincoln!"

Everyone in the crowd laughed at the intensity of her feelings, which immediately defused the potentially explosive moment. We never did change the university's name – but conscious of the importance of black models for the students, we named a fine new dormitory for Frederick Douglass, and plans were made for a Langston Hughes Library. Much later, Thurgood Marshall Hall, a combined residential, dining, and study complex, arose on the campus of what is still Lincoln University.

I should add here that an excess of teachable moments can be counterproductive. Certainly there were times when I deemed it wiser to defuse a crisis than to confront it. Early one morning in the winter of 1967–68, for example, I arrived at the entrance of the Administration Building and found it completely soaked with some kind of red dye. Signs on the building stated that the administration had blood on its hands, somehow related to the Vietnam war and police suppression of racial protests in cities around the country and the casualties resulting from both. I immediately called Bill Osborne, our superintendent of buildings and grounds, and explained what had happened. "Bill," I said urgently, "get some of your men down here to take care of this quickly." Before any students appeared on their way to classes, the red dye had been washed down, and the signs had disappeared. It was the last we heard of that particular issue.

In the summer of 1962, I began a practice of meeting with Lincoln alumni groups. The early meetings found many alumni unhappy for a number of reasons. Lincoln's Theological Seminary, which graduated hundreds of ministers over many years, had been shut down in 1959 due to low enrollment and a shortage of funds. Football had been eliminated for lack of players after the 1960 season, just in time for me to reap the criticism for that deed. The alumni, like alumni everywhere, tended to romanticize the glorious past of both the divinity school (at the turn of the twentieth century) and Lincoln's great football teams (mostly in the 1920s and '30s, before white colleges began recruiting black athletes). Also, the annual Lincoln–Howard football game had been a great social and athletic event that brought blacks together in great numbers in Washington, D.C., and Philadelphia.

Furthermore, Lincoln's decision to become integrated and coeducational undercut Lincoln's proud tradition as one of just two male-only black colleges in America (the other was Morehouse, in Atlanta). And all these complaints, in alumni eyes, were aggravated by the fact that Lincoln at this moment had selected a white Jewish president to replace the only black president in its history.

E. Washington Rhodes, an alumnus and publisher of the *Philadelphia Tribune*, the area's African American newspaper, was especially critical of Lincoln and, perhaps (although he did not say so directly), of me. On the whole, though, throughout the 1960s I was received with open arms and with great hospitality and generosity by the alumni, from Philadelphia to New York, Boston, Baltimore, Chicago, Washington, Atlanta, Los Angeles, and elsewhere. As time went on, I was pleased to find myself accepted as "a Lincoln man."

On one trip into the South, I traveled with H. Alfred Farrell, the Lincoln English professor who doubled as director of alumni relations. Often, when Al and I walked into a restaurant together, we would be eyed from the top down to see what we were up to. In Atlanta, we were able to get rooms only in a black-owned and -operated hotel. Elsewhere on this trip we had to stay almost exclusively at the homes of alumni. In a few alumni homes, we slept together in double beds, since no other arrangements were available. One of those happened to be in Lynchburg, Virginia, where we stayed at the home of Robert Walter "Whirlwind" Johnson, a practicing physician from the class of 1924, football running back, and tennis visionary who had discovered and trained Arthur Ashe on a court next to Johnson's home.

But segregation also thrived in the North – even the enlightened liberal academic North – as I discovered in April 1963 when I was asked to address a meeting sponsored by the Association of Urban Universities and the Johnson Foundation. The participants at the acclaimed Frank Lloyd Wright house Wingspread in Racine, Wisconsin, included college presidents, administrators, faculty doing research on urban problems, and select government and foundation officials. I was the only representative of a black college invited – and, of course, I wasn't black. In other words, at a conference called to discuss urban issues, there wasn't one representative of an urban black institution. (There were no women at the conference, either.)

The topic of my talk was "The Culturally Deprived: Have Urban Universities Discharged Their Responsibilities?" (later published under the title, "Why Don't More Negroes Attend College?"). To increase black enrollment in higher education, I said, would require a smorgasbord solution: desegregation, more opportunities, positive counseling, upgrading of standards at all schools where Negroes are involved, and "convincing the Negro that he may be of service to the broader community and that this community wants him – and not just as a show piece."

In effect I charged that universities and other American institutions had failed to discharge their responsibility to see to it that Negroes were offered opportunities to work, study, and become full-fledged American citizens. My speech provoked more discussion than any of the other subjects addressed at the conference. Several university and government representatives objected that they were themselves sons of immigrants who had managed to adjust to American society and its economy without complaining about their situation. I responded by suggesting that deep-seated prejudice based on skin color, and the drastic historical impact of slavery and legal segregation, made the Negro experience in America different from that that of white immigrants, whereupon one participant took off with a digression on the excesses of New York's black Congressman Adam Clayton Powell Jr., citing him as an example of what blacks would do if given power "too soon."

For many years, Powell had been the most prominent civil rights leader in the United States. He was not totally representative of America's Negro population, and some of the things he was alleged to have done were not much different from activities of some of his white congressional colleagues. Powell had been elected to Congress from Harlem in 1944 as one of only two black members. In 1963, there were five, but as chairman of the House Committee on Education and Labor, he was the most powerful, and the most vocal. He would not let white America forget the wide gap between the American creed of freedom and equality and the actual condition of American Negroes.

The defensiveness of the urban universities' representatives should not have surprised me, since it reflected the attitude of a very large segment of the population. Powell flaunted his power and appeared arrogant to his friends as well as to his enemies; also, he was involved in questionable use of committee funds and in personal affairs with both black and white women while still a married man. All of this made it difficult to defend him. For instance, when charged with improper use of funds on trips to Europe, especially Paris, "with two young ladies," he quickly replied: "two staff members." He also said to critical reporters, "I wish to state very emphatically that I will always do just what every other Congressman and committee chairman has done and is doing and will do."[2] This kind of statement, accusing his colleagues of hypocrisy, did not endear him to them and, later in the 1960s, led to his exclusion from the House of Representatives for two years.

---

[2] Charles V. Hamilton, *Adam Clayton Powell, Jr.* (New York: Macmillan, 1991), 408–409. See this volume for the entire political saga of Powell.

By the time of the historic civil rights march on Washington on August 28, 1963, Powell had been superseded as a black leader by Martin Luther King Jr., as well as by Roy Wilkins (NAACP), Whitney Young (Urban League), and James Farmer (Congress of Racial Equality). And it was King who delivered his stirring "I Have a Dream" speech to close the all-day rally.

Early in my tenure at Lincoln, much of my time (and the faculty's) was involved in revising the curriculum. For instance, I stressed the importance of changing the focus of teaching religion so that it was truly comparative. To that end, I brought to the campus a number of philosophers who, with the religion faculty, developed a respectable program that combined religion and philosophy. A newly instituted January studies program, conducted between the fall and spring semesters, gave students an opportunity to specialize in a field related to their major or to be assigned necessary remedial work. I also helped create an exchange program with nearby colleges like Haverford and Franklin and Marshall so that Lincoln students could go off-campus to take specialized courses in Russian history or economics. We were able to reciprocate by offering courses in the fields of African and African American studies, which few white colleges then offered.

During my tenure, Lincoln established one of the very few black studies programs available. I felt that knowing something about one's own heritage is as important as studying the Classics and Shakespeare. If young Negroes could study their own history and cultural background, I reasoned, they would identify with Lincoln and all of its programs in a more serious manner.

This idea was controversial at the time, and some of our finest alumni felt it was a mistake, believing that an emphasis on black studies would detract from students' preparation for the professions, as well as for work and life in a largely white America. Joseph C. Waddy, a federal judge in Washington, D.C., and a Lincoln trustee, was one alumnus who questioned the launching of this program. I carefully explained to Joe that "teaching African American subjects along with African studies does not have to detract from our offering traditionally oriented Lincoln curricula, but it could very well encourage students' interest in other academic work." In time, our arguments apparently satisfied Judge Waddy and other critics. Today, African and African American studies are accepted, as they should be, along with other specialized programs like women's studies, Jewish studies, and even computer and technology studies.

By the mid-1960s, the federal government was involved in higher education as never before – aiding colleges in the construction of new buildings for the growing student population (caused by the post–World War II baby boom), providing loans and grants to students for tuition and other fees, and sponsoring research and teaching programs. All of these initiatives were part of President Johnson's Great Society Program. Another was the Federal Developing Institutions Program, designed to help predominantly black colleges and other institutions catering to low-income and culturally deprived groups. With the assistance of funds received from this program, President Robert Goheen of Princeton University and I led our respective faculties to cooperate in developing a jointly beneficial project.

Princeton provided us with instructors for several courses previously unavailable at Lincoln, like advanced sociology and anthropology courses, as well as opportunities for Lincoln faculty to engage in postgraduate studies (in some cases leading to the Ph.D.) at Princeton. "This is the first time I have seen the Princeton faculty cooperate in this way on *any* academic project," Bob told me at the time. I believe it was the spirit of those times that caused the research-oriented Princeton faculty to agree to rearrange their schedules so they could leave the Princeton campus one day a week and teach at Lincoln.

None of these ambitious new programs could succeed if Lincoln students were unprepared to take advantage of them. To assure that, we had to supplement Lincoln's standard curriculum and counseling efforts. Like other black colleges, Lincoln admitted many students with poor academic backgrounds and low scholastic aptitude test scores. Taking this into consideration, we initiated a major effort to provide remedial work for those who most needed it. I made the rounds of all of the sympathetic New York-based foundations. In the process I persuaded Fred Crossland, a particularly supportive officer at the Carnegie Foundation, to visit Lincoln to get a better idea of the challenges we faced.

The highlight of Crossland's visit turned out to be lunch at our home with several professors who would be active in the programs. Addie fixed such a good lunch, featuring her specialty, coquille St. Jacques, and the dining-table exchange was so animated that we received a three-year grant from Carnegie. This grant enabled us to establish a program called LIFT (for Lincoln Incoming Freshmen Talent) for high-risk students. It required these students to spend the summer before their freshman year in closely monitored study at Lincoln; they also received special mentoring during the academic year and, if necessary, for an extra summer at the end of the year. It was a successful program, as reflected by improved test scores and graduation rates for this group of students.

To be sure, the most carefully designed curricula and other academic programs can't be effective with students without a quality faculty. Lincoln in those days was a virtually all-black student body taught by a substantially white faculty. So our challenge was twofold: to raise the level of the faculty while simultaneously increasing the number of black faculty faces.

At that time, Colonel Francis Miller, a special assistant in the U.S. State Department, was assigned to deal with the problem of African students who had been displaced from South Africa, Southwest Africa (now Namibia), Angola, and Mozambique because of their antiapartheid or anticolonial activities. A well-placed Lincoln trustee, Wayne Fredericks of the Ford Foundation, arranged for me to drive down to Washington to meet with Colonel Miller to discuss possible solutions. Miller and I subsequently agreed that Lincoln would accept some two dozen of these refugees to start with, orient them to American education, and start them on their way toward earning college degrees.

Having secured a contract with the State Department to develop this "Southern Africa Student Program," I was surprised to discover that the potential program administrators – that is, scholars most interested and qualified on the subject of southern Africa – were white. Black scholars who specialized in Africa were few and far between in the early 1960s. But our new program developed swiftly, so that Lincoln enrolled about one hundred southern African students by 1965, and others were sent to Syracuse University. As a result of their fine American education, a number of students in these programs rose to become very high officials in their developing countries. Although Lincoln's Southern Africa Program was initially led by white faculty, within three years it was directed and managed by Negroes. We had addressed the need by hiring additional black faculty and administrators.

At the same time, I embarked on a personal quest to recruit respected scholars of all races. Over the years, Lincoln's faculty had excelled in producing graduates who became leaders in their communities and in Africa. However, in 1961 the faculty was very small, and we were expanding the student body, as well as choices for students, so that they would be prepared for a new and changed society in which blacks would be able to enter fields previously closed to them. As a result, I spent a great deal of my time recruiting new faculty, at both the instructor and professorial level.

One of my first appointments was John Marcum, already a well-known and published Africanist who had worked with me at Colgate for several years. Later in the '60s, I brought in Herman Brautigam, who had just retired as chairman of Colgate's Philosophy and Religion Department, to aid in developing our newly reorganized combined Philosophy and Religion

Department. I persuaded Charles V. Hamilton, who had been working in the South on voter registration, to come to Lincoln to teach political science. This took some arm-twisting, since Hamilton, a black Ph.D. from the University of Chicago, was on the verge of accepting an offer from a New York State university. I was forced to appeal to his sense of obligation to black students. To this day Hamilton is remembered by Lincoln alumni as a great teacher who brought his practical political experience in Chicago and in the South into the classroom. After he left Lincoln, he occupied an endowed chair at Columbia University for many years.

Another black teacher I cajoled into coming to Lincoln was James Farmer, who, as national director of CORE, was one of the most important leaders of the Civil Rights Movement. Farmer lacked Hamilton's academic credentials but was an intelligent and articulate lecturer with unparalleled real-life experience. Farmer was widely reported to be headed for Washington to run a national literacy program for adults that he had developed and that President Johnson had endorsed. But Farmer had lost favor with President Johnson after he refused to suspend CORE's civil rights demonstrations during the 1964 presidential election and then publicly opposed Johnson's war in Vietnam. As one consequence, Johnson sabotaged the very literacy program he had initially strongly supported, and this embarrassment caused Farmer to resign his leadership post at CORE.[3] This chain of events was a setback for Farmer and the cause of literacy, but it also represented an opportunity for Lincoln.

When I learned of Farmer's difficulty and his newly unemployed status, I visited him and his wife, Lula, in their lower Manhattan high-rise apartment. As we sat around their kitchen table, I described the fine opportunity Jim would have to teach our students and transmit his inspiring message. I convinced him to come to Lincoln and teach two courses each semester, part time, for several years.

In his autobiography, Farmer wrote about his Lincoln experience:

> It was a chance to interact with young black minds at a time when those minds were volatile and angry. Stokely Carmichael had just made "black power" a part of the American vocabulary. The words had galvanized black youth all over the country. The bristling Afro hair-style became a badge of pride, dashikis the attire of ethnicity, the up-raised clenched fist the salute, the medallion on the chain around the neck

---

3 James Farmer, *Lay Bare the Heart: An Autobiography of the Civil Rights Movement* (Fort Worth, Tex.: Texas Christian University Press, 1998), esp. 293–305, for details of this entire episode.

an insignia of blackness. Concealed firearms were almost as common as wallets. Humor was taboo. Jokes were viewed as a betrayal and smiles as demonstration of weakness. . . . [T]he seminars at Lincoln were slam-bang affairs with unfettered give and take.[4]

Philip Foner, who published and lectured a great deal on Negro and labor history, had been red-baited, blacklisted, and hounded out of the teaching profession since the 1940s due to accusations that he was a communist or fellow traveler. But Professor Thomas Jones, chairman of Lincoln's History Department, satisfied me that Foner's scholarship and teaching were widely respected. Among other publications, Foner had written a major biography of Frederick Douglass. Foner was reluctant to leave New York City because of his commitments there. While on a fund-raising trip to New York, I met Dr. Foner in my hotel and induced him to come to Lincoln. In this matter, as in so many matters, the deal-maker was a little thing: I personally offered to purchase half of his Metropolitan Opera season subscription. (Since I already traveled to New York regularly on fund-raising business, it was relatively simple to organize my trips around the opera season for the next two years.) Foner proved to be an outstanding professor and a popular teacher of black subjects, even though he was white. He remained at Lincoln long after I had left and didn't retire until he turned seventy.

Marshall Fishwick, a distinguished art and U.S. history professor, was directing a foundation in nearby Wilmington, Delaware, and agreed to teach part time, and later full time, at Lincoln. He developed an excellent sequence of courses in art and art history. Bernard Harleston, a professor of psychology who had graduated from Howard University and received a Ph.D. from the University of Rochester, was a professor and administrator at Tufts University. I heard him speak at a conference at Howard University, met with him afterward, and persuaded him to visit Lincoln. He was appointed professor of psychology and provost during my last years at Lincoln; later, he served as president of the City College of New York.

Many other senior and junior faculty members, both black and white, came to Lincoln during my presidency, and almost all of them were interviewed and hired by me personally. They were kindred spirits in the sense that they saw Lincoln's role as I did, so my sales pitch to them was relatively easy. Such close involvement by a president in both academic programs and selection of faculty would be very unusual in a larger institution. As a former professor, I had come to Lincoln with the notion that I would not only be the

---

4 Ibid., 306–307.

administrator and fund raiser but the academic leader, as well; that was one of the things that excited me about the challenge of Lincoln. I agreed with the essence of the argument of Harold W. Dodds, president emeritus of Princeton University, who maintained in his 1962 book *The Academic President – Educator or Caretaker?* that a college president could be an effective educational leader as well as an administrator. America's best college and university presidents (with some notable exceptions), I would argue, have been former professors and scholars; they are the leaders most likely to understand and be comfortable with a university culture.

By and large, Lincoln's growing student body seemed pleased with the curricular developments, as well as with the addition of many fine instructors and professors. At the beginning of my tenure, students showed little apparent interest in emphasizing their African roots. Those who did were sometimes derided as "home boys." This was true even though Lincoln had been founded in 1854 to prepare ministers for service in Liberia, and despite Lincoln's long history of enrolling Africans like Nkrumah and Azikiwe, who later became leaders of their countries.

However, this attitude changed quickly as more African students came to Lincoln in addition to those in the Southern Africa Student Program. Also, I managed to secure a Peace Corps training program for Liberia, the first of seven such programs conducted at Lincoln in the 1960s. As the black consciousness movement developed nationwide around 1963, it wasn't long before students developed a strong interest in African studies and black studies. This was the age, as James Farmer noted, when the "Afro" hairstyle became popular, along with the wearing of dashikis and African beads. At Lincoln, perhaps an example of the temper of the times was the fact that, even though the student body was largely black, students felt it necessary to organize a separate black students' association.

This development of black consciousness and black nationalism – what the Harvard psychiatrist Alvin Poussaint characterized as "black rage" – completely changed the nation's racial climate. I felt the 1960s were revolutionary years for race relations precisely because a great deal of progress was being made in trying to bring American institutions in line with our national rhetoric about freedom, equality, and opportunity. I agree with those who have argued that true revolutions only occur after substantial progress already has been made toward reaching the revolutionaries' goals – the so-called revolution of rising expectations. Lincoln was in the forefront of this revolution.

At the beginning of each semester at Lincoln, I addressed the entire student body – at first in the chapel and later, as enrollment grew, in the larger but more rickety old gymnasium. As I look back over these talks, I realize that each one stressed the problems and challenges of the past and present but was, perhaps naively, optimistic about the future. In September 1963, for example, my address was entitled "The Third American Revolution." The events of the civil rights revolution, I argued in that talk, "represent a further development of the first American Revolution which included the struggle for independence from Great Britain. They represent a direct outcome of the Civil War and its aftermath, which constitute the second American Revolution; and they include deep and lasting changes in the political, economic and social institutions and beliefs of this country."

In another semester opening talk, I spoke of a future America "which is diverse, but more unified than ever before, because it has finally dared to grant a great section of its population full and equal rights and opportunities." In yet another, I attacked equally the notions of white segregation and black separatism: "I cannot believe that any large portion of the people of the United States wishes the empty and separate existence of apartheid, and will follow the empty rantings of individuals on the right or the left in this great age of revolution."

As enrollment grew, the proportion of whites in the freshman class grew substantially (although many whites were part-time students or students who transferred after one or two years). In the late 1960s, the total student enrollment broke down at one time as 60 percent black American, 20 percent foreign (mostly African), and 20 percent white American. The faculty changed over the years from white and Protestant to almost equally balanced between white and black, with Protestantism, Catholicism, Judaism, and other religions very much in evidence.

(One unanticipated byproduct of our increased African enrollment occurred when Malcolm X, the controversial black Muslim leader, gave an impassioned speech at Lincoln, surrounded on stage by an array of bodyguards called the Fruit of Islam. Malcolm was charming to me and everyone else, but he committed a substantial faux pas when he praised the African nation of Malawi and its president, Hastings Banda, as models for Africa and for black Americans. Malcolm's black American audiences elsewhere may have accepted this rhetoric without question, but the African students in our audience looked upon Banda as an Uncle Tom and a dictator – the worst example for Malcolm to have mentioned. Still, they failed to challenge him directly on this point – a triumph, perhaps, of good manners over the quest for truth.)

But, of course, achieving balance among various racial and religious groups is no guarantee that the groups will mingle or even get along. For that reason Addie and I made a conscious effort to assure that every social function of any size at Lincoln reflected the composition of an interracial faculty and staff. One black professor complained about this practice, seeing it as conspiratorial. I replied that we were openly and consciously trying to bring some balance to the institution and I assumed that he agreed with what we were doing. After a lengthy debate, he finally conceded, "O.K., I guess you're doing the right thing."

For much the same reason, Addie and I went out of our way to attend all sorts of religious activities, including funerals and memorial services, which were often followed by receptions, lunches, or dinners. Since religion appeared to play such a central role in African American life, I felt it was especially important to attend black services, where I was frequently asked to speak, often without advance notice. I was also invited to give sermons at black and white churches, from the Oxford area to Philadelphia, Harrisburg, Baltimore, New York, and even Los Angeles, and I accepted whenever I could. This was not always easy: Although I was uplifted by the great choirs and powerful sermons in many black churches, as well as by the prayers and speeches, the services sometimes lasted two and a half to three hours. At Philadelphia Corinthian Baptist Church, the emotion generated by the various choirs inspired me to give what I felt was the best speech of my life, even though I was the last speaker in a service that seemed to go on forever. In all these sermons I drew on historical material from my professorial days to stress the importance of a heterogeneous society where all men and women are treated equally. (At Jewish synagogues and before Jewish groups, I often emphasized how brotherhood and self-interest are inextricably linked and emphasized that all minorities, including the Jews, were benefiting from the Civil Rights Movement.)

In those heady days when civil rights seemed to be every American's first priority, I could never be sure what new face might find its way to Lincoln's campus. Early in 1964 I received a call from the head of the United States–South Africa Leader Exchange Program (USSALEP), who asked me whether Lincoln would host a visit by South Africa's deputy minister of Bantu education, a white Afrikaner official of an apartheid state – the very antithesis of black aspirations. I was told that the minister wanted to observe how a black institution in the process of integrating with whites conducted its programs.

This would be the equivalent of inviting a minister of Nazi Germany to a predominantly Jewish American campus in the late 1930s. Nevertheless, I accepted immediately, asking only for several days' advance notice so that I could prepare the campus community – especially our South African students – for his visit.

As it happened, the minister and his wife arrived one fine spring day just before lunch with no notice whatsoever. I could hardly turn them away. (I assumed that the head of USSALEP had simply forgotten to call me.) I took them to lunch with several faculty in the faculty dining room, located in the Student Union building. Somehow, our South African students learned of their arrival and managed to mount signs (visible in the dining room) objecting to their presence. Given the strong feelings of the students in opposition to *any* South African officials, no one knew exactly what would happen if our visitors went out on the campus. I asked the director of our African Center, Professor Richard Stevens, to drive them around the campus and the surrounding area while I met with the students in the student union building to make certain that nothing calamitous would occur.

The students held a raucous meeting. Some shouted angrily that the minister should be kicked off the campus. Others – genuinely curious about what he would say in a black American school where there were many refugees from South Africa – shouted back, "Let him speak." We hastily arranged a meeting in the chapel so students could engage the minister in discussion after he gave a talk about South African education. He was ingenuous enough to expect that Lincoln's black students – and even those from South Africa – would accept his rationalization of apartheid.

To my amazement, the South African students listened to his talk in a fairly polite fashion, although one or two could not resist shouting corrections to his description of the alleged effectiveness of black schooling in South Africa. The discussion that followed proved a great education for the American students, as well as a rare chance for the South African students to debate with the minister – an opportunity they would never have had in their own country. The deputy minister of Bantu education learned a lot, too – for instance, that black South Africans abhorred being described as "Bantu." The bigger winner that day, of course, was the cause of free speech.

My family and I encountered no anti-Semitism on the Lincoln campus and saw little evidence of it elsewhere, except when the Ku Klux Klan from Maryland occasionally crossed the state line into southeastern Pennsylvania, speaking to crowds that gathered on some farmer's land near the border. Although their harassment was directed mainly at blacks, they frequently included Jews in their rantings. Away from Lincoln's campus, anti-Semitism was rising.

On one occasion during my Lincoln tenure I shared the podium with Clarence Mitchell Jr., the Washington director of the NAACP, at a large alumni-sponsored gathering in Washington. What Thurgood Marshall was to the courts, Mitchell was to Congress: He had lobbied so persistently for civil rights legislation that he was often dubbed "the 101st Senator." On this occasion Mitchell warned his predominantly black audience of a new bigotry he saw developing in the Negro community – a development he said he noted with great sadness, since "we have fought too long ourselves against bigotry aimed at Negroes for us to tolerate it in our midst against any other group." He was referring specifically to the growth of anti-Semitism in the 1960s. Looking back at that period myself from a vantage point of more than thirty years, it is clear that anti-Semitism was indeed developing among blacks, and Mitchell was one of the first to notice it.

The business of recruiting commencement speakers and honorary degree recipients, like the business of recruiting faculty and students, was often a matter of finding the key to each individual's heart. Gunnar Myrdal, the Swedish author of the groundbreaking study *An American Dilemma*, was very busy on a visit to Washington when I approached him there to ask him to address our 1964 commencement exercises. He agreed to come if I would present him with a divinity degree rather than one of the more traditional honorary degrees. He felt that *An American Dilemma* was a work of morality and ethics and wanted a doctor of divinity degree to ratify that notion. I agreed to his request but wondered how it would be received by our religion faculty and by the many genuine ministers among our alumni. No one raised a question about it.

I was surprised to discover that a number of ministers (none of whom received honorary degrees from Lincoln) were willing to pay as much as $10,000 to receive an honorary doctor of divinity degree. One popular Philadelphia minister, a Lincoln Seminary graduate, approached me with such an offer. I carefully and respectfully explained our procedures, which precluded any quid pro quo monetary gifts, and he did not pursue the matter further.

One of the honorary degrees we conferred went (in absentia) to Violette de Mazia, director of education and keeper of Albert Barnes's flame at the Barnes Foundation. That foundation had been established in the 1920s in Lower Merion, a near suburb of Philadelphia, as an endowed school for adults to study French Impressionist paintings of Renoir, Degas, Matisse, Lautrec, Van

Gogh, Cezanne, and many others. Old masters like Titian, El Greco, Delacroix, and Corot were also included, as were works of many other European and American painters. In addition, Chinese, Persian, Greek, Egyptian, and American Indian art was shown, as was a collection of primitive African sculpture.

The institution's founder, Dr. Albert Barnes, was a physician and pharmacist who had made a fortune from Argyrol, a patent medicine promoted as a cure-all for many ailments. He had used his wealth and interest to personally study and collect art in France and elsewhere. At first he was ridiculed by the U.S. art establishment for his predilection for Impressionists. He tried to work with the University of Pennsylvania and with the Philadelphia Museum of Art and had intended to turn over control of the collection to the university if it was willing to use his Deweyan, progressive methods of teaching. He became alienated from the University of Pennsylvania and from the Philadelphia Museum and others in the art establishment because of their failure to respect his collection and his art-instruction ideas. But by the time of his death in 1951 it was clear that he was a visionary – albeit a cantankerous one – whose tastes in art were ahead of his time. By the 1960s, his collection was considered so valuable and important that lawsuits had required the main Barnes Foundation building to be opened for viewing by the public on weekends, even though the Barnes Foundation had not been founded as a museum: Albert Barnes had specifically organized it as an educational institution, with a John Dewey philosophy behind its teaching methods – not as a museum.

Barnes's artistic interests included African sculpture, and there were many pieces in his collection. He also admired the work of Horace Pippin, a Negro artist from nearby West Chester, Pennsylvania. As a result, he decided – perhaps as a form of revenge against conservative museums and the University of Pennsylvania – to turn over control of his foundation, including the now acclaimed collection, to Lincoln University to manage after he and his wife died. Whether Barnes was motivated by alienation from Philadelphia's white society or by his reputed friendship with Horace Mann Bond, then Lincoln's president, Barnes appears to have believed that a Negro institution could carry out his will as well as, or better than, a white one.

In the late '60s an opening on the Barnes Foundation's five-person board led to our selection of the first Lincoln-appointed Barnes board member, Dr. George D. Cannon. Dr. Cannon had taken two years of instruction at the Barnes Foundation and concurred with Barnes's philosophy. He had also recently become chairman of Lincoln's trustees. As the other trustees designated by Albert Barnes (including Mrs. Barnes) died, Lincoln replaced them, one by one, so that by the late 1980s Lincoln-designated trustees constituted a majority of the Barnes Foundation board. The linking of the Barnes Foundation to Lincoln was considered a most significant tie for Lincoln, and an honorary degree for Violette de Mazia, director of education at Barnes, was deemed quite appropriate. Lincoln's art professors, from J. Newton Hill (the first Lincoln person to know Albert Barnes before World War II and, coincidentally, Lincoln's first black professor) to those in the 1960s, were thrilled to have a relationship that could benefit their students. At that time, all of the Barnes trustees were preoccupied with honoring the terms of Albert Barnes's will – that is, maintaining the foundation as a school rather than a museum. Only toward the end of the 1990s, as the Barnes Foundation, under the leadership of Richard Glanton, sought a larger audience and staggered under the cost of renovations and protracted lawsuits, did it occur to anyone that such a connection might be more of a burden to Lincoln than an asset.

Every college president spends a good deal of time on the road, raising funds, promoting the school, and maintaining ties with the school's various constituencies. At Lincoln this obligation included two six-week trips to Africa, in 1965 and 1968. We found Lincoln alumni living almost everywhere we went in Africa, particularly in Nigeria, Liberia, and Ghana, and they welcomed us with great cordiality and hospitality, as did heads of state and other prominent individuals. Our sponsoring agencies, the U. S. State Department and the U. S. Information Agency, were delighted to send visitors like us who would have access to high-level officials almost everywhere on the continent.

For example, Tom Mboya, a youthful-looking high official in Kenya who was not a Lincoln alumnus but had a relative studying at Lincoln, was happy to receive me for a lengthy interview. He had organized the Mboya student airlift, which sent Kenyan youth to the United States and elsewhere to prepare them for leadership roles in that newly independent nation. Our discussion ranged over the challenges and opportunities facing these students.

President Moise Tshombe of Zaire, who had no connection with Lincoln at all and was very difficult to see, also graciously granted me more than an hour of his time after personally escorting me into his office ahead of dozens of others – mostly job seekers or favor seekers – who were waiting to see him. He, too, was anxious to discuss education for the young people of the former Belgian Congo, as well as to converse about the future of Africa. I found Tshombe a handsome and pleasant man whose appearance and manner contrasted strongly with the picture of him painted by the foreign press as a power-hungry Machiavellian schemer.

Our finest receptions in 1965 came from Kwame Nkrumah and Nnamdi Azikiwe, presidents of Ghana and Nigeria, respectively. Both received us with great generosity and hospitality and organized dinners and receptions so that Lincoln alumni from West Africa could meet with us. Azikiwe – or "Zik," as he was called – was a 1930 Lincoln graduate who influenced many West African and Gold Coast young men to seek their education in the United States, and particularly at Lincoln; Nkrumah himself had been one of those young men. Zik was a Christian Ibo from the eastern section of Nigeria, but he had worked with Nigeria's northern Muslim tribes, as well as with the Yoruba of West Africa, to unite an independent Nigeria at the close of the colonial period. His statesmanship and diplomatic skills were very much in evidence as we met a variety of Nigerians in festivities arranged especially for us.

One of his cabinet members, Commerce Minister K. O. Mbadiwe, had attended Lincoln as a student and visited with us when he came to the United States with a group of Nigerian dancers heralding the inauguration of Nigerian Airlines. His party for us in Lagos was attended by white and black business leaders, and he was at his jovial best in introducing one or another of these businessmen as "tycoons." The businessmen seemed to take no offense at all at his jocular comments and engaged us in conversation about economic opportunities in the Nigerian nation.

Sadly, when we returned to Africa in 1968 under the same auspices, both Azikiwe and Mbadiwe were out of office because of a civil war in Nigeria, and we were unable to spend any time there.

Kwame Nkrumah, the founder of modern Ghana, was widely considered the George Washington of the twentieth-century African revolution, since Ghana was the first African colony to gain independence. His ties to America and to Lincoln were rich and extensive: He had received his bachelor of arts in philosophy from Lincoln in 1939 and his bachelor of theology degree from Lincoln's Seminary in 1942. He also received a master of arts degree in philosophy from the University of Pennsylvania in 1943 and taught at Lincoln while working on a Ph.D. at Penn from 1943 to 1945. Nevertheless, it was difficult to get an appointment to see him, and not only because attempts had been made on his life.

By the time of our arrival, Nkrumah had become a leader of the unaligned Third World nations that resisted Western domination and Western-style capitalism. He was an advocate of African socialism, a variety of Marxism designed to fit the needs of the new sub-Saharan states. Although a number of African Americans, including several graduates of Lincoln University, had taken up citizenship and residence in Ghana upon Nkrumah's ascendance to the presidency in 1960, he was not friendly to the United States. The State Department's efforts to get me an audience with him during my projected visit to Ghana came to naught. And despite my personal letters to him – sent well in advance of our trip – we received no replies and had no visas for Ghana until we were practically on the plane leaving Lagos, Nigeria. At the last moment, the Ghanaian ambassador to the United States, who happened to be in Lagos at that time, rushed up to us at the airport to personally deliver handwritten visas that would permit us to leave the plane in Ghana.

Imagine our surprise on arriving in Accra to find that President Nkrumah's office had reserved a hotel suite for us. In addition, a car and driver were waiting for us, and Nkrumah had put his personal plane at our disposal so that we would be able to see a good deal of the country, including several of the universities. Nkrumah's generosity made it difficult for us to spend any money in Ghana, despite the financial difficulties we knew the country was suffering at the time.

The day after our arrival, we were granted an audience with Nkrumah in Flagstaff House, Ghana's equivalent of our White House (it was formerly the British colonial government's administrative center). When we reached these headquarters, we were asked to wait until everything was in order. After about twenty minutes, we were accompanied through a door, opened by a remote unlocking system, then through a second and third door, at each of which we were met by armed guards and delays while the door was opened, again by a remote unlocking system.

By the time we reached the president, at the end of this protective arrangement, we anticipated seeing a very large, imposing individual. Instead, here was a modest, small man in a tan Nehru suit, sitting behind a huge desk marked with the word "Osogyefo" (the leader). All of this security apparatus was in reaction to assassination attempts, actual or rumored.

Our conversation was lively. Nkrumah had an alert mind, with many memories of Lincoln University and many ideas about governing his country, democracy, capitalism, and what he called "Consciencism," the title of one of his books. In our conversation he particularly emphasized the shortcomings of capitalism, the importance of the independence of African nations and of their not being beholden to the West. Having read widely in philosophy, theology, and economics, he was a very articulate critic of free-market capitalism. He inscribed a number of his books for us and presented them with his best wishes so that we could better learn his philosophy. As our first interview concluded, his photographer appeared, and the next day we found our pictures in the Accra newspapers, Nkrumah standing with us and smiling broadly.

Nkrumah gave us permission to visit the closed national archives. (I could see no good reason why the archives were closed, other than the Nkrumah camp's paranoia about supposed assassination attempts.) Here we found manuscript copies of his writings while a student at Lincoln and Penn, including his incomplete Ph.D. dissertation (which struck me more like an incomplete master's thesis). His former classmates at Lincoln had told us that Nkrumah had written a doctoral dissertation but that no one on the Penn faculty had felt qualified to judge it, such was the shortage of African expertise on the Penn faculty at that time. In his *Autobiography*, one of the books Nkrumah gave us, he recounts that he had completed all course work for the Ph.D. but did not finish his dissertation because of his teaching responsibilities and his job at the Sun shipyards in Wilmington, Delaware, which he took in order to pay his bills. With his heavy schedule, he became ill and decided to return home to Ghana after studying and working in the United States for ten years. His books, written after his return, indicate that he certainly could have completed an acceptable dissertation if he had had the time and made the effort to complete it.

During our week in Ghana, Nkrumah invited a dozen Lincoln University alumni and their wives from around the west coast of Africa to a reunion dinner with us at Osu Castle, one of Nkrumah's residences. This was an elegant affair, with waiters wearing white gloves and with effusive toasts and speeches. Addie sat at the president's right hand, facing a veranda, and I sat across the long dining table to the right of Mrs. Nkrumah, a tall, regal-looking niece of King Farouk of Egypt, wearing a high bouffant hairdo and a bead-encrusted evening gown. Uniformed guards were stationed in several strategic locations, including the veranda just beyond the French doors. After the entree, as Addie reached for her compact, she noticed an instantaneous movement by two guards reaching for pistols inside their jackets. They were ready to respond to any threat to the president, even from friends and fellow college alumni.

One of the guests at the Osu Castle dinner was another Egyptian, an uncle of Mrs. Nkrumah, who served as president of Cape Coast University in Ghana and treated us in a very cordial manner on our visit to his institution the following day. The university is located on a picturesque site near the sea, not far from the spot where the first slaves from Ghana were once imprisoned and shipped to America. We found its buildings relatively new and spacious, but it suffered from a shortage of qualified professors, which the president of the university was anxious to rectify.

We also visited the University of Kumasi, in the north of Ghana, where we had an audience with the Asantehene (the tribal chief of that area), who treated us to the sloe gin produced in that region for export. Addie and I had flown up to Kumasi in Nkrumah's private airplane, a wonderful small plane with just the two of us as passengers and decorated almost exclusively with photographs of Nkrumah. As we stepped off the plane in Kumasi, a red velvet carpet was spread before us. Nkrumah may have considered himself an African socialist, but his regime struck us as a cross between a monarchy and a dictatorship.

Within a year of that visit, in February 1966, Nkrumah was on his way to Hanoi to visit North Vietnam's president, Ho Chi Minh, "with proposals for ending the war in Vietnam." When he stopped in Peking en route to Hanoi, he was greeted with the news that his regime had been overthrown. In *Dark Days in Ghana*, a book he wrote in 1967 while in exile in Conakry, Guinea, Nkrumah strongly implies that America's CIA masterminded the coup. He was particularly vituperative about the alleged role of Ambassador Franklin H. Williams in bribing Nkrumah's enemies to carry out his overthrow: "It is particularly disgraceful that it should have been an Afro-American ambassador who sold himself out to the imperialists and allowed himself to be used in this way," Nkrumah wrote. "However, his treachery provides a sharp reminder of the insidious ways in which the enemies of Africa can operate. In the U.S.A. the 'Uncle Tom' figure is well known. We have mercifully seen less of him in Africa. The activities of the C.I.A. no longer surprise us."[5]

Franklin Williams, a 1941 Lincoln University graduate, was so upset by this charge that he asked me to intercede for him with Nkrumah and explain that he had had nothing at all to do with the coup. I did write to Nkrumah but did not hear from him; he died in 1968 at age fifty-eight.

Despite Nkrumah's absence and the change of regime, when we returned to Ghana in 1968 we were again treated very hospitably. This time we were able to meet with several dissidents whom Nkrumah had imprisoned, including the Lincoln alumnus Ako Adjei, who, while serving as Nkrumah's minister of foreign affairs (and shortly after receiving a Lincoln honorary degree from me), had been convicted of an attempt on Nkrumah's life. When I found him in 1968, Adjei was practicing law and seemed quite content to be removed from the public limelight. "There was much infighting within Nkrumah's

---

5 Kwame Nkrumah, *Dark Days in Ghana* (New York: International Publishers, 1968), 49.

administration," he informed me. He totally denied the murder attempt charge but suggested that I may have inadvertently caused his problem: The egotistical Nkrumah, he said, resented Adjei's receiving an honorary degree from Lincoln, which had conferred the same degree on Nkrumah a decade earlier.

On this second trip to Ghana, I was asked to give several talks to students and to speak at a large public meeting on the role of youth in developing a new country and writing a new constitution. I did this by referring to the young age of a number of America's founding fathers, including James Madison, Thomas Jefferson, and Alexander Hamilton.

On our two trips to Ghana in 1965 and '68, one of the key people we met with was K.A.B. Jones-Quartey, a Lincoln graduate of the class of 1949. He was a professor at the University of Ghana and was very active in fighting against limits on free expression at the university. He wrote a biography of Azikiwe and gave us an inscribed copy of it in 1965. He arranged several meetings with the vice chancellor (that is, president) of the University of Ghana, Dr. Alex Kwapong, an anthropologist. By 1968, Jones-Quartey was the editor of regular newsletters in Ghana stressing freedom of speech and academic freedom.

President William Tubman of Liberia was also generous with his time and hospitality during our 1968 visit. Since Liberia had been the destination of some of Lincoln University's first graduates in the nineteenth century, and Liberians were enrolling regularly as Lincoln students, the friendliness of those alumni, transplanted and native, was unsparing, whether entertaining us in their homes or accompanying us to significant and historical places and buildings in their country.

Our visits to South Africa, then under the grip of apartheid, were a different story. On our first visit, in 1965, the chief of the U.S. Information Agency met us at the Johannesburg airport and was surprised to find that Addie and I were white; he assumed that America's oldest Negro college would certainly have a black president. It seemed strange that the U.S. Information Agency would be so badly misinformed. He put us up in his home in Pretoria, and after several days there we visited Johannesburg and were able to contact relatives of several Lincoln students. In addition, we met with U.S. officials for briefings; toured the largest black township, Soweto; and met with a group of whites and blacks at the U.S. Information Center – about the only place in the city where interracial groups were permitted.

Addie had a regular visa, but mine was only a "transit" visa (meaning my allowable time in the country was severely limited) – probably because, two years earlier, I had sought permission for Robert Sobukwe, a black South African leader imprisoned on Robben Island, to leave South Africa and receive an honorary degree at Lincoln. Sobukwe represented an earlier incarnation of Nelson Mandela, and South Africa's apartheid government displayed no inclination to permit him to leave prison, much less the country. Presumably, my restricted visa was the government's way of trying to discourage me from such symbolic gestures in the future. Such was the price I happily paid to help keep the world's attention focused on the evil of apartheid. In any case, despite the transit visa, we were able to see a good deal of the countryside, as well as Johannesburg, Pretoria, and other nearby cities.

This was not the case during our second visit, in 1968. The South African government had become even more security-conscious and defensive about apartheid, and clearly it perceived me as someone who was potentially dangerous. This time Addie and I were not allowed to leave the Johannesburg Airport. Instead we were kept overnight in the airport hotel, with our passports and visas retained by police officials, until we boarded a plane for the independent black nation of Lesotho the next morning. Even within the airport we were only permitted to walk around a restricted area.

So we were surprised when an Asian newspaper reporter, having somehow learned of our presence, approached us for an interview. To ensure our privacy, we conducted the entire interview while standing outside restrooms on the second floor, out of sight of any police. Since our passports were being held for our departure, I felt somewhat uneasy during the interview. But I was merely discussing Lincoln University and the purpose of our trip to Africa, so I couldn't imagine how we could be punished. When we next returned to South Africa in 1981, long after I had left Lincoln, both the international and domestic pressure to end apartheid had reached a groundswell. When we last visited there in 1990, the peaceful demise of apartheid was clearly within reach.

Aside from South Africa, on all of our tours in the 1960s we spent time with government officials and Lincoln alumni, in addition to visiting schools, colleges, and universities. In most countries I also gave speeches to student groups and public audiences about American foreign policy and educational opportunities in the United States. On one such occasion, in 1968, in the small nation of Botswana, I spoke in a hall packed not only with Botswanians but also with American Peace Corps volunteers. Much to the embarrassment of the instinctively polite Botswanians, the mostly long-haired hippie Peace Corps volunteers asked very pointed and critical questions about U.S. race relations and America's war in Vietnam. It was clear from their "questions" – which were really speeches criticizing the United States as a racist and imperialist nation – that they were not eager to hear answers that might conflict with their opinions.

Nevertheless, I was able to make my responses heard quite well, since I had the stage and the microphone. "I know there are large warts on the record of American history and in current American institutions," I told the audience, "particularly in race relations, which many Americans are seeking to eliminate." I went on to give a brief history of U.S. racial discrimination and explained some positive things that were happening on the U.S. racial front in the 1960s. Vietnam was more difficult to explain, but I gave both America's reasons for engaging in the conflict there, as stated by President Johnson, and the reasons for the great antiwar opposition in the United States, which drove Johnson from the presidency not long after our 1968 visit to Africa. In any case, the Botswanians were much more interested in the race question and opportunities for education and work in the United States than they were in the Vietnam war.

(I was opposed to the Vietnam war at the time, but I had learned long before, at Salzburg, that for a representative of the United States to speak in very anti-American terms when abroad can be counterproductive around people who expect one to defend, or at least be balanced about, his own country's shortcomings.)

The narrow purpose of our visits to Africa was to recruit students and faculty to Lincoln and maintain ties with Lincoln alumni there. As I look back now, those trips produced an unanticipated byproduct: We returned from each of these tours armed with greater determination to wipe out racial prejudice and discrimination in the United States in any way we could.

Nothing I encountered during my first seven years at Lincoln prepared me for the reaction to the assassination of Martin Luther King Jr. on April 4, 1968. I was meeting early in the evening with a group of African students when we learned of this tragic event. I rushed home, where Addie and I were playing hosts to a potential faculty member and his wife. Quite soon, we heard rumblings of possible retribution against "honkies." In fact, several white deliverymen had already been frightened away from campus by threats that evening.

These threats, like the fury that spawned them, were genuine. The previous month I had heard rumors of substantial numbers of firearms sold to students. Helen Stewart, a university employee who often helped us in our home, reported that she saw three Lincoln students carrying new rifles and cases out of Fagan's Hardware Store in the month of March. A senior employee and neighbor of ours, Tom Murphy, said to me at about the same time, "The dorms are like an arsenal."

I had been sufficiently alarmed to investigate the situation personally. Mr. Adelman, the manager of the Western Auto store in Oxford, told me that there had indeed been a marked increase in the purchase of high-powered ammunition by Lincoln students. He had sold firearms to students in the fall, he said, but now he was refusing to sell them rifles or pistols without their parents' permission. Another store gave me the names of a dozen students and a faculty wife who had bought pistols.

Now, the greatest civil rights leader of our times was dead at the hands of a white racist, and as tensions continued to mount that night, a disoriented student known on campus as Tex rang our doorbell, pounded on the door, and tried to force his way into our home. "Now you've got what you wanted!" he shouted, shaking his fist. "I hope you're satisfied!" To Addie's dismay, I opened the front door, gently pushed him out of the doorway, took him by the arm, and gradually calmed him sufficiently to walk him down the porch steps and suggest we discuss the tragedy "tomorrow."

The next day I learned from the state police that Tex had purchased a rifle from a Sears Roebuck store in nearby Coatesville. From his dormitory window he had a clear bead on our front porch. I could temporize with his fury about the King murder, but not with his possession of a gun. Since I had specific information about Tex, I alerted the dean of students and the college psychiatrist and directed the dean and our single campus policeman to go to Tex's room (we knew he wasn't there) and take the rifle and any ammunition he possessed. They were very hesitant to enter a room without the student's permission, but I told them that this was "a clear and present danger," quoting the famous phrase used by Supreme Court Justice Oliver Wendell Holmes, and I would take personal responsibility for their action. I telephoned Tex's parents in Texas, who sounded quite understanding about what we had done. (The realization that a half-crazed student had been able to purchase a gun helped me become a strong supporter of gun-control laws.)

Meanwhile, I called together the leaders of the Student Senate and the faculty. We unanimously decided to suspend classes four days ahead of the regularly scheduled spring break, out of respect for Dr. King. This proved to be a very wise move, since violence erupted on a number of black college campuses around the country during those days.

Another crisis arose the following year concerning the campus physician. Toye Davis was a black Lincoln graduate who had earned a Ph.D. as well as an M.D., had taught biology at Lincoln, and maintained a medical practice in nearby Oxford in addition to his campus duties. Students had criticized this dual-practice arrangement – unreasonably, I felt – for some time, contending that Dr. Davis should spend more time on campus and be able to cure any and all ailments promptly. Two incidents in 1969 brought the situation to a head.

First, a student collapsed in front of the doctor's office, suffering from a ruptured aneurysm. Students somehow blamed this incident on the university's health service and demanded the doctor's resignation. Then the members of a small campus jazz group got high on drugs, and one of the students suffered a fatal overdose. When an ambulance service – based several miles away – took some time to reach the campus, Dr. Davis and the Lincoln administration were blamed for the student's death, even though there was no evidence that the student had been alive when the ambulance was called.

Dr. Davis had suffered enough criticism to last a lifetime, and after the drug incident he decided to resign. He refused to reconsider his resignation, he said. We quickly purchased a used ambulance for a modest sum in order to make sure that, in the future, Lincoln wouldn't be dependent on an outside ambulance service. And after Dr. Davis's resignation, the chairman of Lincoln's trustees, Dr. George Cannon, and I persuaded a well-regarded alumni physician, Wayman Coston, to come to the campus on a temporary basis from nearby Wilmington, Delaware. Soon afterward we were able to hire a full-time physician, which we did. One more crisis was solved.

The reader of these memoirs may validly wonder why I subjected myself to what must seem like an endless succession of crises, protests, and threats of violence at Lincoln. One answer is that these crises constituted rewards in themselves in that they provided dramatic learning experiences for me and for the students whom I was charged with educating. Another answer lies in the small words of appreciation that often passed my way. At a time of growing anti-white sentiment among blacks, for example, what white person would not be heartened by a note such as this one, which appeared in the October 1968 issue of the *Journal of Negro History*:

> Lincoln University, Pennsylvania, the oldest predominantly Negro college, is engaged in its greatest expansion with an enrollment of 1,100 students now and a goal of 1,200. President Marvin Wachman, easily the greatest leader that Lincoln has had in 115 years, is moving forward with an "Interim Program"...[which] provides for the varying needs of students ... between the two semesters.[6]

---

[6] William M. Brewer, ed., *Journal of Negro History* 53, no. 4 (October 1968): 374.

To discover myself praised in such a way (deservedly or not) by the editor of one of the oldest and most prestigious black periodicals – without even a reference to my race – more than compensated me for any campus struggles I encountered.

The gun episode after Martin Luther King's assassination was one of the few problems I encountered at Lincoln that had anything to do with my being white. Nevertheless, the rise of the black pride/black consciousness movement throughout the 1960s certainly caused me to review the appropriateness of my own role as a white leader of a predominantly black institution. When I introduced my fellow black-college president Dr. Samuel Proctor as a speaker at the Annual Meeting of the Pennsylvania Association of Colleges and Universities in 1968, he good-naturedly referred to me as "Wrong Way Corrigan Wachman" – a reference to my serving as president of Lincoln at a time when blacks were taking over all such positions. He certainly would not have made that comment, even in jest, in 1961 when I became the president. In the winter of 1968–69, a chemistry professor, W.T.M. Johnson, whom I had hired and been friendly with in the early 1960s, openly expressed a desire for a black president. Dr. Johnson had been an integrationist in the early '60s but, like many other blacks, had shifted his stance during the second half of the decade.

When Dr. Johnson called for my replacement, he was unaware that I had already informed Lincoln's Board of Trustees that I was resigning, in good part because I, too, felt that the university needed a black president. Also, after eight years as president, I felt that I had lived through two cycles of Lincoln's development and had probably given as much leadership as I could.

In retrospect, Dr. Johnson's call for a black president may have been a case of "Be careful what you wish for; you may get it." He and other Lincoln faculty members later sued my successor, Herman Branson, for violating their First Amendment right of free expression. (In 1978, some faculty members picketed a campus appearance by former U.S. President Gerald Ford, even though Branson, through the university's lawyer, had warned them not to. One of the picketers placards read: "Tell Branson about democracy." The lawyer's mailgram to the faculty leaders had stated that they would be subject to penalties "up to and including dismissal." Carlton Trotman, professor of English, was in fact dismissed, resulting in the suit, which the faculty ultimately won. Subsequently, Branson seized on Johnson's low class enrollments as an excuse to remove him from teaching his favorite advanced courses and, ultimately, to dismiss him. Since I was a consistent advocate of freedom of expression, such a tactic against a faculty critic would not have occurred to me. But if it had, it would have been very difficult for me as a white president to carry out such a strategy, given the mood of the era. Branson, as a black president, suffered no such qualms.)

Almost from the day I arrived at Lincoln I was approached with offers to run other institutions. One such offer came in 1965 from the New School for Social Research, an adult and graduate school in New York City. I had been recommended there by the New York civic activist August Heckscher, president of the 20th Century Fund and a New School board member, who knew of my experience at Salzburg, Colgate, and Lincoln. I met with him and a committee of the New School's board and decided that, despite my initial interest in this unique institution, it would be difficult to work with the chairman. More important, I felt it would be inappropriate to leave Lincoln after only four years in office. Besides, Addie, with her small-town background, was not anxious to move to New York City. For all these reasons, I took myself out of that race very quickly.

By 1968, my feelings were quite different. The common passion and commitment to a multiracial (albeit predominantly black) college was eroding. That, in turn, jeopardized the spirit of community and unity among most blacks and whites on the campus that was so dear to me and many of my colleagues. This was driven home to me in March 1968 when I received a heartfelt three-page, single-spaced letter from Philip Bell, the white Quaker chairman of Lincoln's Department of Economics, whom I had recruited from Haverford College. Bell had grown up on the edge of Harlem, had joined an all-black church, and had taught at Fisk University, a fine Negro College in Nashville. "I write this letter with a heavy heart," he wrote. "It seems clear . . . from recent faculty meetings that in the eyes of many of our black colleagues, no white person *can* be sufficiently sympathetic, *can* understand the black man's position today, regardless of how much racial or religious discrimination he has had to stand up to in his life and work."

I was not as gloomy about the situation as Bell, which is perhaps merely a reflection on my own incurable optimism. But there was no question that the ideal in which liberals like Bell and I believed – the struggle for a color-blind society – was no longer the first priority of most civil rights activists. It was time for me to move on. I had several offers of professorial and administrative positions from other universities, and I now began seriously to consider them. But I had no desire to leave Lincoln abruptly. Martin Luther King's assassination on April 4 further deterred me from sharing my feelings with others in the university. Also, Addie and the girls loved Lincoln and resisted the idea of leaving, despite the growing aloofness of some of the girls' black friends as the mood on campus changed.

In the same year that I received Bell's letter (1968), I was approached by Colgate University's president, Vincent Barnett, who offered me an endowed chair in American studies, Colgate's first endowed chair in that field. Returning to Colgate would have been like a homecoming. The offer seemed a wonderful opportunity to get back to scholarship and teaching, with a bearable teaching load and an opportunity to do some writing. But I felt it would be inappropriate to abandon Lincoln in the midst of two assassination crises – of King and Robert Kennedy – not to mention the continuing tensions over civil rights and the Vietnam war. Consequently, I told Barnett that I couldn't consider leaving Lincoln until the summer of 1969, at the earliest.

That was agreeable to him and others at Colgate. But in the meantime I was contacted by Paul Anderson, president of Temple University in Philadelphia, about coming to his university as vice president for academic affairs. Presumably, Temple courted me because I possessed some understanding of community relations and race relations, and some practice in dealing directly with students of different races and religions – high priorities for an urban university. Temple was also attracted by my experience as president of a private but state-aided institution who had dealt with Pennsylvania governors and legislators. Temple had long been a state-aided private institution (like Lincoln) and had only recently changed its status to "state-related." This meant that it received greater financial support from the state, in both operating and capital funds, which enabled it to substantially reduce its tuition and to expand its enrollment and academic offerings. My background, along with the fact that I had been a professor long enough to make modest contributions to scholarship, appealed to Temple's officers and trustees, as well as to deans of its various colleges. Faculty members and students who served on the search committee told me personally that they felt I was the right person for the job and strongly encouraged me to throw in my lot with Temple.

I was intrigued by this offer because of what Temple University represented in my mind: a great heterogeneous city university, deeply involved in the race question as well as numerous other urban and related social issues. What's more, during our years at Lincoln, Addie and I had become involved in cultural and civic activities in Philadelphia. I was serving on various committees and boards in the city, including nonprofit boards and the board of directors of the Philadelphia Savings Fund Society, a large mutual savings bank.

While both the Colgate and Temple offers were on the table, we returned to Colgate for a visit and for a talk I gave to the Phi Beta Kappa Society. We still harbored very warm feelings about Colgate, but on this visit we found ourselves somewhat less excited than we thought we would be. Our years in the civil rights cauldron at Lincoln had transformed both of us, but Colgate's intellectual climate seemed not to have changed much since we had left there to go to Salzburg ten years earlier. The issues debated and discussed were important in the relatively calm academic setting of Colgate but seemed less relevant to the real world in which we lived at Lincoln and would live and work in Philadelphia. After that visit, I became more open to negotiations with Temple. I met with board members and with the vice presidential search committee, which included deans, vice presidents, faculty, and students. These were thorough and intense discussions and gave me the opportunity to analyze my suitability for the position. After those discussions, I was given a firm offer in writing.

Addie and I discussed the Colgate and Temple offers at great length. Among the Philadelphians who served as my sounding board, Walter Phillips, who had convinced me to go to Lincoln, stands out. He sympathized with my nostalgia for Colgate but felt that I would be able to exert much greater influence in Philadelphia, and at Temple. Temple, he said, needed more than a good academic administrator; at that moment, it needed someone with my experience in race relations, as well.

In the spring of 1969 I accepted Temple's offer, with the understanding that I would not only be the chief academic officer but would have a tenured history professorship, which I could occupy after serving a few years as vice president. When I called Vince Barnett at Colgate to thank him for his generous offer and explain my reasons for going to Temple rather than Colgate, he was very understanding: after all, he, too, was a former professor who had faced similar choices. Then I informed Lincoln's trustees, faculty, and student body of my plans.

To my astonishment, a delegation of black student leaders visited our home and tried to persuade me to reconsider my resignation. They wanted me to stay on at Lincoln into the indefinite future. "You are no longer a white president first, but *our* president," one of them said, "and you have led Lincoln through difficult times." After bantering with them on small matters – sports, the condition of the university, and so on – I finally told them what I sincerely believed: that our decision to move on would pave the way for a new president who would lead Lincoln to new heights. I promised that I would help Lincoln in any way I could, including in its search for a new president. "I am moved to the bottom of my heart by your backing and will never forget it," I said, "nor will I forget the encouragement offered by students over these past several years." I believe they left with good feelings about how our personal relationships had developed and how Lincoln had changed for the better during their undergraduate years.

My last hurrah at Lincoln occurred at my last Lincoln commencement, in 1969. U.S. Chief Justice Earl Warren was soon to retire. What better speaker for my farewell Lincoln commencement, I reasoned, than the author of the 1954 *Brown* decision that ended school segregation? I sent an invitation to Warren and then wrote to Thurgood Marshall, by then an associate justice on the Supreme Court, to put in a good word for us, thinking that he would accompany the Chief Justice to see him honored by Marshall's alma mater. Marshall did not respond, perhaps because of his negative reception by black students at the University of Wisconsin, where black nationalist students made disparaging comments not only about Marshall but also about Whitney Young (called "Whitey" by some of the nationalists), and even the deceased Martin Luther King Jr.

Receiving no reply from Chief Justice Warren, after a decent interval I invited Carl Stokes of Cleveland, the first black mayor of a large American city, and the Reverend Jesse Jackson, a leading civil rights activist who had been close to Martin Luther King Jr. I hoped for an acceptance from one of the three invitees; if two of them accepted, I figured, one could give the baccalaureate address and the other the commencement speech.

Lo and behold, shortly before we were to send our program to the printer, all three accepted – including Warren. On a sleepless night, my solution came to me in a flash. Why not have Reverend Jackson give the baccalaureate address on Sunday morning and Earl Warren the commencement address in the afternoon, to be followed by Carl Stokes, who would assume my normal responsibility and deliver the "charge" to the graduating seniors? This worked out very well. My final commencement, held outdoors on a very warm and sunny day, was an unforgettable occasion with an overflow audience, just like my first commencement with Martin Luther King Jr. in 1961.

When I accepted the offer from Temple, Addie and I looked for a house in the city close to the university. But we couldn't find one that fit our purse strings and our needs, so we settled in Abington Township, a Philadelphia suburb. It was convenient to schools and public transportation and was an easy drive to Temple. In effect we made the same decision that millions of other Americans were making, and in the process we joined another great socioeconomic movement of the second half of the twentieth century: the suburbanization of America.

I left Lincoln on January 1, 1970, remaining in my office until the early hours of New Year's Day to clear my desk and write notes to my secretary and to the provost, Bernard Harleston, who would take over as Lincoln's acting president for the spring semester of 1970. Then I drove to our new home in Abington Township, where Addie and our daughters already resided. In terms of miles, the drive was not far from the campus where we had spent the better part of a decade. But in other respects, the new life was a world away.

Temple:
The Urban University

J ANUARY 2, 1970, WAS A COLD, windy morning in North Philadelphia. I left my car in the parking lot and walked across Broad Street to the corner of Montgomery Avenue. It was 7:45 A.M., and hundreds of students and faculty were streaming out of the subway station a block away and getting off buses at the doorstep of Conwell Hall, Temple University's primary administration building and nerve center. This scene presented a sharp contrast to Lincoln's rural campus, where I had lived only a hundred yards from my office, with not a single high-rise building in sight.

At the outset I perceived few similarities between these vastly different institutions. My new job as vice president for academic affairs bore little resemblance to my former position as president of Lincoln. For example, at Temple the English Department alone numbered well over one hundred professors, more than Lincoln's entire faculty. Lincoln had exactly 1,131 students when I left; Temple, when I arrived, had 30,000.

Yet I quickly discovered one common characteristic: At Temple, as at Lincoln, student activism was the order of the day; the main difference concerned the scale and complexity of the activism. Temple students couldn't invade my home as Lincoln students had, but within one week of my arrival at Temple I was confronted with two sit-ins, one in the hall right outside my office door and the other in a small gymnasium, one floor above me. The issues were the university's expansion into surrounding neighborhoods and displacing residents, and demands for the admission of more black students and the hiring of more black faculty. Imagine my surprise to discover a familiar face among all those in the packed gymnasium, looking determined and daring anyone to oust him. It was Tony Monteiro, a recent Lincoln graduate who had once had a face-off with my daughter, Lynn, when she ripped down some of his posters demanding that Lincoln change its name to Frederick Douglass University.

"Tony, what are you doing here?" I asked.

"I'm a graduate student at Temple," he replied sheepishly. "It's good to see you again."

We bantered a bit about the comparison between the two universities and noted that some of the issues and tensions between students and administration were similar. Despite the great difference in the size of the institutions, we agreed that, with good will, the disputes at Temple could be quickly resolved.

Tony Monteiro later ran for Congress on the Communist Party ticket but soon gave up politics entirely and resumed graduate studies. Eventually he received a Ph.D. at Temple and became a professor in social science at the Philadelphia College of Pharmacy and Science (now University of the Sciences) and, for one year, a visiting professor at the University of Pennsylvania.

The other sit-in, outside my office door, was led by Milton Street, a part-time student who owned one of the many lunch trucks that sold cheesesteaks and hoagies on campus. He later became a controversial elected member of the Pennsylvania House and Senate – "the Chutzpah King of Philly politics," the *Philadelphia Inquirer* columnist Tom Ferrick called him. And, of course, Street's less contentious brother John, a Temple Law School alumnus, went on to become president of Philadelphia City Council and, in January 2000, mayor of Philadelphia.

Milton Street and Tony Monteiro were good examples of students who led sit-ins and other types of protests in the '60s and '70s on issues ranging from advocating civil rights and opposing the Vietnam war to objecting to cafeteria food and dormitory rooms. Though some issues were more significant than others, there was never a shortage of causes to rally around.

The sit-in led by Monteiro was temporarily settled by an agreement brokered by my staff and me to have a joint student–administration group clarify the issues and recommend changes in university policy. More serious and lengthier demonstrations occurred later in the spring of 1970, after U.S. troops invaded Cambodia, and especially after National Guardsmen in Ohio killed four student demonstrators at Kent State University on May 4.

In the midst of one of these protests, an Army Reserve unit drove a tank down Broad Street, the main thoroughfare running through Temple's campus, prompting demonstrating students to climb on the tank and take it over for a short time. That incident had comic overtones – some students taking themselves seriously, others joking about the entire affair. Fortunately no one was injured, nor was any property damaged. But another military presence on campus, the Reserve Officer Training Corps (ROTC), was a constant target of antiwar students. They wanted the ROTC removed altogether, and they were especially indignant that academic course credits were being given for ROTC work. Because of the community's interest in this issue, even the Board of Trustees was involved in the subsequent agreements. Faculty members and deans of several of the colleges met with me to work out the final compromise, in which the ROTC remained on campus but credit toward graduation for its courses was eliminated, except in those individual colleges that specifically had reason to grant credit for them.

Equally vehement objections were declared against another campus presence, the National Institute for the Administration of Justice (NIAJ), which trained working policemen. Protesters felt that police were racist and heavy-handed against minorities, and Temple should have nothing to do with them. Those protests simmered, but the NIAJ was not dismantled; instead, with my support, it was soon transformed into a very respectable Department of Criminal Justice with a full agenda of teaching, research, and service to the community. I was very interested in having programs of this sort, which addressed a necessary community issue while at the same time stressing the intellectual side of police work in an academic setting.

There were so many protests and demonstrations in my first year at Temple that, it seemed, all of us top administrators were constantly working to resolve issues they presented and to make sure the campus remained as stable as possible. In fact, sometimes I felt that we ought to bring in cots and sleep in Conference Room 3B in Conwell Hall because we were there so many evenings and weekends.

My experiences at Lincoln in the hectic 1960s helped me cope with the challenges that confronted us at Temple in the '70s. The demonstrations at Temple were often similar to the famous '60s protests at Columbia University and the University of California at Berkeley, but ours made fewer headlines, perhaps because Temple was basically a commuting institution, with many students going home or to jobs after classes. Media attention changed, however, in August–September 1970, when the Black Panther Party chose Philadelphia as the site of its nationwide Revolutionary People's Constitutional Convention.

The Black Panthers had been founded in 1966 in Oakland, California, by Huey P. Newton and Bobby Seale to promote a new militant black philosophy. Where Martin Luther King Jr. had counseled peace and interracial brotherhood, the Black Panthers projected a frightening image of armed young men who would respond in kind to any violence committed against blacks.

A month before the September 5 opening of the convention, the Panthers' Philadelphia coordinator found himself unable to secure a meeting place downtown and was looking for alternatives. Several politically active Temple professors suggested Temple's recently built gymnasium, McGonigle Hall.

At about the same time, Temple's president, Paul Anderson, received a call from Reverend Paul Washington, a Lincoln University graduate who was rector of the Church of the Advocate, only three blocks from Temple's main campus. Father Washington asked that McGonigle Hall be made available for the convention. When asked how much the Panthers would be involved, Washington replied (according to Anderson), "Some," giving no indication that the Panthers would actually be running the whole show. Mindful that our African American neighbors supported the convention, and that Temple had a strong commitment to serving the larger community, Anderson agreed to allow the use of McGonigle.

This decision was no doubt a relief to many local white politicians and civic leaders who were eager to steer the Panthers away from Philadelphia's downtown business district. But it did not mollify the city's bombastic police commissioner (and later mayor) Frank Rizzo, who loudly insisted that *no site* in Philadelphia should be made available for any convention that included the Black Panthers. Pennsylvania's lieutenant governor and several prominent state legislators also proclaimed their disapproval.

Temple, warned State Representative Richard A. McClatchy, might "endanger further subsidies from the state legislature," which he said was "alarmed by the rising tide of anarchism already rampant in American society." In a public letter to Anderson, he added: "I am shocked and dismayed at your permission to let the Black Panthers use Temple University's facilities to spread their hate, venom and special brand of racism. To allow a state-related university that is subsidized by tax-payers' funds [to offer McGonigle Hall] without charge to such a Fascist group under the guise of freedom of speech and community cooperation borders on the heights of the ridiculous."[1]

Anderson replied to such criticism: "Our decision has nothing to do with the endorsement of the Black Panthers or other groups at the meeting. But it does pertain to a belief in a free and open society. It does pertain to a belief in free speech. It does pertain to an attempt to be a good neighbor in our local community. For these reasons, we are standing by our decision."[2] With other members of the president's cabinet (but not all), I thoroughly agreed with Anderson's position.

Matters became even more complicated when violence erupted in Philadelphia just one week before the convention was scheduled to begin.

---

[1] *Philadelphia Sunday Bulletin*, August 16, 1970.

[2] *New York Times*, September 2, 1970.

During an armed attack on a guardhouse in Philadelphia's Fairmount Park, a policeman was killed and another injured. A day later, elsewhere in the city, two policemen were shot and wounded. Although no evidence implicated the Panthers in these attacks, the police raided three Panther "headquarters," ostensibly to confiscate illegal weapons. In two of these houses, Panthers resisted police with gunfire. In the third raid, the police took six men out of the house, stripped them, and searched them; a photograph of the six naked black men lined up facing a wall – the quintessential picture worth a thousand words – was published in newspapers throughout the United States, further fanning black fury as well as white concern about police racism in Philadelphia.

Fourteen people were arrested in those raids, but none of the charges filed against them had anything to do with the killing and wounding of police officers. (Five other suspects were subsequently rounded up in connection with the Fairmount Park shootings.) However, in the minds of Philadelphia police and many other citizens, the Panthers were responsible for the apprehension and panic in the city.

At the same time, many feared that denying the Panthers a convention site would provoke further violence. Prominent business leaders, seeking a peaceful resolution, advocated calm and reason in dealing with the issues and requested a meeting with Commissioner Rizzo. Rizzo refused, asking, "Where were these people when those bastards were printing . . . garbage about killing the pigs?"[3]

Panthers and delegates from other antiestablishment groups began arriving in Philadelphia in large numbers during the last week of August. For several days just before and all during the convention, President Anderson's cabinet met almost around the clock. As vice president for academic affairs, I worked with the president; the vice president for finance, John Rhoads; and the vice president for university relations, James Shea, on how to arrange seating for more delegates than the 4,500-seat gymnasium could hold. We also dealt with media relations and fire department and security matters. Insurance issues were worked out with the Pennsylvania attorney general and Governor Raymond P. Shafer's staff. (Because of the fear of violence, it was very important to the attorney general and the governor for us to have insurance to cover any negative possibilities.)

When all the problems finally had been resolved, Jim Shea explained to the press how the "philosophical decision to permit use of McGonigle Hall for

---

3 *Philadelphia Daily News*, September 5, 1970.

Saturday and Sunday, September 5th and 6th, was made."[4] President Anderson forthrightly declared that "America's strength is in her openness, her tolerance and her restraint," and that "we must agree... that ideas... be tested on the anvils of open discussion."[5] Faculty and student activists, who had often attacked Anderson on other issues, now applauded him for resisting pressure from politicians and the police. Temple University also received kudos from business and civic leaders for making sure that the Revolutionary People's Constitutional Convention took place away from Center City in an air-conditioned building, where the oppressive summer heat would not exacerbate existing tension. The entire affair demonstrated that sticking to a university's principles is good pragmatic strategy. If one's position is carefully explained, even those who disagree will understand and respect the final decision of a president and the university's officers.

The convention went off without serious incident. True to their word, the Panthers permitted no weapons inside the arena and policed the convention very effectively. As expected, the keynote speaker – Panther Supreme Commander Huey P. Newton, recently released from jail on a manslaughter charge – unleashed his fiery rhetoric on the crowd but, fortunately, did not provoke the violence that so many had feared. We all breathed a sigh of relief and felt that our reasonable tactics (as opposed to Rizzo's confrontational tactics) with the convention leaders, including the Panthers, had paid off.

Shortly after these Labor Day weekend events, Jim Shea and I, along with other Temple representatives, attended the trial of about a dozen students who had been apprehended by police for minor infractions during the convention. We were surprised and pleased when the city's chief prosecutor, Richard Sprague, asked the judge to dismiss all charges against the students and went on to praise Temple for its efforts in handling the entire affair. We later learned that, while Temple personnel were struggling with containing the convention, Mayor Jim Tate and other city officials were spending that same holiday weekend at the New Jersey shore.

All of us were happy to leave these events behind, to have fall classes begin on a peaceful note, and to return to regular work at Temple. For me, serving as vice president for academic affairs proved to be stimulating, invigorating, and strenuous. As president of Lincoln my responsibilities had been similar to those of a large university president but also included involvement in

---

4 *Philadelphia Inquirer*, September 5, 1970.

5 *Philadelphia Evening Bulletin*, September 5, 1970.

academic and scholarly matters. At a university the size of Temple, these functions are divided: The president handles external relations, including fund raising and contacts with government, community officials, and agencies, and serves as chief spokesperson and planner for the entire institution. The vice president for academic affairs (now called the provost) deals most directly with all deans, and often with department chairmen and faculty, to develop academic and professional programs.

Chairing the Council of Deans and working individually with deans of Temple's fifteen schools and colleges was absorbing. Although all fifteen deans were white males in 1970, they represented a broad spectrum of ages and backgrounds. There were deans in their thirties and others in their sixties. Their specialized interests ran the gamut from medicine, law, music, and art to literature and social work. But their personal characteristics, I found, mattered less than their respective academic disciplines. If I knew which college the speaker represented, I usually could predict the response I would receive to a university-wide issue. Obviously, each dean looked first at how a university-wide regulation or policy would affect his school, with its particular specialization. Organizing these deans into a cohesive group concerned with the entire university, and not just with their own programs and faculties, was a continuing challenge.

The academic vice president was also responsible for programs as diverse as athletics, student affairs, admissions, the Registrar's Office, the Special Recruitment and Admissions Program, and the Afro-Asian Institute, as well as the aforementioned ROTC and Criminal Justice programs. So I had a full plate at all times. Moreover, the position presented me with my first experience with professional schools such as law, medicine, and dentistry. I hadn't realized, for example, that overseeing the medical school would require me to know so much about a variety of subjects, such as hospital-building code violations, nursing shortages, and Temple University Hospital's monumental debt resulting from unreimbursed care for the poor. It did not require a medical degree, however, to see that the hospital posed great financial problems for the university and that the hospital's aging facility itself would soon have to be replaced. Dealing with the programs and personnel in each professional school and the hospital served as my initiation into the problems of a large urban institution.

Although the vast majority of Temple students were white, race – my primary area of expertise up to this point – was central to practically every issue we dealt with in the early '70s. During my tenure at Lincoln, I had often made it a point in off-campus speeches to explain that Lincoln then had more

Strolling on the campus of Temple University as the new president, 1973
Courtesy of Temple University

Wisconsin State High School Champ, Milwaukee, 1934

All photographs not otherwise attributed are from the author's collection

BOTTOM LEFT: *The beginning of a "sports career," with brother Harold standing by, Milwaukee, 1923*

BOTTOM RIGHT: *Collegiate Racketeer, Evanston, Illinois, 1933*

*Corporal Wachman on a free
day with Addie, Galveston,
Texas, 1943*

*"Ma" at age seventy with
Harold and his wife, Lillian,
Long Beach, California, 1944*

Civilian faculty colleagues at Biarritz American University, a U.S. Army institution, Biarritz, France, 1945–46.
LEFT TO RIGHT: Charles R. Wilson, Colgate University; James Ranck, Hood College; Vernon Cooper, Montana State University; Paul Clyde, Duke University; Harold Davis, Hiram College; William Halperin, University of Chicago; Rhea Smith, Rollins College

Katie and Lynn (on left) on the stairs of their "Castle," Schloss Leopoldskron, Salzburg, Austria, 1959

"The American Economy" faculty, Salzburg Seminar, Salzburg, Austria, 1960.
LEFT TO RIGHT, WITH WIVES: *Tibor Scitovsky, University of California; Clair Wilcox, Swarthmore College; Alvin Hansen, Harvard University; George W. Taylor, University of Pennsylvania; Leland Hazard, Pittsburgh Plate Glass Company and Carnegie Institute of Technology.*
FOREGROUND: *Marv and Addie and Assistant Director Robert Bjork and Mrs. Bjork*

Inauguration as president of Lincoln University, with Walter M. Phillips, chairman of the Board of Trustees, doing the honors, Lincoln University, Pennsylvania, April 1962
Taken from *Lincoln University Bulletin*, Spring 1962, with permission of Lincoln University

Birthday party for Langston Hughes (fourth from left), Bedford-Stuyvesant, New York, 1966

FROM LEFT: *The Wachmans; Robert E. Lee, D.D.S. (Lincoln, class of '41), who moved to Ghana when Nkrumah became president; President Kwame Nkrumah; Mrs. Nkrumah, Accra, Ghana, 1965*

Meeting with Kenyan students, Nairobi, 1965

Commencement speakers Chief Justice Earl Warren and Cleveland Mayor Carl Stokes, Lincoln University, Pennsylvania, 1969

From the *Evening Bulletin*, June 2 (the author's collection)

Lunching with students at Leo's popular food truck. Temple University, Philadelphia, 1973
Courtesy of Temple University

Dancing with Addie at Temple University Inaugural Ball, Philadelphia, March 30, 1974
Courtesy of Temple University

Giving tennis tips to neighborhood youngsters, 1974   Courtesy of Temple University

Student rally protesting state legislature's delay in funding student financial aid and Temple University's appropriation, 1976   Courtesy of Temple University

Tennis with Bill Cosby, Cherry and White Day, Spring 1979   Courtesy of Temple University

Daughter Lynn whispering to her father at his final commencement ceremony at Temple University, Philadelphia Convention Hall, May 27, 1982   Courtesy of Temple University

The six Wachman siblings at reunion in Long Beach, California, 1984.
LEFT TO RIGHT: *Harold, Lillian, Minnie, Helen, Marv, Anna*

Addie and Marv walking on Forbidden Drive in Wissahickon Valley Park, Philadelphia, 2001

"Hats off to the graduating class of 1982"
Courtesy of Temple University

black male students than any other college or university in Pennsylvania. Furthermore, Lincoln and Cheyney University (which was then a state teachers' college) together had more black students, male and female, than all the other institutions of higher education in the state combined. As a result of persistent and committed effort, by the mid-1970s I could claim that Temple had come to have more black students than Lincoln and Cheyney combined, and substantially more than other large universities in the state.

This turnaround was one example of the truly remarkable demographic changes occurring in many American universities. At Temple these changes inevitably resulted in issues of perceived discrimination against blacks in the student cafeteria, controversies related to development of the Afro-Asian Institute, and disputes about our Special Recruitment and Admissions Program (which brought in students in need of substantial remedial work). During my three-and-one-half years as vice president for academic affairs, I experienced the exhilarating feeling that I was at the center of everything important happening at the university, as well as dealing with issues at the core of America's domestic problems and the world's human challenges. The notion of making even the slightest dent in these difficult human issues was always gratifying.

Among the predominantly white faculty, some members felt Temple was lowering its admissions and academic standards in order to appease aggressive blacks. Others felt the university should concentrate on research and graduate and professional studies so that it could avoid the racial turmoil in the undergraduate student body, which was becoming more and more integrated. (This was a period, remember, when whites were often insensitive to the sort of discrimination, rebuffs, and slights endured by blacks.)

At one Faculty Senate meeting, in the fall of 1970, I was called on the carpet to explain what the members perceived as special treatment for Temple's black students. In an emotional presentation, I made it clear that I felt many of the black students' grievances were indeed valid. Now that the university had recruited large numbers of minority students, I argued, we had an obligation to examine their needs and address them. These incoming students deserved to be made comfortable enough on campus to be able to succeed in their studies.

"All other issues are insignificant compared to the black–white human relations question," I said, reading from notes I had prepared specifically for the Senate meeting. "Our country had a sad history when it came to our largest racial minority. At the very least, it has not lived up to American principles of equal treatment and equal opportunity. Now, in 1970, along with other institutions of higher learning (UCLA, the University of Wisconsin, and the

University of California at Santa Cruz), all of whom are struggling with similar issues, we are being confronted with the obligation to make good on our country's promises. We have no true historical precedents for this new set of circumstances, although there are some examples in our immigration history for us to heed. Probably, we must go through a difficult period in order to build a stronger university and United States. We are paying now for our history, national and institutional. Now we need to compensate, which means we must move faster than we are ready to move, financially and psychologically. If we use reason and good judgment, and get some additional, effective personnel, we may be able to make the necessary adjustments. Neither whites nor blacks have made the adjustments yet; all of us must try, or each small hill will become a mountain to overcome during the coming year and thereafter. Great opportunities lie ahead for us."

I delivered this speech with passion, and several of my faculty friends later told me that if I wanted to get my points across, I should be emotional more often. Except on matters of race, I found this difficult, since I have always tried to treat even serious issues in a calm and rational manner. I believe that I was able in this meeting to provide needed perspective to the faculty. In fact, I believe I succeeded in changing many people's minds, which led to less criticism of the direction in which the university was going.

I had not come to Temple University with any notion of becoming a president again. In fact, I had hoped eventually to return to full-time teaching and writing. So it was quite a jolt when I received phone calls from the chairmen of two universities, followed by a call from the chairman of a fine nonprofit institution in Philadelphia, the Academy of Natural Sciences, each seeking my candidacy as president.

I immediately advised the Academy, a Philadelphia museum and research institution, that I did not wish to leave campus life and work. The universities were a different matter. Wayne State University in Detroit was interested in me as president for some of the same reasons that Temple had recruited me as vice president. And I was pulled toward it because of its similarities to Temple. The chairman of Wayne State's trustees and several members of the search committee interviewed me in a private room at the Bellevue-Stratford Hotel in Philadelphia, and subsequently invited Addie and me to Detroit. There, we were wined, dined, and questioned by the trustees and the full search committee.

Not long after that, Melvin C. Holm, chairman of Syracuse University's presidential search committee, flew to Philadelphia to interview me. Our interview took place on his private plane while it sat on the tarmac at Philadelphia International Airport. Addie and I knew Syracuse from our fifteen-year association with Colgate University, just fifty miles away, and I was well known in the Syracuse area not only as a professor and college administrator but also as a tennis player. Several weeks later, we were flown to Syracuse on the chairman's plane.

As we walked to the steps of the small jet, the handsome young pilot greeted us with obvious delight. "You may not remember me," he informed Addie, "because I was not one of your best students in Hamilton High. But you were my English teacher over twenty years ago!" Addie easily recognized him and gave him a warm hug as we boarded the plane.

When we arrived in Syracuse, I had a full day of interviews and discussions with faculty and the trustees; Addie also met with the trustees. Then we were taken through the president's house, where we would live if I accepted their offer. Holm was anxious for us to see improvements that had been made to the fine old president's residence and to tell us what more *could* be done to the great attic if we wished.

I was flattered by these job offers. The discussions and interviews I had at Wayne State and at Syracuse made me examine my own aspirations and my feelings about what I would like to be doing for the rest of my professional career.

For very different reasons, both of these presidential job offers were very tempting. But shortly after we returned from our visit to Syracuse, yet another job prospect opened up. In early 1972, Paul Anderson announced that he would retire from Temple's presidency in June 1973 when he turned sixty-five, the university's normal retirement age for a president. William Spofford, chairman of Temple's trustees, had learned that I was being sought for the presidencies of Syracuse and Wayne State, and he called me soon after Anderson's retirement announcement. Spofford appealed to me to remove my name from consideration by other institutions; there was great enthusiasm among board members, he said, to name me Anderson's successor.

Only then did I consciously realize that I had been secretly hoping for an opportunity to remain at Temple. With its heterogeneity, its broad set of programs and colleges, and its emphasis on issues facing urban America, Temple was my kind of institution. I already knew Temple's challenges and problems firsthand, and I felt close to its faculty. I felt comfortable there, and Addie and I had come to appreciate Philadelphia's cultural diversity. So I withdrew my name from consideration by Wayne State and Syracuse.

Temple's search committee was chaired by the distinguished U.S. Appeals Court Judge William H. Hastie, who had been the first African American to hold a gubernatorial seat in the United States (as the presidentially appointed governor of the Virgin Islands) and then the first black federal judge. Hastie and his committee interviewed me and reviewed my record. The search procedure for a new university president usually takes about a year – sometimes longer. This one took three months. As far as I know, the search committee and the board did not seriously consider anyone else. In his formal report to the full board of trustees, Judge Hastie declared:

> We are convinced that he has the capacity and the will to lead Temple to new heights as a great urban university, while preserving the ideals that have characterized the university from its modest beginnings. ... All sixteen members of this Committee firmly believe that Dr. Wachman is the best person to lead Temple during the decade ahead.[6]

I was overwhelmed by these sentiments and by the support not only of faculty, students, and trustees, but even of those community leaders with whom Temple had had a rocky relationship. One of the community leaders was Father Paul Washington, who wholeheartedly supported me as someone who understood the needs of the community and the minority students. The faith these people expressed in me reinforced my determination to make certain they never felt they had made a mistake.

I was formally elected president of Temple on May 9, 1972, but continued to serve as vice president for academic affairs for the following fourteen months, until my presidency became effective on July 1, 1973. The trustees' meeting at which I was elected was held in the student dining room at Temple's suburban Ambler campus, about fifteen miles north of Temple's main campus, because I was scheduled to present the board with a long-range plan for that bucolic campus. Before it became part of Temple University in the late 1950s, Ambler had been the site of the Pennsylvania College of Horticulture for Women. My proposal involved developing Ambler from a branch campus with a maximum of six hundred to seven hundred students – all freshmen and sophomores studying liberal arts and horticulture and landscape architecture – into a broad-based, four-year undergraduate branch of the university, offering at least 2,000 students a wide range of undergraduate courses, and perhaps master's level courses in business and other fields. I felt strongly that the population growth in Montgomery County justified Temple's

---

[6] *Temple Times*, vol. 2, no. 15, May 18, 1972.

expansion of Ambler's facilities, so I had already formed a planning council for Ambler, which conducted extensive demographic and market studies for the area. Their findings were the basis for the plan I had devised. At the May 1972 meeting where the trustees elected me president, they also accepted my plan for Ambler.

Over the following six years, Ambler grew to a full-time student enrollment of 2,500, and an evening school population of close to 3,500, for a total of 6,000 students. From a two-year basic studies and horticulture program, the campus developed into a four-year branch of the university. Master's degree programs in certain areas, notably business, were also introduced. Basic science courses were offered there, but full science programs were not mounted because it was too expensive to duplicate science facilities already available at the main and health-sciences campuses. Instead, we established a shuttle bus service for science-oriented Ambler campus students so they could commute between Ambler and Philadelphia's main campus. Students in other fields, like English, history, political science, and business, were able to take all of their courses at Ambler. This was helpful for those who were unable to commute into the city.

Another campus launched during my last year as vice president for academic affairs was Temple University's Center City campus (TUCC). The Westinghouse Corporation owned and operated a downtown high-rise building. Because it housed a local radio and television station, it was known as the KYW building, and it contained a small theater (where the popular Mike Douglas program had been televised) that was easily adaptable for graduate-student theater productions. Westinghouse planned to move its station to a new and modern facility on Independence Mall, near the famous Liberty Bell, and was trying to figure out what to do with its old building.

After considerable negotiation, Westinghouse decided to donate the building to Temple, since our School of Communications and Theater could make good use of the facility, including its wiring and communications equipment. (Of course, Westinghouse was able to take advantage of tax incentives in making this gift.) Temple's School of Communications was one of the top two or three in the nation, with outstanding departments in theater as well as in radio–television–film. To own a building right in the heart of the city where those disciplines, together with journalism, could be taught was very attractive.

But given the university's perpetually strapped financial condition, some people at Temple, including several trustees, felt we should sell the building or, at the very least, rent out the first floor or two and get the benefit of the income. I argued strongly that we should use the entire building, for fields like continuing education, communications, and business administration. As we had done for Ambler, we conducted a demographic and market study for Center City. The results reinforced my belief that we should use the entire building. I felt we should have a large visual presence in Center City as we launched this program. At the very least, I felt, we should try it for a few years – including especially the potential commercial space on the Walnut Street ground floor. That would provide a window to Temple right on a main thoroughfare in the heart of the city. Our university relations people, led by Vice President James Shea, agreed with my position. As a result, we adopted the policy of trying to make the building pay for itself by bringing in income not only through tuition, but also through theater performances and other activities.

We began classes there in the academic year 1973–74 with about 600 part-time students, some of them actually full-time Temple students, taking part of their loads in communications and journalism at that site. Within a few years, more than 9,000 people were taking courses at this downtown campus. A master of law program was developed for practicing attorneys who could come out of their offices in late afternoon, take courses nearby, and then catch the train home just three blocks away. The School of Business and Management soon became a major user of these downtown facilities, with banks and other businesses often sponsoring their employees as students and renting rooms in the building for meetings and conferences. Liberal arts and fine arts courses also became attractive, particularly for adults living in apartment buildings around Rittenhouse Square and other Center City neighborhoods.

Because so many of Temple's alumni live and work in the Philadelphia area, and a high percentage work "downtown," we moved the headquarters for our General Alumni Association into the former KYW building, as well. It became a convenient meeting place not only for alumni, but also for committees of the Board of Trustees. TUCC became so successful that additional space was required, making it necessary to rent most of a much larger building across Walnut Street. That building eventually took over as the primary facility for Temple's Center City operations. In those two buildings, not only credit courses, but all manner of non-credit courses – in real estate, the stock market, court reporting, and even dancing – were offered. Also, a senior citizens' organization called TARP (Temple Association for Retired Persons) was formed.

In short, Temple's Center City campus proved to be not only a window but a gateway to the entire university for Center City residents and professionals. The Ambler and TUCC experiences indicate the value in carry-ing university programs to locations where people live and work, especially for urban universities catering largely to commuting students.

Before taking office as president, I had begun to refer to Temple as "The Peo-ple's University." This slogan was not original; it had sprung from Temple's humble beginnings in Russell Conwell's ministerial study in 1884 and then had faded away. But it characterized my own philosophy of what Temple was and should be. A few faculty members felt I was advocating open student admissions or tagging Temple with a Marxist label. But what I meant by the term was that the university should appeal to all sectors of society, and be proud of it.

I struck this pose partly in response to a sometimes amusing, sometimes serious discussion among faculty members who yearned to see Temple be-come the "Harvard on the Delaware" (as in Philadelphia's Delaware River). Those who seriously advocated this notion believed that Temple, now state-related and more active in research, should emphasize graduate and profes-sional schools, using the undergraduate schools mainly to provide teaching experience for Ph.D. candidates.

I felt that we should strive for quality education and quality research activity in every field on both the undergraduate and the graduate levels. Our public support, it seemed to me, depended on the recognition that we were a broad-access institution, not a limited-access one. I repeatedly indi-cated my pride in Temple's heterogeneity – the fact that we enrolled students of all economic, racial, and religious backgrounds. I was convinced that we could attain high levels of achievement with such a student body. My expe-rience at Lincoln, in particular, indicated the potential of young people who don't necessarily score well on standardized tests or who may come from underprivileged backgrounds. I also argued that there was no inconsistency between operating large, broad-based undergraduate programs while oper-ating a medical school that could accept only 180 students out of an applicant pool of 5,000, a law school that could take about 380 out of a pool of 3,000 or 4,000, and a clinical psychology doctoral program that could admit no more than a dozen graduate students each year. In fact, I felt that such a range of programs demonstrated our strength and service as an urban university.

During the final months of my year as president-elect, an opportunity presented itself to put my beliefs into practice. Pennsylvania's Department of Welfare announced plans to build an entirely new facility for multiply hand-icapped, mentally retarded individuals called Woodhaven. In Pennsylvania, care of the mentally handicapped had been a burning issue for years. Experts argued against "warehousing," a term used to describe the practice of shutting away the retarded in sometimes deplorable facilities, often for life, so that they would not trouble their families or society. Along with many others, I was revolted by that practice.

The Woodhaven Project, located in Philadelphia's Northeast section, was the state's response to "warehousing" charges. At Woodhaven, residents would live in small, cottage-type facilities and receive a high level of attention from mental health professionals on site; they would also maintain close ties with community-based organizations and their own families. I met with Pennsylvania's secretary of welfare, Helene Wohlgemuth, and expressed my enthusiastic support for the project. That meeting led to the negotiation of a contract in which the state turned over complete responsibility for operating the Woodhaven facilities to the university. Such an arrangement appealed to state officials, including Governor Milton J. Shapp, because the state lacked personnel to run the program; it appealed to me because I felt that a state-related "People's University" should combine practical work in the field with the theories, statistics, and analyses taught in the classroom and published in scholarly journals.

Woodhaven's primary relationships with Temple began with the Special Education Department in the College of Education and with the School of Social Administration. Eventually, however, Woodhaven drew on the talents and skills of Temple faculty and students from fourteen different departments in six schools. The operation became a model of how a university and government can work together for the public good.

When I took over as president of Temple on July 1, 1973, many faculty and alumni expected the university to plan a formal inauguration ceremony. But since I had served as academic vice president for three and a half years, and since I had already had an elaborate presidential inauguration at nearby Lincoln University, I was already known to much of the greater Philadelphia community. Temple had received considerable favorable publicity at the time I assumed office, and I had been quoted a good deal in the newspapers. Also, I was serving on important civic committees and organizations and was well known to the movers and shakers of the Philadelphia area. I felt an elaborate inauguration would be both unnecessary and wasteful. Furthermore, I was not enchanted with pomp and ceremony. "Inaugurations cost as much as commencement exercises," I remarked at a meeting of the Faculty Senate, "and I can think of a lot of areas at Temple where the money can be put to better use."

As a consequence, my "coronation" took place on March 30, 1974, nine months after I had assumed office, at the General Alumni Association's annual Founder's Dinner. It cost the university almost nothing. My address that evening focused on Temple's founder, Russell Conwell, and his century-old dream of making higher education available to everyone who had the required intellectual ability and the will to work toward its development, regardless of caste or class. I also incorporated into my speech some ideas from "The Urban Involvement of Higher Education," a formal paper I had presented in Washington a month earlier at a special meeting of the American Council on Education. I reminded the audience that the sons and daughters of America's immigrants in the late-nineteenth and early-twentieth centuries had looked to Russell Conwell's university as a beacon of opportunity. Now that Temple was approaching its one-hundredth anniversary, I suggested, another group of students had come knocking at Temple's door.

"These new persons come not from the shores of Italy or the muddy villages of Eastern Europe," I remarked, "but from the dusty fields and towns of the American South, and from the barrios of Puerto Rico. And as it did for generations of urban immigrants before, Temple University is meeting the special needs of these new groups in their struggle for upward mobility."

My intent in this speech was to point toward a necessary expansion of Temple's academic programs at home and abroad and to wrestle, as my predecessors had, with a definition of the urban university. It was also my aim to prepare Temple for an increase in the number of minority students, to help the university work through its difficult financial problems and become one of the nation's great teaching and research centers.

After more than four years of close association with the university, I was more certain than ever that Temple and I were suited for each other. I liked the egalitarian purpose of Russell Conwell's dream, its unpretentious style, the informality associated with the institution, and even the gooey cheesesteak sandwiches offered by the ubiquitous campus food trucks.

I had long been accustomed to describing life and work as a balancing act. When asked what I hoped to accomplish at Temple, I often responded with a question: "How do we, as a university, balance the traditional, the academic, and the professional with the matter of service to the immediate and broader community? It is a question of balance."

But the first crisis I had to deal with as president had little to do with Temple's goals and programs. Rather, I was confronted with a fiscal problem at Temple University Hospital that could have plunged the entire university into bankruptcy.

In 1974, the hospital's accumulated debt was more than $25 million (the equivalent of $128 million at this writing, adjusted for inflation) and climbing daily. Located in the heart of poverty-stricken North Philadelphia, the hospital had taken on the task of meeting the health care needs of poor people living in its surrounding neighborhoods. At that time, the hospital was a 530-bed teaching and referral center that also served as family physician for 200,000 indigent people in the surrounding area. It was essentially a private facility performing a public service, yet receiving virtually no direct government aid for patient care and being drained financially in many ways. It housed the city's second busiest emergency room, with 45,000 cases a year. Only Philadelphia General Hospital – a city-owned facility – treated more cases. But many of the people who needed this kind of treatment at Temple Hospital could not afford to pay for it and were not covered by insurance, resulting in an annual loss to the hospital of $1 million. Shortly before I came to Temple, the university had threatened to close its emergency room if more funds from the city were not forthcoming. This backfired when the bellicose police commissioner, Frank Rizzo, said he would break doors down to get the sick and injured into the hospital for treatment. Now Rizzo was mayor.

Outpatient clinics at the hospital represented another financial drain. In 1974, these clinics recorded about 100,000 patient visits, most of them from people covered by Pennsylvania Medical Assistance. In those days, the cost of a clinic visit, including X-rays and lab tests, averaged $18. Yet the state reimbursed Temple only $6. For the hospital, the difference translated into another $2 million in yearly losses.

Finally, the hospital was bled by an additional $2 million annually for in-patient care, a category that included "over-stays" by elderly patients who could not find a nursing home to accept them, as well as private insurance plans that did not pay for the full costs of hospital stays. Year after year, hospital and university officials, even when complaining about lack of city contributions for emergency care, had accepted the losses as a cost of doing business in a community where such care was sorely needed. As I indicated in several speeches, "Each year, like a cancer left untreated, the indebtedness grew larger."

"It is a burden so oppressive that it threatens the very future of my institution," I told the Pennsylvania Senate Appropriations Committee on

May 1, 1974. I explained that in the days of Russell Conwell, Temple University Hospital was known as Good Samaritan. I played on that theme as I brought our enormous problem to the attention of the committee. "Like the biblical Good Samaritan," I said, "Temple Hospital still serves those in need. Yet today it is the Samaritan, not the person he helped on the road to Jericho, that lies bleeding and beaten." I asked for a meeting with the legislative leadership "to see if we can develop a feasible plan to reduce the hospital debt." I emphasized that public health care "is a public responsibility."

We at Temple had worked diligently to alleviate the problem. In one effort, three top Temple officials – A. Addison Roberts, chairman of our trustees; Dr. Paul Kotin, vice president for health sciences; and I – met with Governor Milton Shapp in his home in a Philadelphia suburb. While sitting around his kitchen table, my colleagues and I argued that the state should take over operation of the beleaguered hospital – or, better yet, make the entire Health Sciences Center (comprising Temple's hospital, medical school, dental school, pharmacy school, and College of Allied Health) into a separate state-owned institution. Those suggestions were not adopted, but Governor Shapp was very interested in them, and his understanding and help were vital in the solution that was worked out later.

Events moved very quickly after we met with the governor, but during the time we were working on various tactics to resolve the hospital's predicament, the university was forced to borrow heavily from three major banks. Temple already had a line of credit with these banks for short-term borrowing. However, with an accumulated hospital debt quickly approaching $30 million, the debt was obviously no longer short term. Nevertheless, the banks were tolerant at first, probably because of the university's relationship to the state.

Ultimately, however, notwithstanding my attempt to dissuade him, John Bunting, chairman of the lead bank, First Pennsylvania Banking and Trust Company, sent a letter to me on May 21, 1974, declaring that the situation at the hospital "has now reached the point where we must advise you that it will not be possible for us to renew your loans after the end of this calendar year. This position, which also reflect(s) the position of the Philadelphia National Bank and the Girard Bank, is forced upon us by the accumulated and continuing deficits of the hospital. We realize that to a large extent this financing problem is beyond your control, but feel that it cannot continue to be met by bank borrowings. Resolution of the problem must come from State and/or City funding with your commercial banks providing support only to the extent that working capital funds are required.... We feel that a soundly financed Temple University and Hospital are critical to the Philadelphia community and the commonwealth, but we cannot continue the present course of financing deficits by bank loans."[7]

In the end, this letter proved to be important when the university went public with the hospital's plight. I felt it was essential to bare our soul to the faculty and staff, and to the public, before the deficit grew much larger and the problem continued to fester. I had no doubt that we would eventually solve this problem and receive support, but it was necessary to move quickly and with full force.

Armed with Bunting's letter and graphs and statistics, we held a press conference on June 11, 1974, in Erny Amphitheater at the Temple University Hospital. A large delegation of press, radio, and television attended the conference. I laid out for them the crucial role that Temple University Hospital played in providing health care for a large section of Philadelphia's population, and the dire consequences – including closing the hospital or bankrupting the university – if substantial outside funding was not provided.

Our plea found receptive ears. During my presentation, Jim Logan, vice president for finance, sat next to one of the television newswomen, Jessica Savitch, and heard her whisper, "Something's got to be done to avoid this tragedy!" Later that day, I was interviewed by various media representatives and was quoted in the press, on the radio, and on television regarding our impossible financial situation, which had been caused by our providing millions of dollars' worth of *un*reimbursed and *under*-reimbursed care for the poor and low-income public.

Having attracted the public's attention, we then successfully pushed the legislative leaders to appoint a special Commonwealth Blue Ribbon Committee to work with Temple to solve the hospital's financial problems. This panel included the majority and minority leaders of the House and Senate Appropriations Committees, Pennsylvania's secretary of health, and community leaders. With the approval of the Blue Ribbon Committee, Temple hired a Boston-based consulting firm, Institutional Strategy Associates. Scores of possible solutions were studied, including detaching the hospital from the university corporation, merging with other hospitals, or "selling" (really "giving") the hospital to some other for-profit or nonprofit organization.

After burning the midnight oil drafting possible resolutions and statutes to be considered by the committee, David V. Randall, Temple's government

---

7 John Bunting to Marvin Wachman, letter, May 21, 1974, in the author's files.

relations director, and I engaged in shuttle diplomacy between Philadelphia and Harrisburg. We met with individual members of the committee as well as with other executive and legislative leaders.

The Blue Ribbon Committee recommended a statute that was finally enacted on October 8, 1975. The statute authorized the state to acquire Temple University Hospital for $30 million – the total accumulated deficit up to that time. This action was taken with the proviso that the hospital be leased back to Temple for $1 per year so that Temple could continue to manage its operations. As Senator Richard Tilghman, a panel member, stated, "We're not going to be stuck running that hospital!" The $30 million would come from the sale of Commonwealth bonds. Actually, the legislature had approved the sale of bonds a number of years earlier to finance construction of a new clinical teaching building (fancy words for a new hospital) in our Health Sciences Center.

By the end of 1974, a huge hole had been dug by the state in the ground behind the existing hospital buildings, "to make sure," as Senator Henry J. Cianfrani Jr., chairman of the Senate Appropriations Committee, put it to me, "that there will be no turning back in actually building that hospital for Temple." However, despite the senator's promise and the excavation, the plans for construction were put on hold while the hospital's debt was eliminated and the operation of the hospital reorganized.

The complicated settlement included the establishment of a fifteen-member board of governors to oversee the hospital's operation. Its first chairman, Fitz Eugene Dixon Jr., a lifelong Republican who was actively involved in implementing the settlement, stated years later that if it had not been for the role of the Democratic governor, Milton Shapp, "the whole damn university might have gone down the tube." Shapp himself had acknowledged that he could not have effected this solution without active support from two Temple alumni in the Pennsylvania General Assembly: Speaker of the House Herbert Fineman and Senator Cianfrani. All of this is no doubt true. But I also have no doubt that our public relations blitz was the tool that commanded the attention of the governor and the legislators in the first place.

The state also agreed to provide an additional $2.5 million for hospital operations in 1975 to help cover the cost of unreimbursed patient care. The consultants hired by Temple had said it was doubtful that the hospital could continue to serve the needy without extra Commonwealth support – a clear recognition that "public health care is a public responsibility." The $2.5 million provided by the state became an annual supplement that continued for many years.

The financial plight of Temple's hospital and the medical school often took up the bulk of our annual appearances before the Pennsylvania legislature's appropriations committees. Of course, many issues arose at these hearings that had nothing to do with our hospital or medical school. On one occasion, for instance, I was asked my opinion of Temple students' pushing for the establishment of a pub on campus for students age twenty-one and older. A state senator went on for quite a while about the evils of serving beer to students. When he concluded his discussion and posed a question to me on this subject, I simply replied, "Senator, you're asking the wrong person. I'm from Milwaukee." The entire hearing room erupted with laughter, and he pressed me no further. Ultimately, Temple did authorize the serving of beer in a small restaurant on its main campus. Appropriations hearings were almost always deadly serious, but a little humor, from time to time, helps not only the committee but the applicant seeking funds.

On another occasion, after Temple had resumed playing football against Pennsylvania State University, one state senator offered to build a new football stadium for Temple if we could just "beat Penn State!" One never knew what kinds of questions would be asked, or statements made, in these hearings, but they certainly kept us on our toes. Even when we were discussing a serious, specific funding issue, comments like that one sometimes best demonstrated what was really on a politician's mind.

Fitz Dixon was not only central to the deliberations and activities regarding Temple University Hospital, and other university matters, but he and his wife, Edie, had become extremely important to Addie and me in our lives as Temple's president and first lady. During my fourteen months as president-elect I had been trying to make a decision regarding our family's home, knowing that our social life would change upon my assumption of the presidency.

Our existing home in Jenkintown Manor was a very comfortable three-story stone house, where our two teenage daughters could live on the third floor (after we put in a new bathroom) with some privacy, and Addie and I could use the first floor for entertaining. Since Temple University, unlike most other colleges and universities, lacked a president's house, we originally considered building an extension to the living room for entertaining large groups and visiting dignitaries. As Addie and I planned this addition, Fitz Dixon called to say that he and his family were moving out of their home in the beautiful rural area of Erdenheim – just beyond Philadelphia's northwestern boundary.

Through his Widener and Elkins ancestors, Fitz Dixon was heir to two nineteenth-century streetcar fortunes. He explained to me that his maternal uncle, George Widener, had died, and under the family estate arrangements Dixon's family was required to move into the Widener home, located on a five-hundred-acre farm that raised Black Angus cattle and sheep. Fitz said that the home his family was leaving would eventually go to whichever of his children married first, but it would probably be about five years before that happened. He then suggested that the Wachman family occupy the house in that interim period, with no rent charged to Temple University.

At first, Addie and I were reluctant to accept that kind of offer from one of the university's trustees. But Fitz Dixon persuaded us to at least come over and look at the house. We did that one Saturday morning and were delighted by its warmth and style. It was certainly large enough for our small family, as well as for entertaining; in addition, it included an indoor–outdoor swimming pool next to the house and a large rear patio that looked out on the Dixon/Widener Race Track, where race horses were trained. The offer was so generous, and the home so comfortable, that we accepted almost immediately. We moved into the home in the fall of 1973.

The house was perfect for a college president, with plenty of parking space and large living and dining rooms for entertainment, including the Sunday afternoon fund-raising concerts given by musicians from Temple's School of Music. There was a pool house with separate dressing rooms for men and women and its own kitchen. The privacy it offered proved valuable to me, as president, whenever I wished to conduct private conversations concerning sensitive personnel issues.

In the basement, there were billiards, table tennis, dart games, and other activities for children and adults. Committee meetings could be held at the house, away from city pressures – an important benefit because the farm-like atmosphere exerted a calming influence on everyone. No matter what the issue under dispute, who could remain angry while sitting on a veranda looking at beautiful horses jogging around the track, or after taking a refreshing swim in the indoor–outdoor pool?

After five years, the Dixons' son, George, married and moved into the home, while the Wachmans found another fine residence in Philadelphia's lovely Chestnut Hill section. Although the house was not in such magnificent surroundings, we continued the pattern of entertaining faculty, trustees, and students in a manner befitting a college president.

Despite all the professional, administrative, and social activities connected with a college president's job, I never quite gave up the notion that I was still a teacher and professor. I especially enjoyed being invited, from time to time, to give a lecture or lead a class, and I relished participating in discussions with faculty and students about curricular changes and students' needs. In all my years as Temple's academic vice president and president, I don't believe I ever missed a Faculty Senate meeting. As president, I invariably reported at monthly Senate meetings on the state of the university, the issues before the trustees, and the challenges confronting the university. The questions or comments made by some professors at these meetings could be brutal, accusing the university (and, indirectly, me) of filling up their classes with incompetent students, or belittling the time and energy I devoted to the hospital's financial problems. Nevertheless, I always appreciated being involved in debates about significant academic/educational issues.

In the mid-'70s, on my initiative, Gerald Kneiter, president of the Faculty Senate, and I co-chaired a Commission on the Future of Temple University. This commission consisted of key faculty members, administrators, and several students. Our charge was to plan for the next decade of the university's operations. The commission and its staff also became the self-study body charged with preparing for the once-in-a-decade visit of an accreditation team representing the Middle States Commission on Higher Education.

The accreditation team was drawn from a cross-section of professors and administrators from similar universities. For nearly three days this nine-member evaluation team examined our comprehensive self-study report and interviewed faculty, staff, and students across the university in order to form a judgment as to whether Temple was fulfilling its published mission and goals. The team's report was issued in 1977, midway through my administration. It was remarkably favorable.

"We were particularly impressed," the team wrote, "by the degree of consensus that the basic goals of Temple University must be a combination of two quite distinct features: that Temple must be a people's university, a populist institution, stressing broad access and a willingness to serve its community, but that it can best fulfill this mission within the context of a heterogeneous system of public higher education by stressing quality. Temple University can on the whole be pleased with the heterogeneity of its student body, particularly at the main campus. It appears to be successful in continuing the much-quoted

Conwellian tradition [of providing] a relatively open path to quality educational programs."[8]

I couldn't have been more gratified by this statement. It proved to me that the goals I had set for the university at the beginning of my administration were being realized. Having served on a number of accreditation teams over the years, and knowing the serious way in which members of those teams operate, I was obviously pleased. There are those in the higher education world, especially in large universities, who look down on the accreditation process and feel they are above it. I have never felt that way and still believe that any college or university needs an external and objective view as to whether or not it is meeting its goals. The accreditation process provides that.

As time went on, the quality that had impressed the Middle States team began to earn Temple a national reputation that was reflected in our research grants. Temple's external funding for research and programs more than doubled from 1973 to 1981, growing from $26 million to $58 million.

The medical school and hospital had fine programs in cardiology and cardiothoracic surgery. They were strengthened considerably by the addition to their staff of Dr. Jacob Kolff, one of the pioneers in performing heart transplants and in the development of artificial hearts. In a large university, it is not normal practice for the president to be involved in the appointment of professors; that is left to the faculty, the department chair, and the dean of the school or college. In Dr. Kolff's case, however, the dean of the medical school asked me to interview the candidate and help recruit him. There was significant competition for someone of Dr. Kolff's stature, and his ability to bring in substantial government and private grants for his work explains why the medical school wanted me to help out in this case.

Dr. Kolff was impressed by our medical school and hospital, as well as by the work of the science departments and the engineering school. In our conversation, I stressed to him that the presence of many other medical schools and hospitals in Philadelphia, all with top-notch scholars and clinicians, would help him in his work. Dr. Kolff came to Temple in the late 1970s and, with his colleagues, established a thriving program in cardiothoracic surgery, including what later became one of the nation's largest adult heart transplant programs.

---

[8] Middle States Association of Colleges and Schools, Commission on Higher Education, "A Report of the Temple University Middle States Evaluation Team," Ernest A. Lynton, chairman, April 13, 1977, Board of Trustees file, Temple University, Philadelphia.

Important work was also done by Temple doctors Arthur Schwartz and Daniel Swern, who experimented with the hormone DHEA as an organic product to prevent cancer. More than twenty years later, Dr. Schwartz and his team continue to work on DHEA and other molecular forms to cure diabetes. Other members of the medical school staff developed important scientific and medical research in fields like thrombosis and hemostasis (led by Dr. Sol Sherry), recombinant DNA, the causes of aging, skin cancer, environmental pollution, arthritis, the relationship between drug addiction and crime, and multiple sclerosis. I had a personal interest in sports medicine because of several tennis injuries I sustained, one of which required elbow surgery. So when one of the first sports medicine centers in the country was established in Temple's Department of Orthopedics, I was among its strongest supporters and even helped recruit its staff.

Temple's reputation as a center of scholarly endeavor was enlarged by the continued growth of activities begun in the late 1960s during Paul Anderson's presidency. One such activity was the development of quarterlies like the *Journal of Ecumenical Studies* and the *Journal of Modern Literature*; another was the growth of Temple University Press, which by 1981 had published 216 books. One of these works, *The Secret Police in Lenin's Russia*, earned a Western badge of honor as *samizdat* literature in 1975, when it was banned at the Moscow Book Fair. An indication of the strength of the press's publications was that its books increasingly received regular reviews in such national media as the *Washington Post* and *New York Times*.

The accomplishments of individual faculty during that time are also worthy of notice. In 1981, History Professor Russell F. Weigley was nominated for a National Book Award for his major work *Eisenhower's Lieutenants*. "For a detailed account of the war in Europe," declared the *New York Review of Books*, "it is probably the most thorough we shall ever see."[9] In the same year, a young Temple English professor, Susan Stewart, was nominated for a Pulitzer Prize for her first book of verse, *Yellow Stars and Ice*, and one of her colleagues, David Bradley, received the prestigious PEN/Faulkner Award for his best-selling historical novel *The Chaneysville Incident*. A year later, another English Department professor, Toby Olson, received the PEN/Faulkner Award.

Within Temple's many schools and colleges, important academic activities bore witness to a growing drive for excellence. The College of Liberal Arts, while struggling with the issue of the worth of the humanities and liberal arts in a world of vocationalism, strengthened its course offerings through such

---

9 *New York Review of Books*, September 24, 1981, 55.

innovative and interdisciplinary programs as intellectual heritage, the master of liberal arts degree, and a revamped honors program. I was more than happy to assist in the fund-raising required to support these new programs and was particularly pleased when I was able to secure grants from the Mellon Foundation for use in strengthening our freshman and sophomore courses in the liberal arts.

In 1974, after years of failed attempts, the undergraduate college was finally able to initiate a Phi Beta Kappa chapter – a significant symbol of excellence, important to students and faculty. John Hope Franklin, pre-eminent scholar of African American history and, at that time, president of Phi Beta Kappa, came to Philadelphia to preside over the installation. Dr. Franklin had been a personal friend of mine since my Salzburg Seminar days and stayed at the Wachman home during his visit.

Until the 1970s, it was unusual for college campuses to be unionized, except for a few urban institutions where unions represented nonfaculty employees. In 1970, Temple had only three campus unions, all of them representing maintenance employees and skilled workers. But by 1977, the university had to bargain with fourteen unions, including, after 1973, the American Association of University Professors (AAUP). This union represented some 1,400 faculty, librarians, and academic professionals in all Temple schools except law (which later organized its own group), dentistry, and medicine. In large part, this broad union development at Temple resulted from the state legislature's passage, in the late 1960s, of a very important piece of legislation: Act 195, The Public Employees' Relations Act, which permitted almost all categories of employees in state-related institutions, including faculty, to unionize.

Negotiations between administration and faculty to reach their first collective bargaining contract had begun toward the end of President Anderson's term of office. There were interminable sessions with the Pennsylvania Labor Relations Board (PLRB), in which university and faculty attorneys jousted over whether department chairpersons should be included in the bargaining unit, and whether all schools and colleges should be required to have union representation. The administration naturally sought to exclude chairpersons, since they were administrators. The department chairpersons themselves, many of whom were more concerned about job security and benefits than about the institution's well-being, felt otherwise. One of them testified: "I have no administrative or management responsibilities, except to make sure there are enough paper clips in the office." This from a chairman who did almost no teaching and managed a department of dozens of faculty, plus graduate assistants and secretaries!

As vice president for academic affairs at that time, I served as administration spokesman at PLRB hearings on these issues. As I discussed the process in a 1975 speech, "For both sides, in the first round of negotiations at Temple, there was one overriding question: How do you take the touchstone of the industrial labor contract and re-shape it to fit the academic community, while still preserving as much as possible that delicate quality called collegiality?"[10]

Much to my chagrin, at just about the time that the state hearing examiner was finally becoming acquainted with the difference between academic units and manufacturing company production units, he was, for unknown reasons, removed by the PLRB. A new examiner, who appeared to have had all of his experience in hearing steel union cases, was appointed. We did not get very far with him. He rejected the administration's requests to exclude chairpersons. He and the PLRB also disregarded the administration's argument that the professional schools' faculty were members of the University Faculty Senate, and that the deans of those schools served on Temple's Council of Deans and reported, as did other deans, to the vice president for academic affairs.

The negotiations persisted for about a year until a settlement was reached in 1974, at which time Temple and AAUP signed their first faculty labor contract. In the process, Temple became the first major, multipurpose university in Pennsylvania to have a faculty union. This contract wielded a large impact on faculty–administration relationships and also on the power and influence of the Council of Deans and the Faculty Senate. By formalizing the natural adversarial differences between faculty and administration, it removed a good deal of the flexibility that deans had always enjoyed in dealing with personnel matters.

"Without any question, I believe the negotiations produced some very innovative solutions to serious questions about collective bargaining in higher education," I readily conceded in my talk on "collegiality and collective bargaining" at the annual meeting of the Pennsylvania Division of the AAUP in March 1975. "I think it also helped engender mutual trust between faculty and administrators – those two sides forever passionately involved in a love–hate relationship, with or without a union." On the other hand, I said, "I cannot stand here today and say that every college or university faculty should have

---

[10] Speech at the annual meeting of the Pennsylvania Division of the AAUP, March 1975, in the author's files. A shortened version of the speech was published in *Pennsylvania Division AAUP Newsletter*, vol. 20, no. 2, June 1975.

collective bargaining. I simply do not believe it. Whether or not an institution can benefit from faculty unionization or collective bargaining depends upon many variables."[11]

Negotiations for that first faculty contract were largely conducted by attorneys. However, as years passed, attorneys played little, if any, role. Instead, Robert Harrington, who had negotiated all of the nonfaculty union contracts, was brought in from the university's Personnel Office to work with administration and faculty on subsequent AAUP contracts. Bob was a good-natured Temple graduate and former basketball player who was soon promoted to associate vice president for personnel. He turned out to be a genius at labor relations. Somehow, he quickly gained the confidence of his adversaries, as well as university administrators, labor mediators, and arbitrators. As Leroy Dubeck, a physics professor who served as chief negotiator for the AAUP, observed, "Both sides had become more self-reliant, and an atmosphere of cooperation in solving problems had developed over the years." Although the administration had to deal with several strikes by other unions during the '70s and early '80s, none involved the faculty union. Our experience demonstrated that it was very important to keep highly emotional people – as well as those who were overly legalistic – out of the negotiations. Pragmatic discussions, with an understanding of what the opposition felt, were exceedingly important.

In fact, the faculty union and Temple's General Alumni Association worked together with the administration in lobbying the state legislature in 1977, when the university experienced one of its most serious financial crises. The fiscal year 1977–78 began on July 1, 1977, but the Pennsylvania General Assembly had not yet agreed on a budget. As a result, Pennsylvania's state-related and state-aided colleges and universities watched helplessly as the months dragged on without a resolution. I canceled out of a General Alumni Association trip to London because I was afraid to leave Pennsylvania before appropriations were agreed upon; I had to be ready to testify in Harrisburg on Temple's behalf at a moment's notice. By October 1977, Temple was existing on tuition and borrowed money, with interest on its loans costing $4,400 a day. I debated members of the General Assembly on television regarding the needs of the state-supported colleges.

Finally, there was a breakthrough, but not before the university had been forced to pay hundreds of thousands of dollars in interest payments on short-term loans. During the discussions in Harrisburg, Speaker Herbert Fineman, our Temple alumnus, argued that Temple should be compensated for these

---

[11] Ibid.

outrageous interest payments. But such compensation never materialized. To make matters worse, at the close of 1977, because of the state's fiscal condition, Governor Richard Thornburgh rescinded $1 million of Temple's appropriation, as he had done with many other state-supported institutions. That forced the university, with great reluctance, to increase tuition modestly for the spring semester of 1978.

By the mid-1970s, I had become aware of three very substantial changes affecting the administration of higher education: unionization (discussed earlier), regulation, and litigation. The notion that colleges and universities were cloistered, ivory-towered, self-regulating, and self-policing institutions was fast disappearing. The old principle, in loco parentis – by which colleges and universities acted as parents for students, operated as they saw fit, and did what they felt best for their institutions and their students – was almost dead. In the mid-1960s, as I recall, the courts first began seriously to consider cases contesting college regulation of students. In one case, in a Catholic college, a senior student married his long-time girlfriend and was refused permission to graduate, because the institution had a regulation against student marriage for undergraduates. That rule was voided by a court decision – only one example of a number of cases in which courts overruled decisions made by the administrative officers of colleges and universities.

I have never been a fan of in loco parentis, but I know that in some cases the courts intervene in university personnel matters that the judges don't understand. If the court does its homework well, its involvement can be helpful all around, since university policies must be consistent with the policies of government.

In the same period, federal aid to education on a massive scale was initiated to assist institutions in dealing with the nation's burgeoning student population. Federal efforts included funding for new dormitories and other campus facilities, providing scholarship and loan assistance to students, and supporting a great deal of research and program activity on campuses across the country.

This government financial help inevitably led to government regulation. In exchange for federal funding – which just about all colleges, public and private, accepted to some degree – colleges were required to abide by new federal affirmative action standards for admission of minority students: Title VII for employees, Title IX for student athletes, and all kinds of directives (like occupational safety and pension regulations) that were originally intended for business and industry and hadn't previously been applicable to educational institutions.

During the 1960s, the number of court cases involving educational institutions was still quite limited. As president of Lincoln, I was involved in only two court cases during the entire decade. But at Temple in the 1970s and '80s it appeared that we were involved with some kind of litigation almost every day. And Temple was typical of what was happening at universities around the country. It is quite appropriate for students and faculty to exercise their legal rights. My point in mentioning these changes is simply to indicate that university administration has become more complicated because of them. I have discovered over the years that whether I agree or not with the decision in a case depends most often on a judge's reasoning.

In one case at Temple, a doctoral candidate in the field of education had served as a teaching assistant. At the end of one semester, his department discovered that he had enrolled himself in courses that he taught himself, and had given himself "A"s. When the chairman realized what had happened, he called the graduate student/teaching assistant into his office, verified the facts, and then set up a hearing with the appropriate departmental committee. As a result of the hearing, the student was dismissed from the doctoral program, and from his teaching position. He took the case to court, and won a reprieve, on the basis that adequate due process had not been provided.

Ultimately, the university decided not to fight this case, because the monetary compensation was minimal and much less costly than the legal fees required to appeal the court decision. (The College of Education had given him due process through an additional hearing, but that didn't satisfy the court.) Also, as we had guessed, the student did *not* attempt to return to the department to complete his doctorate. Obviously, the ill will he had generated in the department would have made it difficult for him to work closely with any member of the College of Education faculty.

In a second case, a student sued the Psychology Department and (of course) the president of the university because she had not been admitted into the Ph.D. program in clinical psychology. The independent professional accrediting agency approved only a limited number of students for admission to that program, and the complaining student lacked the excellent grades and relevant experience of those accepted. She lost that case, but the legal expenses the university incurred in fighting it were sizeable.

A third case involved a student who had flunked out of Temple's law school three times but had been given permission to re-enter the first two times because of extenuating circumstances. When he was dismissed for the third time, he sued on the ground that his poor grades were due to circumstances beyond his control. In filing this suit, he inadvertently proved the wisdom of the law school faculty, because he sued the university from the wrong jurisdiction, and his case was thrown out of court. Obviously, he had learned very little during his three stints in the law school. But the larger point is that, in previous times, filing such a suit would have been unthinkable.

In keeping with the growing complexity of Temple was its steady development from local beginnings, in 1884, into a national and international institution. I felt that a true university, reflecting the Latin cognate from which the word came, had to embrace more than just its own region or state, or even its own nation. My commitment to the international aspects of education, of course, had taken root during my teaching days at the GI University in Biarritz, France, at the end of World War II; at the University of Maryland's program in Trieste and Germany several years later; during my direction of the Salzburg Seminar; and through my African travels for Lincoln University. Well before coming to Temple, in a commencement address at Central State University in Ohio in April 1966, I had reflected that the word *university*

> represents in the finest sense a universality, an openness to ideas, and a continuous search for the truth. It also represents transcendence over parochialism and national chauvinism in the development of attitudes and in the process of training young people for life and service.
>
> A university cannot justify that label in this era, unless it represents all types of people – of various races, religions, nationalities, and backgrounds. And it cannot justify the label unless it attacks the problems of these people getting along together in a constructive fashion through its curriculum, its co-curricular activities, and through the vital process of simply living together.[12]

Temple University actually began its foreign "outreach" long before I arrived. Faculty exchanges had taken place for many years, and students had sometimes been encouraged to study abroad for a semester or a year. But the late '60s witnessed a new emphasis on overseas activity at Temple. In 1967, the university authorized its Tyler School of Art to launch a "year abroad" program in Rome. Charles LeClair, dean of Tyler, had discovered a vacant mansion on the Tiber River near central Rome, and he subsequently located all classrooms, studios, and the library in that building. In the '70s, that program was expanded to include the liberal arts and eventually, from time to time, communications and theater, engineering technology, architecture, and law.

---

[12] From the author's commencement address at Central State University, Wilberforce, Ohio, April 17, 1966, in *Journal of Human Relations* 16, no. 1 (1968).

Between 1973 and 1982, Temple established new programs on practically every continent. A business administration program was begun in Brazil. Liberal arts programs opened in Paris and Dublin, the latter under the direction of the Temple poet, translator, and scholar Thomas Kinsella. Faculty and students from Temple's communications and theater programs, as well as the medical school, participated in programs in London, and Temple's Human Services Center developed a joint program with the University of Haifa in Israel. In addition to summer classes in Rome, the law school subsequently established educational programs in Ghana, Greece, and Israel and engaged in faculty exchanges with those nations.

Perhaps most aggressive of all in seeking international links was the College of Education. Its faculty seemed ready to go anywhere. As a result of initial contacts made by a Temple alumnus, Jack Lutz, who had been working in Africa, I authorized investigating the feasibility of introducing an ambitious teacher training degree program in Nigeria, to be sponsored by the United Nations Educational, Scientific and Cultural Organization (UNESCO). The result was the establishment of the Temple–Abraka Program in the Nigerian state of Bendel.

Beginning in the mid-1970s, the College of Education sent its graduate faculty members to Abraka College to provide course offerings leading to the master of education degree. Before the Temple program was created, teachers at Abraka and elsewhere in Nigeria had to leave the country to pursue graduate education. The Temple plan – which was much less costly for them, more convenient, and of high quality – made so much sense that UNESCO and the United Nations Development Program (UNDP) funded its beginning years, and the Bendel state government funded it for two additional years after United Nations funding expired.

In the summer of 1980, a group of us, including Jay Scribner, dean of the College of Education, and Temple trustee Henry Nichols, a well-known black minister from Philadelphia and previously president of Philadelphia's Board of Education, traveled by plane to Lagos and to Benin, the capital of Bendel State. From there we took a lengthy van trip over almost impassable dirt roads, eroded by ruts and pools of water, to reach Abraka. We were there to participate in the first commencement exercise held overseas by Temple – perhaps the first by any American university in Africa.

Under a shed, in an outdoor morning ceremony held on a hot, humid August day, I conferred degrees on sixty-two proud students who had successfully completed Temple's graduate program at Abraka College. In the fall, another thirty-seven students completed their studies. The program was such an unqualified success that several other states in Nigeria contacted our College of Education about the possibility of having Temple set up similar programs for them. Only Nigeria's political turmoil at that time kept Temple from mounting programs like Abraka's in a number of other Nigerian states.

The College of Education was also involved in another creative effort, this time in Europe. Temple's Research and Program Development Office received an RFP (request for proposal) from the U.S. Army for a major educational program involving tens of thousands of American military personnel across the continent of Europe. Formulating a response required that I fly to army headquarters in Frankfurt to refine and develop the proposal, including curriculum and budget. My task in Europe was simplified by Milton Rock, an active Temple trustee and managing partner of the international management consulting company Hay Associates, who offered me the use of Hay's Frankfurt office. Hay personnel provided the secretarial, copying, and communication support that was essential to our meeting the army's technical and deadline requirements. After two weeks of negotiations on details with the army, our submission was accepted over competing bids from other universities. The army granted us a $23 million contract, and I was then able to return to Philadelphia.

The task of the Temple European Army Mission – or TEAM, as it was called – was to train members of the armed forces assigned to NATO bases across Europe, from Great Britain to Turkey, in reading and mathematics skills so that they could function more effectively. The army, entirely dependent on volunteers, had recruited many soldiers with Hispanic backgrounds who knew little English. Others, products of inner-city as well as suburban school districts, had somehow graduated from high school without mastering fifth-grade English and mathematics. Without language and computational skills, they were of little value to an army that was increasingly dependent on technical equipment.

Temple's responsibility was to send faculty and administrators to Europe in order to hire and train qualified teachers, and to design educational materials for their use. This was probably the army's largest single contract of its kind with any American university. I felt the TEAM program was not only an opportunity for the university to serve its nation, but also to give Temple faculty an excellent setting in which to develop methods that could be used to improve basic education back in the United States.

At about the same time that the TEAM program was well under way and the Temple–Abraka Program culminated, Temple's interest in Asia was gaining momentum. In Philadelphia we had been enrolling a fair number of

Japanese students and increasing numbers of Chinese students from Taiwan. In 1976, officials of the Republic of China on Taiwan had invited me and three other university presidents to visit their country. They labored under the mistaken notion that college presidents had a great deal of influence with American leaders in Congress and the White House. We four college presidents and our wives were treated royally and were honored by the opportunity to meet with presidents and other officers of major universities, as well as with top government officials. In addition, we were flown to the ship-building port of Kaoshiung in the south of the island, the atomic energy plant at Keelung in the north (headed by a graduate of Penn State, whose president, Jack Oswald, and his wife, Rose, were with us), the beautiful Taroko Gorge in the west (where the bulk of indigenous Taiwanese live), and to Quemoy, the garrison island just off the mainland coast. We all came to appreciate what the Nationalist Chinese had done to build up the economy and the national structure of the Republic of China, even though democracy certainly was not yet the norm on that island in 1976.

The People's Republic of China on the mainland, at that time, was pursuing scientific and educational contacts abroad and seeking international exchanges, following the disastrous decade-long nightmare of Chairman Mao Tse-tung's Great Proletarian Cultural Revolution. After Mao's death in 1976 and his replacement by the reformer Deng Xiaoping, the Chinese were looking for stability and endeavoring to build upon successful training and development programs in other countries. Temple already had a Chinese heritage, of sorts: Temple's founder, Russell Conwell, had traveled through China in the nineteenth century as a foreign correspondent for the *Boston Herald Traveler*. More important, we had a contemporary connection in our Chinese-born professor Mann Chiang Niu, a molecular biologist.

With my assistance, Dr. Niu had returned to China several times shortly after Richard Nixon made his historic visit there in 1972. As a result of these early trips, Dr. Niu had become well connected to the post–Mao power structure of the People's Republic. With Dr. Niu's help, Temple had honored Deng Xiaoping during his triumphant tour of the United States in 1979, when the United States formally re-established relations with China. The television anchors Walter Cronkite and Tom Brokaw were among many notables in the audience when I presented the diminutive and affable Deng an honorary doctor of laws degree at Blair House, just across the street from the White House. At that time, Deng was considered a reformer and "liberal" who advocated broad freedoms in China, particularly in the economic and educational areas, and in that hopeful moment the honorary degree was widely applauded. With that good-will gesture Deng became an official Temple University alumnus. He seemed to enjoy receiving a small replica of the Temple owl mascot, and he did not forget his new "alma mater."

That same year, Temple's College of Education worked with Ohio State University to create a program to teach English at Beijing University and at the Huazhong Institute of Technology in the city of Wuhan. In June 1980, officials of the Chinese Academy of Sciences invited me to bring a Temple delegation to tour China and visit a number of their universities. Our nine-person delegation – representing the fields of education, chemistry, engineering, anthropology, geography, English as a second language, and university relations – spent most of June 1980 touring six cities in China and visiting universities.

On our delegation's June 1980 visit to China, we were invited to meet with Deng Xiaoping in Beijing's Great Hall of the People, on Tiananmen Square. This remarkable gathering (the first time Deng had ever met with delegates from an American university) took place in Room 115, the same meeting hall in which Mao had entertained high-ranking foreign guests. Sitting in a large, upholstered chair, dressed in a gray uniform, sipping jasmine tea, and chain-smoking his favorite Panda brand of Chinese cigarettes, the four-foot, eleven-inch Deng chatted with me and my fellow travelers for more than an hour.

To my surprise and enjoyment, at one point Deng steered the conversation into a discussion of the American Civil War and a famous book about it that he said he had read and enjoyed very much: *Gone With The Wind*. The book was fast becoming a best seller in Communist China, and I casually mentioned that a movie had been made from the novel, with Clark Gable as the leading actor.

"They are making a movie out of this book?" Deng asked, with great interest, through one of his two interpreters.

"It *was* a movie," I responded "quite a few years ago. I'd say about 40 years."

"The novel is well written," Deng remarked. "In China, there was a debate about the book because some people said it favors the slave owners in the South. We wanted to publish the book, so the criticism doesn't matter to us. The public should be given a chance to read it and make up their own minds."

My clearest recollection of Deng Xiaoping lay in his repeated statement that his generation had to give way to younger people, and he wanted to give up his leadership role. "Life-time appointments are tantamount to feudalism," he said. Yet he didn't exactly practice what he preached. He was seventy-six when I heard him make that statement, and nine years later he was still in control when the Chinese army violently dispersed student demonstrators in Beijing's Tiananmen Square.

At that point, some Temple students and faculty recommended withdrawing Deng's honorary degree. But in retrospect, Temple was wise not to burn its bridges to China. In January 1999, Temple established a law school program in China, and when Minister Wan Xue Yuan of the State Bureau of Foreign Experts visited the campus, my having granted the degree to Deng was once again applauded. It was rather surprising to me that the way a national leader is regarded can change so rapidly, from one extreme to another, even among scholars at a large university. Ultimately, however, a college president, after seeking as much balanced advice as possible, must follow his own counsel, regardless of the feelings of some impetuous faculty or students.

The Deng degree was an important gesture, but only a gesture nevertheless. The real seeds of our China relationship were planted during our 1980 tour there. Sitting around a large conference table, sharing the ever present green tea, I negotiated a sister relationship with one of China's key institutions of higher learning, Nankai University in Tianjin (Zhou Enlai's alma mater). We also worked out an arrangement with a teacher training school, Tianjin Normal College.

Within two years of our visit, more Chinese students and faculty than ever before were working at various levels at Temple; one Temple undergraduate was completing a full year of her studies in China; and two Temple faculty were teaching full time at the former college that had become Tianjin Normal University. Also, a member of Temple's staff was leading a study tour on the mainland. Furthermore, a nine-member Temple group was touring China as part of a Fulbright fellowship program, and Dr. Joseph Schmuckler, chairman of Temple's Science Education Department (who had been on the original trip in 1980), was preparing to make his third trip to Tianjin to aid the Normal School faculty in teacher education in China. Opening up mainland China made it possible to supplement or replace activity on Taiwan – where, for instance, doctoral students in Chinese history had been previously required to work exclusively.

Students from mainland China as well as Taiwan continue to enroll at Temple on the undergraduate and graduate levels to this day. But more important than Temple's activities there was my establishment of a full-fledged Temple branch in Tokyo in June 1982, a few weeks before I stepped down as president.

With the Pacific rim of Asia becoming exceedingly important econom-
ically and politically, some of us at Temple envisioned setting up a center
in Tokyo to give Temple faculty further opportunities to experience life and
work in an Asian country and cultivate ties with Japanese academics. Many
Japanese felt that their universities and for-profit language institutes were not
doing a good job of teaching English, so our original idea was to set up an
English language center and later expand it into liberal arts and business subjects. To develop and direct this program, I selected William F. Sharp, history
professor and head of Temple's undergraduate honors program. Bill Sharp
and I searched all over Tokyo for appropriate office and classroom space before finding the right location for our first headquarters in the Shiba section
of the city.

Negotiations with Japanese government officials for the establishment
of Temple University Japan (called TUJ) were complicated (necessitating
several visits to Tokyo) and took almost a year. Japanese authorities were
as reluctant to accept an American educational institution as they were to
approve foreign competition for their commercial products. Finally, with
the help of several Japanese educators, we were able to convince Japan's
Department of Education that we did not seek Japanese formal accreditation
but would maintain the high standards dictated by U.S. accrediting bodies.

Our efforts culminated in ceremonies at a large Hyatt Hotel in Tokyo in
June 1982, when several hundred potential Japanese students came to learn
about our program and to register for classes. We had been able to organize a
Japanese board of directors composed of interested business and educational
leaders. Technically, this board contracted with us for Temple's services, much
as an American university board would operate. The board was staffed by
our original Japanese contact person in Tokyo who, unfortunately, thought
that the initial tuition payments belonged to him personally and absconded
with them. Despite this rocky start, Temple University Japan developed into a
very successful program, both academically and financially. It has been valuable to the students who have attended the classes in language, the arts, and
business, many of whom have subsequently transferred to Temple University in Philadelphia or to other American colleges. Full degree curricula there
expanded remarkably in the 1980s and '90s. TUJ also turned out to be strate-
gically important to Temple faculties in law, business, and other fields as they
began to develop new programs in China and Korea.

In 1997, to help celebrate the fifteenth anniversary of the founding of
TUJ, I was invited by my successor, President Peter J. Liacouras, to speak
at commencement exercises in Tokyo. Two hundred and eighteen graduates

received Temple degrees in Tokyo that year, including sixty-seven with master's degrees in economics and education, and three with doctorates in education. Except for the doctoral students, about twenty masters, and a handful of B.A.s, all the degree recipients were Japanese. It was a gala occasion, American-style, with all participants robed in academic caps and gowns and Japanese graduates speaking in fluent English about their experiences. Following the ceremonies, hundreds of family members of the graduates joined us at a colorful reception and buffet.

In 2002, when TUJ marked its twentieth anniversary, I was again asked to speak at its graduation. Robert J. Reinstein, dean of Temple's law school, who was in charge of Temple's programs in Japan, China, and Europe, also cajoled me into giving the commencement address to the graduating class of the master of law program we had mounted at Beijing several years earlier. This program serves the many Chinese lawyers who are eager to learn more about Western-style law and to be able to handle international cases. For several years, some thirty-two young lawyers and practicing judges have been admitted to our program each year and completed the equivalent of a two-year study program in law, leading to a master's degree. The program includes one semester of residence in the United States (normally a summer), and has been funded and is growing. Reinstein's invitation brought me back to China at age eighty-three, twenty-two years after opening our initial mainland programs in the People's Republic.

When I arrived in Beijing, I found that I was regarded as somewhat of a celebrity by the students and their families. All of them seemed to know that I had awarded an honorary degree to Deng Xiaoping in 1979. Consequently, almost every graduate, and his or her parents, wanted to be photographed with me after the commencement ceremonies. My address – translated into Chinese by the co-director of our program, Mo Zhang – focused on the role the law school program was playing in China's economic development and its relationship with other countries. I emphasized the important role the graduates would play in China's new era of membership in the World Trade Organization and in the increased entrepreneurial activity that was sure to follow. I stressed that the graduates represented the "wave of the future," because their country was becoming more and more involved in complex economic matters.

Temple's growing presence overseas has in turn attracted more foreign students to Temple's campus in Philadelphia. Even by the '70s, when I became president, the changing nature of Temple's student body was visible to anyone visiting our classrooms or roaming the streets of the main campus.

The subsequent development of the new School of Engineering, the growing respect for the School of Communications and Theater in the United States and abroad, and the continuing strength of Temple's graduate and professional schools all made the university attractive to a great variety of foreign students of all ages and backgrounds. During this same period, it also became clear that Temple's medical school had great drawing power for international scholars and clinicians, giving it and the Temple University Hospital a decidedly cosmopolitan outlook. On my watch from 1973 to 1982, the number of foreign students and visiting scholars at Temple grew from about 400 to 1,400, representing eighty-five nations. Since 1982, that number has continued to grow.

This growth inevitably pushed Temple's General Alumni Association to expand its international agenda. Addie and I were invited to participate in a number of trips during my tenure as vice president and president. Two of the outstanding trips we led were to Greece and to Israel, where the university's School of Law offered programs, and where alumni lived and worked. These alumni trips gave us a chance to verify and take pride in the truth of one of the university's slogans, "Temple Grads Are Everywhere!" In Greece, in 1972, I had the opportunity to present the General Alumni Association's Order of the Owl Award to U.S. Ambassador Henry Tasca, class of '34. With tears in his eyes, the ambassador told us that he would never forget Temple University for "giving a poor kid like me, from the streets of South Philadelphia, a chance to get an education and serve his country."

In Israel, we met and celebrated with a diverse group of alumni in the King David Hotel in Jerusalem. Among these were *Time* magazine's Jerusalem reporter, Marlin Levin; members of the Israeli government; and graduates who had recently migrated from the United States. After one exhausting day of traveling by bus, hiking, and visiting Israel's biblical sites, we finally checked in at our hotel in Tiberias, on the Sea of Galilee. It was midnight by the time we went to bed. Shortly thereafter, we were awakened by a long-distance call from Philadelphia. It was the student editor of the *Temple News* who wanted to know what we were doing, and what the weather was like.

A few days later, when I returned to the campus, I was greeted with headlines in the student newspaper that read, "Temple President Basks in Sun in Israel while Students Freeze in Philadelphia." Actually, it was fairly cool in Israel in March 1976, although warmer than Philadelphia at that time of year. My only real problem with the 1976 editor was that he invariably mixed up the financial figures for the Temple Hospital, which we had to correct.

In my dealings with student editors over the years, I found it best to be as open as possible. It's wise not to hide anything from them but, instead, to take the trouble to inform them and correct any errors they make.

In the late fall of 1976, I was invited to Nigeria by an old Lincoln friend and alumnus, K. O. Mbadiwe, who had been a cabinet member in Nigeria's first civilian government in the '60s. He wanted me to come to his home town of Arondizogue to dedicate a new rural hospital. He and I were to participate in a fund-raising drive for the Ojike Memorial Hospital (named for another Lincoln alumnus, Robinson Mbouri Ojike, class of 1943) and to try to establish a relationship between it and the medical schools of the University of Nsukka and Temple University.

I insisted that Dr. Roger Sevy, dean of our medical school, accompany me on this trip. Our visit led to short-term consulting relationships and Temple's assistance in procuring necessary medical supplies and equipment for the new hospital, but nothing of a sustained nature. Dr. Sevy and I recommended that cooperation with the nearby University of Nsukka would be more reasonable and fruitful for the Ojike Memorial. Both Dr. Sevy and I spoke at the elaborate ceremonies dedicating the new facility; sang, danced, and ate with young and old Nigerians at the festivities; and traveled to the University of Nsukka to explain the needs of the Ojike hospital. We then went to other cities to meet with prominent individuals around the country in order to help Mbadiwe get financial support for the Ojike hospital. Everywhere we went, the ebullient Mbadiwe shouted "Timber! Caterpillar! Caliber!" as he came upon old friends. I have no idea what this meant, but he and his two American guests were invariably greeted with enthusiasm and champagne toasts before we sat down to the business of fund raising. K. O. had such a warm and persuasive approach that no one turned us down.

At Arondizogue, we met Mbadiwe's nephew, Dr. Chukwuemeka Mbadiwe. A young physician performing his required national medical service in the Muslim northern section of Nigeria, he was visiting his home village. "Emeka," as he was called, was very interested in coming to America to specialize in surgery but did not know how to meet the requirements demanded by U.S. medical and government agencies. At our invitation, he came to Philadelphia the following summer; he stayed at the Wachman home while Dr. Sevy and I arranged for him to get proper certification and to secure a residency at one of the hospitals affiliated with Temple University Medical School.

Emeka remained in Philadelphia, eventually became chief resident at Hahnemann University Hospital, and earned his specialty credential in surgery. His wife, Evonne, came to the United States a bit later and earned a master's degree in French from Temple; they had two children while living in Philadelphia. After eight years, they returned to Nigeria, where Emeka became the chief surgeon for the Police Hospital in Lagos, and Evonne managed to get a government job in the field of education.

Their return to Nigeria was not the happy ending they had hoped for. The couple had been in the United States too long to be able to tolerate either Nigeria's military government or the lack of basic hospital supplies and equipment in Lagos. As a result, Emeka came back to the United States to work in the Crozier-Chester Medical Center near Chester, Pennsylvania, while living in Wilmington, Delaware, where his entire family is now located. Even though the Mbadiwes had previously experienced at least one episode of racial harassment here (young white teens burned a cross in their yard in Philadelphia), they loved living in the United States and preferred it to Nigeria. Their experience and success was another example of the positive effect of Temple's outreach programs.

While Temple was becoming more international in its makeup, activities, and outlook, it was also becoming increasingly diversified at home. It was attracting and recruiting more "nontraditional American students," a term applied to blacks, Hispanics, Asian Americans, older adults, and the handicapped. With our encouragement, the percentage of these students within Temple's total enrollment grew substantially during the '70s and early '80s (and continued to increase after that time), as did the number of minority and women faculty. As I noted in my President's Annual Report for 1980–81, Temple's record in these areas "can be matched by few institutions of higher learning in the nation."

The commencement exercises of 1976 demonstrated the type of institution Temple had become. That graduating class included Melvin Gessleman, who, at eighty-two, was the oldest recipient of a bachelor's degree in Temple's history; David Hartman, the first blind medical student in the twentieth century in the United States; and Frank Bowen, a twenty-five-year-old black quadriplegic who was confined to a wheelchair after a freak high school football accident left him paralyzed. These remarkable people represented the fulfillment of Russell Conwell's dream of educational opportunities for all.

It was especially gratifying for me to see the increased enrollment of handicapped, as well as minority, students. With my approval, David Hartman had been admitted as the 181st member of a medical school class whose prescribed number was 180, so that no one would feel he or she was being denied admission in favor of a "questionably" admitted student. Professor Prince Brigham, an assistant dean of the medical school, had agreed to be Hartman's mentor and liaison with the medical staff to make certain he was capable of pursuing a medical education.

David amply demonstrated that he was up to the challenge. On one occasion, he was making the rounds with other students at St. Christopher's Hospital for Children, the pediatrics hospital for the Temple University Medical School. I happened to be in the department chairman's office that day while the students were there discussing difficult cases. There was considerable noise outside the chairman's open door, and before anyone with full sight could move, David stood up, walked to the door, and closed it, much to the amazement of everyone else in the room.

As he advanced through medical school, David often joked that he was thinking of becoming a neurosurgeon (in fact, he was training to be a psychiatrist). "All of us are handicapped in one way or another," David remarked at his 1976 commencement. "My handicap just happens to be blindness."

Some years later, in 1989, Dr. David W. Hartman was presented the Louis Braille Award in Philadelphia. At that ceremony, I noted, in introducing him, that David never considered himself different from his classmates. He said that the term *handicapped* was misleading because "it caused people to focus on the handicap and ignore the individual." David Hartman taught us all a great deal about the potential of the "handicapped." As I look around the Temple campuses today while writing this memoir, I can see how the number of handicapped and the diversity of students on the campus have increased, and I realize how much they have enriched the climate and the intellectual excitement of the university.

By the early 1980s, in keeping with its goals of encouraging handicapped and minority representation on campus, Temple had hired almost one hundred full-time and thirty-two part-time black faculty members – more than any other institution in Pennsylvania. Many other minorities, including Hispanics and Asians, were also well represented on the faculty. In addition, Temple enrolled and graduated more black students than any other university in Pennsylvania. The 1981 Ethnic Category Report of the state's Department of Education put Temple's total minority student enrollment at 20 percent, including almost 5,000 black students.

Temple's law school, with its Special Admission and Curriculum Experiments (Sp.ACE) program, earned a national reputation for fairness in student recruiting. Long before the U.S. Supreme Court struck down minority quotas in the famous California *Bakke* case in 1978, Temple's law school had sought to correct imbalances in the legal profession without the use of quotas. It did that by going beyond the criteria traditionally used to assess the potential of students applying to law school.

In the fall of 1975, for example, the law school admitted four hundred students from an applicant pool of 3,200. Of these, 75 percent were accepted through the regular admissions process, which put great emphasis on the four-hour Law School Admission Test (LSAT). The remaining 25 percent were admitted through Sp.ACE; twenty-six were black; six, Hispanic; five, Asian American; and sixty-six, considered exceptional candidates under one or more of the Sp.ACE categories, such as overcoming economic deprivation, relevant work experience, leadership potential, or physical disability. The Sp.ACE guidelines proved to be highly reliable predictors for success as law students. (Peter J. Liacouras, the law school dean who was instrumental in establishing this program, eventually succeeded me as president of Temple University.)

Temple's medical school produced a similar record of accomplishment. According to the National Medical Association, throughout the 1970s Temple ranked third in the nation in enrolling African American medical students. Only Howard University and Meharry Medical College – predominantly black institutions – enrolled more. (Coincidentally, Charles S. Ireland, a Lincoln University graduate, was the administrator of this Temple program.)

In 1981, the Pennsylvania Human Relations Commission reported that Temple was preparing 75 percent of the state's Hispanic elementary school teachers, and Temple and Cheyney State College (now Cheyney University) together were training half of Pennsylvania's total supply of black secondary school teachers. During the 1970s, Temple appointed its first black vice president, Dr. Bernard C. Watson, and its first black dean, Dr. Ione Vargus of the School of Social Administration. Dr. Vargus was soon followed by additional women deans, including Dr. Norma Furst, dean of students; Dr. Mary Lee Seibert, dean of the College of Allied Health; and Helen Laird, dean of the School of Music.

Despite this record, as well as hundreds of success stories among Temple's African American graduates, Temple was accused of racist policies on several occasions during my tenure as vice president and president. No one ever leveled the criticisms or allegations of racism directly at me; nevertheless, I felt them personally.

One of these attacks came in 1976 from a black professor of African American history, Dr. Lawrence D. Reddick. He had reached the mandatory retirement age of sixty-seven for professors and was required, by university policy at that time, to step down. (In the mid-1980s, Temple and other publicly supported universities changed their retirement policies due to new federal legislation.) Reddick did not want to retire, and he resented our hiring a replacement for him. He was further upset when the chairman of the History Department, although appointing Reddick as a member of the committee to name his successor, did not select him as its chairman.

When his personal entreaties to his department chair, dean, the vice president for academic affairs, and the president failed to yield the special treatment he wanted, Dr. Reddick launched a campaign in which he accused the entire university of racism. Taking his accusations to the state legislature's Black Caucus, he organized a group of dissident black students and employees to join him in making outlandish charges against Temple, such as "Affirmative action at Temple is a sham," and when you are on the faculty, "if you're white, you have fifty times more of a chance to be given tenure at Temple."

In view of Temple's record, it was difficult for me to believe that anyone would take such charges seriously. Nevertheless, as David Randall, our state government lobbyist, was soon to inform me, Dr. Reddick's group had obtained a formal hearing before the black state legislators. Fearing that Temple's state funding might be jeopardized, Randall called me in Boulder, Colorado, where I was presiding over meetings of the National Center for Higher Education Management Systems. His urgent call left me no choice but to drop everything and fly immediately to Harrisburg, our state capital, to add my voice on this issue.

My appearance before the Black Caucus consisted of a full five hours of listening to complaints, and then another three hours of giving my own testimony. "The charges are ironic," I said. "Temple University's record is outstanding in Pennsylvania ... and one of the top two or three in the country as far as minority affairs are concerned. We're not perfect, but we don't have to be defensive about anything. ... We have some weak spots, but we've made tremendous gains in the last ten years, particularly the last six and a half years. ... If you're looking for an institution that is racist, you're looking at the wrong institution."

The Black Caucus chairman wanted me to respond in writing in several days to the complainants' "demands." However, the legislators did not endorse the demands, and most of them were highly supportive of what I had said, and of our accomplishments.

Despite that support, the leaders of the Black Caucus decided to hold an open public session on our main campus in the fall of 1976 for the airing of additional complaints. In the highly charged racial atmosphere of the time, they no doubt felt it necessary to sponsor public discussion of the complaints and issues. For several hours, I responded to all charges. In something akin to a grand jury hearing, I sat in the pit of the Ritter Hall Kiva Auditorium arena with the legislators on stage before me, acting like prosecutors and jury. I defended the university and its record and apparently satisfied "the jury." The matter was pursued no further, and we soon received our $66 million appropriation from the state.

A biracial committee (four blacks and four whites) of the College of Liberal Arts had been appointed by the dean and faculty to investigate Professor Reddick's charges. His complaints had been widely publicized in the black news media, as well as in major daily newspapers. After investigating the facts and conducting hearings, the Liberal Arts Committee concluded that there was "clear room for improvement in minority hiring, but that Temple's record in regard to minorities – students, faculty, employees and administration – is far superior to other institutions."[13] In 1978, a similar committee, created by Temple's Board of Trustees, carefully considered more material about faculty recruitment, promotion, and tenure, and reached similar conclusions.

Nevertheless, charges of racial discrimination resurfaced in 1981. These came from disgruntled faculty and students in the Pan African Studies Department of the College of Liberal Arts. Begun in 1970 after heated debate in the Faculty Senate, the department was originally called the Afro-Asian Institute. It was given considerable independence, as its original leaders had resisted its becoming a conventional academic department. In teaching and publications, they stressed advocacy for minority rights and self-determination for Third World countries. They opposed granting tenure to members of their faculty and insisted on using their own criteria for faculty appointments, consistent with the advocacy aims of the program.

The first director of the Afro-Asian Institute was Sol Gethers, whose background was in social work. It didn't take long for Gethers and his faculty and students to feel like second-class citizens in the university. As vice president for academic affairs, I encouraged them to adopt normally accepted academic standards for courses and faculty appointments so the program would be treated equally with other departments by students and faculty in the university. I argued that such changes would lead to both better quality and higher enrollment, not to mention stability. I worked diligently with the director of the institute and the dean of the College of Liberal Arts to transform

---

[13] "Report of the Affirmative Action Committee/College of Liberal Arts," 1976, Temple University Archives, Temple University, Philadelphia.

the institute into a regular academic department, subject to College of Liberal Arts and faculty requirements.

With support from the College of Liberal Arts as well as the university administration, the institute (soon renamed Pan African Studies) grew. In the academic year 1975–76, it reached a peak size of 1,300 class enrollments and twelve full-time faculty members. After that, enrollments declined, probably because the department wasn't offering courses that attracted students who had their eyes on degree requirements, and because the department made little effort to encourage white students to take its courses. By 1980–81, its enrollment was barely six hundred, and the chairman of the department resigned.

At that juncture, a small group of Pan African faculty demanded that the university appoint as chairperson one of their short-term assistant professors, a young woman who did not meet the college's qualifications. When the dean rejected their "nomination" and selected a three-person interim management group to run the department instead (in accordance with College of Liberal Arts regulations), they objected strenuously.

In addition to their demand to appoint their own department chairperson, some members of Pan African Studies wanted Yosef ben-Yochannan to receive a presidential appointment as professor of African history, with an eight-year full-time contract (from 1981–89), a six-year part-time contract (through 1995), and an option for renewal subsequent to that time. Ben-Yochannan had been hired as an instructor just days before the start of the fall 1980 semester. He began teaching under a one-year contract as a dean's appointment, which is not subject to the same kind of rigorous scrutiny as presidentially appointed faculty who work toward tenure through teaching, research, and service. Ben-Yochannan was unable or unwilling to verify his academic credentials, including allegedly having received a doctorate from the University of Havana in Cuba. Had he been able at least to do that, he might have been considered a candidate for a tenure-track position.

In the midst of debate on these two issues, as well as on four or five others, flyers were distributed around the campus calling me "Public Enemy #1" and threatening to block all traffic on Broad Street, the main public thoroughfare running through the campus (shades of the '60s!). At the same time, a small group of students attempted a coup by occupying the office of the dean of liberal arts. They did not succeed in that gambit, but they then tried to take over the campus radio station, WRTI, by forcing their way into its studios and offices, breaking a glass door, and damaging furniture. The campus police arrested two of the students at the radio station, and criminal trespass and conspiracy charges were levied against them.

Some of their fellow students demanded that the arrested students be given "complete and unconditional immunity," as should "any and all students who have been involved in the struggles for the survival and development" of the Pan African Studies Department.

"My response to the demand for immunity is unequivocal," I said. "We cannot have a dual system of university governance and discipline. Any student, regardless of his or her motives or background, is subject to the responsibilities and campus regulations that apply to all other students at Temple. If a student violates the law, he is subject to the penalties established by legal authorities. If he violates university regulations, he is subject to our penalties as well."

Pan African students brought all of these issues to the attention of black elected officials in Philadelphia's City Council, as well as the state legislature. This culminated in a meeting at City Hall in which Pan African group leaders and Temple administrators, including Dean George Wheeler of liberal arts, presented their positions to the politicians.

As a result of the attempted coup, two Pan African student leaders had been banned from the campus. At the City Hall meeting, Academic Vice President John Rumpf agreed to let them register and attend classes if they returned as "peaceful and non-disruptive" students. The Pan African group replied that it was satisfied with that solution, even though Dr. Rumpf said that the university would not drop charges or change university disciplinary committee plans. No other issue was settled at that meeting.

I was out of town at the time of the City Hall meeting and later learned that it had concluded with this statement by the chairman, Councilman Lucien Blackwell: "It appears we have learned 'something' from today's meeting, but no final or major decisions can be made until Dr. Wachman returns."[14]

As soon as I returned to Philadelphia, I met with Councilman Blackwell alone in his office. I explained to him, in greater detail, the university's position on all issues, including our doubts about the legitimacy of Yosef ben-Yochannan's credentials. At that meeting, I brought along several of ben-Yochannan's publications, showed them to Blackwell, and made clear that they could not possibly have passed muster by any respectable academic committee. After that meeting, I heard no further objection from Blackwell, or other black political leaders. The Pan African Studies Department settled down under its interim management, and life and work at Temple went on.

---

[14] From "Notes on Meeting with Black Elected Officials in City Hall, September 1, 1981," James M. Shea, recording secretary, copy in the author's files.

All of this may prove again that fairness in sticking to principles, and taking the time to explain the basis for administrative decisions and actions, pays off.

In addition to having a broadly representative student body, faculty, and administration, an effective university should maintain a close relationship to the surrounding community. But the outlook and goals of members of an urban community are often much different from those of the university personnel in its midst. Impoverished residents of neighborhoods that surround a university often regard that institution as representative of wealth, privilege, and "the establishment" – even a deliberately nonexclusive university like Temple. The "urban involvement" of which I had spoken and written at the outset of my presidency proved to be exceedingly important to carrying out the mission of Temple University. But maintaining good community relations is a complex matter. It may be even more complex and challenging for a university like Temple that strives very hard to relate to its community.

In the late 1960s, prior to my arrival, Temple expanded enrollment and services at both its Main and Health Sciences campuses on Broad Street. University officers and concerned community leaders engaged in intensive discussions of the problems this expansion created for Temple's surrounding neighborhoods. The discussions culminated, in 1969–70, in what was called a *charette* (an architectural term for lengthy, last-minute work on building designs). Agreements were reached on projected building heights, parking spaces, and community employment. The dialogue continued into the 1970s, aided by Temple's strengthened Office of Community Relations, as well as by the university's heightened sensitivity to neighborhood hopes and fears.

At Temple, "community involvement" was defined broadly. It meant assisting the immediate neighborhoods in setting up a Town Watch to deal with safety, and having our Center for Social Policy and Community Development offer training for housing rehabilitation specialists for the City of Philadelphia. Good community relations also involved turning over to the city's Board of Education most of a large building on the edge of the campus, for $1 a year, so the board could establish the outstanding Carver High School of Engineering and Science. It included the work of dental clinics at Temple's Health Sciences Center, which by 1981 were handling 88,000 patient visits – many of them from poor and needy people. Service to the community also included expanding Temple's Long Term Care Gerontology Center, one of only nine in the United States.

Good community relations were especially fostered by Temple University Hospital, whose service to neighboring residents in North Philadelphia was discussed earlier in this chapter. When the hospital established a Board of Governors, it was exceedingly helpful to have members from the neighboring community sitting on that board. At some level, in all of these efforts, I was either leader or participant, since I regarded them as serious obligations for a university located in an impoverished area of the city.

Simply opening up our own facilities to residents whenever possible was a boon to the community. With funds provided by the William Penn Foundation and other donors, Temple also reconstructed an old playing field and turned it into a first-class Astroturf facility that was then opened to the community at a festive dedication ceremony. One of the community leaders present urged the young people, eager to use the facility, that they should take care of it as if it were their own. "Use it, but don't abuse it," she cautioned. And our young neighbors *did* handle the baseball diamond and football field with care.

Our gymnasium and swimming pool were also opened to nearby residents whenever possible, particularly during the summer months. Summer basketball leagues played in McGonigle Hall every year. Sonny Hill, organizer of those leagues, always made sure to express his appreciation for use of the air-conditioned, first-rate basketball arena whenever he spoke at the games. Also, we organized community days at Temple's football games, and free tickets and bus transportation were provided for young people in surrounding neighborhoods. We hoped that our good neighbor policy would inspire area youth to enroll at Temple and would help their families recognize us as cooperative friends. Because of the university's expansion and the many disputes with the community this created in the 1960s and early '70s, these programs played a vital role in changing the community's attitudes toward Temple.

Whether warranted or not, considerable, and probably disproportionate, attention must be paid by university presidents to athletics. Alumni and the public often judge the quality of a university by the reputation of its sports teams, and they hold the president responsible for creating top-notch athletic programs. There were times when I felt that running a university wouldn't be very difficult if one didn't have to contend with big-time football. Of course, if there were no medical school or hospital, it would be even easier!

After some fine winning seasons in the 1930s, Temple had deemphasized football and played in a lower "college" division. Throughout the '40s and '50s, the football teams suffered losing seasons almost every year. During one period in those decades, Temple's football team lost nineteen games in a row – often by large margins – while playing against much smaller liberal arts colleges like Susquehanna, Muhlenberg, Hofstra, and Gettysburg. In the

1960s, Temple football teams fared somewhat better but still recorded largely losing records. They certainly didn't perform as well as alumni, students, and the public thought they should. The de-emphasis period of Temple's football gave the comedian Bill Cosby, Temple's famous alumnus, many hilarious stories to tell in the routines he created about the years he played on those losing Temple teams. But in 1970, Ernest Casale, the athletic director, had had enough. "If we're going to lose," he said, "we ought to lose to institutions that are similar to ours, in size and educational programs."

Casale convinced my predecessor, Paul Anderson, and the Board of Trustees that upgrading athletics, starting with football, would benefit the university without jeopardizing Temple's high academic standards. Ernie's high regard for academics came naturally: He taught mathematics at Temple and continued to do so when he became Temple's baseball coach and even after he became athletic director.

I supported Ernie in upgrading football from the college division of the National Collegiate Athletic Association (NCAA) to the top university division (now called Division 1A). But we both agreed that this shift should not lead to lowering academic expectations and achievements for football players, or to excessive expenditures. Neither we nor, earlier, Paul Anderson anticipated the tremendous growth of interest in sports, and the increased cost of mounting a big-time football program during a period of greatly expanded television coverage. Nor did we foresee what appeared to many to be the professionalization of college football, with more players leaving school to join a professional team before completing their undergraduate work. By the end of the twentieth century, these developments necessitated multimillion-dollar subsidies from most universities each year. The only exceptions were a few dozen schools that had top-level football teams and were able to fill hundred-thousand seat stadiums with paying spectators.

Once Casale's plan was approved (by Paul Anderson and the trustees), his first step, in 1970, was to hire Wayne Hardin, formerly a successful coach at the U.S. Naval Academy. Wayne turned out to be the winningest football coach in Temple's history. Playing a highly competitive schedule, Temple won better than its share of games in the '70s and early '80s, highlighted by a 10–2 record in 1979. The team won a nationally televised game in Honolulu that year and defeated the University of California in the Garden State Bowl at New Jersey's Meadowlands Stadium. These were signal accomplishments at that time, since the plethora of Saturday television broadcasts of all manner of college football games had not yet arrived, nor had the extremely numerous post-season bowl games.

One of the outstanding features of our football schedule during this period was the opportunity to play in Tokyo in two successive years, 1978 and 1979. These "Mirage" Bowls, entirely subsidized by the Mitsubishi Motor Company, attracted capacity crowds and gave Temple such a high degree of visibility that, when we started a branch campus in Tokyo in 1982, Temple was already well known there to many young people and their families. The Temple band and cheerleaders accompanied the team on these trips and paraded down Tokyo's main streets. Team members were interviewed on Japanese national television. Young people reached up to the windows of the team bus with pens and papers, seeking autographs. All this prompted a young Temple quarterback to remark: "This international playing is what it's all about."

Although I have emphasized Temple football, I should add that the men's basketball program in the 1960s, '70s, and '80s was outstanding. The legendary Harry Litwack coached the team in my early years at the university, and the soon-to-become-famous John Chaney took over when I retired in 1982.

Temple's football team was not alone in benefiting from international exposure. In 1981, led by another fine coach, Don Casey, Temple played basketball against UCLA one evening in the Suntory Bowl in Tokyo. On a second night, Temple played against a Japanese all-star team. These were fine experiences for the athletes and all the students who traveled with them. Moreover, these trips did not take the students away from their studies for lengthy periods, were financially self-supporting, and gave the university fine publicity, both in the United States and abroad. For these reasons, I gave these games my enthusiastic support.

Despite my support for Temple teams, I have never felt that big-time football and basketball were necessary for a first-class university. The University of Chicago and New York University are just two of a number of elite urban universities that dropped football and subsequently succeeded in building better academic institutions. Following our fine record in the 1970s and early '80s, Temple's record in football declined, and the cost of the program, including university subsidies, increased. Although sports may attract students and bring publicity to the university, especially in the sport sections of newspapers, costs and effects on the academic programs must be considered, particularly if the subsidies become excessive. I know Temple is grappling with these issues, and I wouldn't want to second-guess the decisions of my successors. A neighboring suburban university, Villanova, which had a fine football rivalry with Temple, dropped the sport for financial reasons but then revived it, due to alumni pressure, albeit in a category just below the top level.

That may be a route that Temple would wish to follow, but the cost savings may be insufficient to justify making such a move.

As a former college and tournament tennis player, I was especially interested in tennis, but also in golf, gymnastics, swimming, and other sports, which were sometimes classified as "minor" compared with football and basketball. Ernie Casale and I agreed that the broader the range of athletic activities offered to students, the better. We shared the belief that a university's athletic program should be part of the educational experience for students, and its success should not be judged solely by how well it is able to train student athletes for professional sports. This may seem Pollyannish in light of the recent changes that have occurred and the finances involved in televised games and tournaments. But we held to those beliefs in the 1970s and early 1980s, even though many Temple football and basketball alumni were "graduating" to professional teams.

For a good deal of that time, we were fortunate to have as chairman of the Board of Trustees Fitz Eugene Dixon Jr., an avid and generous sports fan with beliefs similar to ours. At one time, the crew coach, Gavin White Jr., wrote to Dixon asking if he would lend the team $10,000 to purchase a new shell. "I won't lend you the money, but you can buy it," Dixon replied, pulling out his checkbook when he next saw Gavin. (Dixon and his wife, Edie, supported all of Temple's teams, including the women's teams.) The new shell permitted Temple's crew to row competitively in the Henley Regatta in England. This was a great opportunity for members of the crew, and their participation was another small way for an urban university to give some of its students a broad international experience. Other sports, like women's and men's tennis, golf, soccer, and women's lacrosse, also fared well. In fact, the lacrosse team won the national collegiate championship in 1982 and has repeated its fine record since that time, playing on a par with the best college teams in the country.

The greatly increased nationwide interest in women's sports during the '70s struck me as only part of a broader cultural change regarding women's status. For example, the '70s marked a greatly expanded enrollment of women in the nation's law schools, and a growth in the number of women entering the legal profession. It was also the decade when the percentage of women entering classes in medical schools rose from 1 or 2 percent to between 25 and 30 percent.

I can recall attending meetings in the 1960s (when I was president of predominantly black Lincoln University) concerned with increasing the number of minorities *and* women in medical schools. At those meetings, many male doctors and medical administrators argued that substantially raising the number of women medical students was not appropriate, because medical education was very expensive and lengthy, and women were likely to leave the profession soon after graduating to devote themselves to marriage and child-rearing. Such arguments were shattered in subsequent decades, as were the arguments opposing "excessive" concentration on women's athletics.

Before the '70s, no strictly athletic scholarships were offered to women at Temple, and collegiate women's sports were governed nationally by the Association of Intercollegiate Athletics for Women (AIWA), not by the NCAA. At that time, many women still did not desire to emulate the highly competitive practices of major men's sports, which often seemed to have little relationship to academic programs and standards. But those attitudes were changing significantly, and young women were demanding equal access to intercollegiate sports, as well as matching subsidies and financial assistance. Temple had always fielded strong women's teams in gymnastics, tennis, and track and field, but the financial support they received certainly did not match that provided to men.

Despite changes in attitudes and greater assistance provided to women by Temple in the '70s, many women still felt that progress toward equity with men was too slow. The federal government's new Title IX mandated gender parity in institutions receiving federal funds. Such parity was impossible to achieve overnight. Since Division I football teams have as many as 125 squad members, including 90 to 100 scholarship athletes, the number of male athletes and the financial subsidy of men's sports compared with women's was still skewed. Temple responded to changing attitudes about women and to Title IX as fast as its athletics officials felt they could. Women's athletics were transferred from the College of Health, Physical Education, Recreation, and Dance to the Athletic Department, and a well-qualified woman was appointed to the newly created position of women's athletic director. The university improved women's facilities, including increasing locker space and providing newer equipment. It also began to offer athletic scholarships to women and gave more equitable financial support to women's teams. By adding sports like volleyball and soccer to women's teams, and paying more attention to women's basketball, the university achieved a more balanced approach to women's sports, more consistent with its approach to men's sports (excluding football), and more supportive of women's aspirations.

Nevertheless, in 1981 several women sued the university (*Haffer v. Temple*) for unequal treatment under Title IX. A number of other universities across the United States were similarly sued. A settlement of the *Haffer* suit of 1981, satisfactory to all parties, was not reached until 1989, at which time the plaintiffs felt that the additional scholarships, the increased interest and investment in women's basketball and other sports, and the increased subsidies in general for women's sports were reasonable.

One of my more difficult human situations as Temple president reached a climax in 1981. Dr. Barrows Dunham, a distinguished Temple philosophy professor, had been dismissed by the university after invoking the Fifth Amendment during the McCarthy-era congressional witch hunts of the early 1950s. Barrows had apparently once belonged to an organization that was labeled pro-communist, and he didn't wish to discuss, in public, the organization or any of its members. His dismissal was based upon a state law requiring institutions that received state funds, like Temple, to fire any teacher who invoked his constitutional protection against self-incrimination. Later he was cited for contempt of Congress, a charge overturned by the courts in 1955. As a result of his dismissal, Dunham was forced to eke out a small income by writing and teaching part time in a community college.

Some twenty-five years later, in the late 1970s and in 1980, a graduate student, Frederick Zimring, and a number of concerned faculty took up Dr. Dunham's cause and brought it to my attention. By then, Dunham had reached retirement age. I was very sympathetic to his plight, since I felt strongly that professors should be able to join whatever organization they wished and hold any political views they felt proper, as long as their affiliations and political views did not affect their teaching. However, it was a sensitive situation because several Temple trustees – including a previous president, Millard Gladfelter – still felt that Dunham could have avoided the entire matter by being more forthright in his testimony before a congressional committee and with officers of the university. They argued against university action on his behalf. To complicate matters, while I was opening up this issue with the board, Dunham sued a student who had written a disparaging letter about him in the student newspaper at our Ambler campus. As I told Dunham's lawyer, "It will be impossible to provide any redress for your client as long as he attacks the free speech rights of a student, the same rights he had asked for himself in the '50s."

Considerable negotiations followed between the university's attorney and Dunham's, and the libel suit was dropped. As a result, I was able to persuade the trustees that Temple had indeed done an injustice to Dunham in the '50s, since the law requiring Temple to fire him was unjust and probably unconstitutional. The board then granted Barrows Dunham the title of professor emeritus as well a modest lifetime pension for him and his wife. Professor

Dunham's colleagues and friends held a party at his home to celebrate the accomplishment. There I remarked to the faculty and others that "the university has laid to rest a painful vestige of the McCarthy era."

In the late '70s, Temple's School of Dentistry had been threatened with loss of accreditation because of its inadequate physical facilities. Its main building, which had been converted from a World War II Packard automobile assembly plant, had to be replaced. Fortunately, state funds for a new Temple Hospital building had already been authorized but put on hold, so there was a possibility they might be available to us. David Randall, our Harrisburg lobbyist, and I worked with members of the General Assembly to secure legislation to permit Temple to use some of those funds for a new dental building. Once again, we shuttled back and forth to Harrisburg, on one occasion persuading Fitz Dixon, our board chairman, to fly us there in his private plane and exert his influence on key legislators. When the appropriate bill was passed and signed by the governor, we immediately began planning for a new dental building. This structure saved our accreditation status, even though the building was not completed until after I retired from the presidency. (The new Temple University Hospital was subsequently funded in a complex manner that included a state grant, federal funds, municipal tax-free bonds, and corporate and individual gifts.) The new hospital and dental structures, along with Allied Health/Pharmacy and Faculty/Student Union buildings, which were all completed in the 1970s, greatly improved Temple's presence on North Broad Street.

Although these buildings were constructed primarily with state funds, substantial gifts and grants from private sources were vital to completing them, and to improving the entire campus environment. For that reason, I was determined to strengthen Temple's development office – that is, its fund raising – before we launched a capital campaign. My first step was to search for a new vice president for development, a position that had been left vacant for three years at the close of Paul Anderson's administration. There were a number of fund raisers, and an acting leader of the Development Office, but it seemed to me that we needed to bolster that office substantially. Dr. Anderson had felt that state assistance was much more important than private funds, so he wasn't as anxious to fill the vice presidency as I was.

In 1976, after a national search, we appointed Lee Wenke, then associate vice president at Southern Methodist University's School of Humanities, to be our new vice president for development. After adding several other development officers, we were ready for a large drive. Under the leadership of Board Chairman Fitz Eugene Dixon Jr., Trustee John C. Haas, and alumnus

R. Anderson Pew – all heirs to famous Philadelphia fortunes – the university launched its Centennial Challenge Program to raise $60 million by 1984, Temple's one-hundredth anniversary. It was the most aggressive development campaign in Temple's history – indeed, the only one worthy of the name. Incredible as it may seem, Temple had engaged in no major development effort since the early twentieth century, when Russell Conwell embarked on a campaign to raise $1 million, not an insignificant sum at that time. For most of the period since Russell Conwell's campaign, Temple had somehow muddled through on a combination of tuition, state aid, and occasional gifts.

During our campaign, it was encouraging to discover that Temple and its mission were highly regarded by major corporations and foundations, as witnessed by the significant gifts and grants they made. These were especially helpful because they came in the midst of what was widely dubbed the "New Depression" in higher education. It was a period marked by general decline in student enrollment, soaring inflation, rising energy costs, and reduced federal and state support. Despite those conditions, we not only reached our goal; we exceeded it.

In all, the university raised well over $80 million for academic programs and campus upgrading. That figure included grants from the Pew Memorial Trust, the Haas Trust, and the Widener Trust. It also included a fine gift to the university's School of Communications and Theater from the Annenberg Foundation, and another one for campus improvement from the Kresge Foundation.

With funds provided by the trust of George D. Widener – that is, Fitz Dixon's family – during the campaign, we were finally able to erect a fully equipped science building on our Ambler campus. This was a valuable structure for both faculty and students, enabling them to keep abreast of important scientific advances, especially in the fields of horticulture and landscape architecture. Since the Widener name had already been given to another building on the campus, this new building was named Dixon Hall in honor of Widener's grandson, Fitz Dixon, who had worked hard to obtain funds for the science building from the trust. Also, Fitz was particularly interested in the development of the Ambler campus.

Unfortunately, the money we had raised for capital and operating purposes failed to cover all our needs. Financial difficulties in the clinical practices of professors in the medical school, who also staffed the hospital, had an impact on both the hospital and the university. As early as 1970, I had heard criticism of the accounting methods of these clinics. At one budget meeting of the Board of Trustees, John Rhoads, then vice president of financial affairs, remarked, "I have just received figures, by phone, about the income from the clinics, and I cannot confirm them."

After I became president in 1973, I received audited reports indicating that checks that had never been deposited were found in the desk drawers of doctors or secretaries. The relatively new vice president of finance, Jim Logan, complained, "We have no oversight whatsoever on the finances. The doctors bill patients, the money is sometimes sent in, and from time to time a secretary comes down to the Bursar's Office and deposits, say, ten thousand dollars with no accounting of where it has come from."

It was clear to me that tighter controls were needed. Jim was determined to change the procedures in the clinics, as was I. No one accused the physicians of wrongdoing – just sloppy and inadequate bookkeeping. When Logan pressed for control over clinical practice funds, many professors expressed great resentment, and some of the physicians demanded his scalp.

At about this time, Paul Kotin, Temple's vice president for health sciences and dean of the medical school (with general oversight of the hospital), left the university for a generous and challenging offer in the commercial world. I felt that Kotin's portfolio had been too large, and that two new appointments were necessary to fill his old position. Following thorough searches, Roger Sevy, a long-time professor and department chair in Temple's medical school, was selected as dean of the medical school, and Edward Noroian, head of a large Pittsburgh hospital, was appointed executive vice president of the hospital. As soon as they had settled into their positions, I appointed them, along with Jim Logan, to function as a three-man committee to work out a solution to the operation and control of clinical practice funds.

This small committee and its staff studied more than sixty practice plans throughout the United States before finally proposing a contract between the university and the clinical physicians. The contract provided the doctors with an opportunity to receive quarterly departmental bonuses. Gross expenses of clinical practices were to be deducted from gross revenues; of the net figure, the university would receive half, while the other half would be earmarked as bonuses for the physicians. This was a complicated change and would require the university to hire administrators to handle the practice plan, including net income earned off campus. It also meant that if bills were sent immediately, and checks received and deposited promptly and regularly, bonuses, over the normal pay of the physicians/professors, could raise their total incomes substantially. However, "the quid pro quo," as Jim Logan said, "was that physicians accept the financial control system."

Discussions among the vice president of finance, the dean of the medical school, and the executive vice president of the hospital went on for months. In protecting his area of responsibility, each of these officers, and each clinical department head, had a different point of view. Doctors were especially concerned about losing control over the income they generated as well as the management of their departments.

At one meeting, around a conference table at the medical school, one doctor/professor with a large outside private practice was finally convinced by the arguments. "O.K.," he said, "let's give the practice plan a try." At another meeting, on a beautiful fall day, sitting on the veranda of our home and looking out at the horses jogging around the Dixon/Widener race track, a group of doctors and administrators appeared almost ready to enter into an amicable agreement on details of the plan. But it seemed, at times, that we would never get everyone on board to successfully conclude this complex process.

Finally, after more months of negotiations, the key physicians with extensive outside practices (who would have to report a good deal of that outside income), as well as the chairmen of the largest clinical departments, swung over to the side of adopting a practice plan. This successfully concluded a major effort by a number of doctors and by Logan, Sevy, and Noroian, and proved to be a very fruitful arrangement for the physicians, the hospital, the medical school, and the university. With the new ability to promise bonuses on top of normal salaries, it became possible to recruit other top-notch physicians to Temple. At the same time, the cash income could be regularly accounted for and allocated, and the dependable cash flow could assist the university in managing its multimillion-dollar budget. In fact, in the '80s and early '90s, the practice plan produced surpluses that aided the university in balancing its budget.

But if the medical school and hospital were to continue generating income and cutting costs, one other key issue remained: the cost of doctors' medical insurance. Jim Logan and University Counsel David Randall developed a plan to set up a self-insurance trust for medical malpractice liability, thus saving the university a great deal of money when conventional malpractice insurance rates rose dramatically shortly thereafter. Logan was also the driving force behind the creation of Genesis Ltd., an ingenious reinsurance company to handle claims for property damage, general liability, and workmen's compensation. Genesis, created in tandem with other colleges and universities, was organized in Bermuda as an off-shore stock company designed to insure nonprofit institutions that were co-equal owners in the company. It's a good demonstration that, contrary to popular stereotypes, universities often harbor a wealth of entrepreneurial creativity right on their own campuses.

Even with the many campus unions with which the administration had to deal, by and large Temple enjoyed a fine cooperative spirit. But this spirit was sorely tested by the traumatic issue of faculty retrenchment.

Over the years, Temple had experienced severe budgetary problems caused by inflation, the skyrocketing cost of energy, hospital deficits, and a decline in its percentage of state aid. But between 1978 and 1981, the most serious concern was falling enrollment. This was caused mainly by a steep decline in the number of high school graduates in the Philadelphia area, but also by a sagging economy. From Temple's historic high peak in 1977 of about 36,300 students (full and part time), enrollment dropped to about 31,500 in 1981. The resulting loss of revenues severely squeezed the institution. All areas of the budget were examined for potential cost savings and efficiencies. Some 1,200 nonacademic positions were eliminated, most by attrition. In 1979, we closed the university's popular summer music festival on the Ambler campus. It was impossible to justify an annual half-million-dollar deficit at the festival at the same time we were raising tuition and holding employees' salaries down.

Because conditions continued to worsen, in the spring of 1979 we were forced to take the drastic step of sending "provisional retrenchment" (that is, potential layoff) letters to a number of tenured faculty members in the schools and colleges that had experienced the most severe enrollment declines. They were to take effect in eighteen months. Fortunately, that fall enrollments increased in some colleges, and deans and department chairs were able to make satisfactory staff adjustments by replacing temporary, nontenured faculty with those on tenure. As a result, the termination letters were rescinded.

However, enrollment in some of the colleges continued to decline, and by 1982 Temple's financial crisis had reached a critical stage. The College of Education, for example, had lost several thousand students over five years. Compounding this problem was the fact that faculty in that college were almost completely tenured – that is, theoretically assured of their jobs until retirement. Some colleges, like the College of Liberal Arts, could adjust their teaching staffs because many of their instructors were hired on a year-to-year basis. But in view of the substantial enrollment decline in the College of Education and several other colleges, it would have been irresponsible to continue supporting excessive complements of professors in departments with very few students. Faculty numbers, obviously, are related to student numbers, and a university with limited financial resources cannot long support faculty with only two or three students in some classes, and none in others.

During my last year as president (1981–82), budget projections showed that if I did not take immediate action, my successor would face a substantial deficit in his very first year. I therefore called a special meeting of the Faculty Senate on February 18, 1982, in the Kiva Auditorium of Ritter Hall. Before a standing-room-only crowd, and flanked by John Rumpf, vice president for academic affairs, and James Logan, vice president for financial affairs, I painted a picture of our grim financial situation.

"It is very clear that because of our income situation, life cannot go on as usual at Temple in the next several years," I said. "Without personnel cuts, the total deficit next year would be about $8 million or more; the second year, double that; and in the third year, triple." If left unchecked, I explained, the accumulated deficit could soon reach almost $50 million. There was no way I would let that happen to the university and to my successor. "Consequently, we will have to take stringent measures to overcome this crisis," I continued, and I asked the faculty for their cooperation and support.

Further reduction of nonfaculty employees would come first. After that, a number of nontenured, annual faculty contracts would not be renewed. But retrenchment of some tenured faculty would also be necessary, and the union (AAUP) contract with faculty clearly stated the steps that had to be taken in order to accomplish that. We followed those steps to the letter.

As a long-time professor myself, I was especially reluctant to send retrenchment letters, as was John Rumpf. Although we carefully observed all legal and contractual requirements concerning notice and consultation, the need to lay off faculty (albeit with eighteen months' notice) caused a major uproar among professors in Temple's affected colleges and was the cause of passionate luncheon discussions in the Faculty Club. Beyond the faculty, no great objection was raised, either within the university or outside it. This may have been because everyone had been made aware of Temple's financial situation, layoffs had already been made in nonacademic positions, and the targeted faculty members would receive a full eighteen months' notice.

After the decision was made, but before retrenchment letters were sent, John Rumpf and I did everything we could to find other positions for faculty who might be receiving the letters. We worked with deans and department chairs of those colleges and departments that would be adversely affected. We often appeared together before college assemblies to explain the situation, where we always asked for alternative suggestions from the faculty. At other times, I was invited by the dean or faculty chair to appear alone and to discuss the university's problems with faculty representatives. We used every possible device to keep the number of retrenchment notices as low as possible, including transferring faculty to other Temple colleges with fewer tenured faculty members.

John Rumpf and I argued that the faculty and the deans had received plenty of warning about the fiscal problems, going back to 1979, when we had been able to reverse a smaller retrenchment exercise. We had repeatedly consulted with those concerned, including the Faculty Union Executive Committee. Also, the administrative staff had been trimmed, and administration operating costs reduced substantially, before any cuts in academic personnel had even been considered. And working with Temple AAUP officers, we had put into effect an early retirement program. This program, by making it possible for some of the older, senior professors to retire, would leave positions vacant for other faculty to fill.

Nevertheless, Philadelphia newspapers and radio and television stations zeroed in on the retrenchment report, using headlines like "Pink Slips Going Out at Temple." One group of faculty in Temple's College of Education paid for a polite "Dear Marvin" advertisement in my family's neighborhood newspaper, the weekly *Chestnut Hill Local*, in which they asked me to reconsider plans to retrench their reading specialists. Despite those media headlines and notices, there was not much outside pressure to reverse the steps that the administration, with the full support of the trustees, was taking.

After all, the AAUP at Temple had become a union, with specific procedures regarding the granting of tenure and possible retrenchment of tenure appointments, and the faculty had become, in the minds of many, similar to any union bargaining for wages and terms of employment. The theory behind tenure, of course, had originally been to make certain that professors had complete freedom to speak and pursue truth without jeopardizing their jobs. Today, tenure has become a financial issue more than a free speech issue.

These unhappy events took place during the spring of 1982, my final semester as president. I had announced my impending retirement in 1981, well over a year before its effective date of July 1, 1982. When I became president, I knew that Temple's retirement age was sixty-five. Despite that official policy – as well as the fact that pension contributions of the university and myself were based upon my retiring in 1982 – Fitz Dixon as chairman of the trustees asked me to stay on for two more years, until Temple's centennial celebration in 1984. I declined his kind offer for several reasons. After planning on retirement and looking forward to engaging in activities with a less structured schedule, I was reluctant to remain in office beyond the prescribed retirement age. Also,

I felt that if I were to stay on beyond age sixty-five, it would set a precedent that would make it much more difficult to retire subsequent presidents at the customary age. Finally, Temple's Centennial Challenge Program had already reached its $60 million goal and would accumulate more than $80 million by 1984 without my continuing as president.[15]

The trustees then conducted a national search for a replacement. After a strenuous and at times controversial debate concerning the merits of an inside versus an outside candidate, they selected the dean of the law school, Peter J. Liacouras.

Some faculty groups, including the Collegial Assembly (the equivalent of the Faculty Senate of the College of Liberal Arts), felt that the president-elect should be consulted about retrenchment, since he would inherit the situation. It was their assumption – and perhaps their hope – that he would oppose the retrenchment, not realizing that Liacouras and his advisers (some of whom were trustees) wanted me to go ahead with our plan before he took office so he wouldn't have to deal with our failure to act.

Since some faculty occasionally called me a "professors' president," many of them presumed that deep in my heart I was on their side in opposing retrenchment. One of the AAUP leaders, Professor Leroy Dubeck, commented that "it is the perception of the AAUP leadership that President Wachman, just three months away from retirement, was unable to dissuade the board from this course of action." But there was no doubt in my mind that Temple's financial future was at stake, and that action had to be taken before the AAUP contract expired on June 30, 1982 – the same date set for my retirement. I had repeatedly and truthfully said that it would be irresponsible to leave Temple's staffing and financial problems for the next administration to deal with. It was nice to know that some of my adversaries in the union felt that I was on their side, but that did not make me feel any better about what had to be done. Delaying the layoffs – and leaving the impending deficit in the hands of my successor – was something that never occurred to me.

Ultimately, I sent fifty-eight letters under the retrenchment clause of the AAUP contract. Of those fifty-eight, fifty-two went to tenured faculty (including two who held dual tenure appointments, in two separate departments, which meant that they were able to retain one of their positions), and six to nontenured faculty. I briefly delayed sending these fateful letters in order to

---

[15] Federal policy changed shortly after I retired, making illegal any mandatory retirements in universities based solely on age. Also, universities, including Temple, more commonly began using multiyear contracts for presidents rather than annual appointments.

complete as many individual departmental transfers of faculty as possible. Long after my retirement, the university continued its efforts to place affected faculty in alternative positions or to ease the pain of retrenchment through early retirement programs. By October 1983, when the eighteen-month notification period expired, only four faculty had not been taken care of by Temple in some way, and those four had all secured positions elsewhere.

Remarkably, in the midst of these many concerns, Bob Harrington, associate vice president for personnel, was able to negotiate a new three-year contract with the faculty union before I left office. Considering the administration's heated arguments with the union when retrenchment became a large issue, that was quite a feat. The agreement that Bob worked out with the faculty union leaders meant that my successor would be free of at least one problem for the first three years of his administration. Bob's success proved that we were correct in removing lawyers, and administrators who were too emotional, from the faculty union negotiations.

Several years later, Bob calculated that the changes we had made to streamline administrative services and reduce nonfaculty and faculty personnel saved the university $30 million. It also avoided a potential series of fiscal deficits in subsequent years. We had steered the university through one of its financial storms and calmed the waters for the incoming administration. As I prepared to depart, I felt very good about Temple's future.

In light of these accomplishments, I was both puzzled and disturbed by statements that appeared in Philadelphia newspapers some years later. In 1986, the *Philadelphia Inquirer* referred to Temple's "near bankruptcy" and the "near catastrophic" situation that confronted the new university administration when it took office in July 1982.

My response was immediate. The letters I wrote made it clear that auditors' statements for both fiscal 1982 and fiscal 1983 showed surpluses for the university, and that Temple's financial status was absolutely solid by the time I retired as president. "In addition," I stated, "the difficult and necessary steps (including the reduction of total staff of the university by 2,500) had [already] been taken before July, 1982, in order to avoid any financial crisis during subsequent years, and to give the new administration a running start."[16]

Nevertheless, similar misleading statements surfaced again during the 1999–2000 academic year, the year of my successor's retirement. This time I was reluctant to set the record straight, fearing that I might appear to be questioning the many accomplishments of Peter Liacouras during his presidency.

---

[16] *Philadelphia Inquirer*, June 22, 1986, editorial page.

But it was still distressing to me, and to the many others who had worked so hard to secure Temple's financial future, that no mention at all was made of the drastic measures we took during my administration's last days to avert future financial difficulties.

My last commencement exercise as president took place at the Philadelphia Civic Center on May 27, 1982. Once again, it was thrilling to stand in front of that huge crowd of 10,000 people. There, amid the sea of black-robed graduates, were representatives of the university's fifteen schools and colleges, as well as hundreds of separate departments within those colleges. The graduating classes included blacks, whites, Hispanics, Asians, and representatives of every possible religious denomination. Delivering the commencement address was an emotional climax to my career at Temple. I had been the featured commencement speaker only once before – in 1977, when, at almost the last moment, the comedian Bill Cosby (probably our best-known alumnus) backed out of giving the commencement address, ostensibly because of a scheduling conflict.

Fitz Dixon and other board members had wished to bestow honorary degrees upon Adeline and me at the 1982 exercises. Addie declined because she felt such an honor should be reserved for individuals who had accomplished something outstanding in the academic world. As for me, I would have been embarrassed at receiving an honorary degree when previous presidents had not. Instead of awarding the two of us degrees, the Board of Trustees agreed to accept my recommendation to give such degrees to three individuals with whom I had worked at great length at Lincoln and Temple – John Marcum of the University of California, Bernard Harleston of City College of New York, and Joseph First, chairman of Temple's Academic Affairs Committee throughout my tenure.

My commencement speech was fairly philosophical and touched on issues that concerned me: the growing specter of nuclear warfare, racism, the poor job that elementary and secondary schools were doing in providing students with basic education, and the need for greater public support of higher education. Much of my talk centered on information I had gleaned about the graduates themselves from a questionnaire they had been asked to complete. Among the more than 6,000 graduates were representatives of many foreign countries, as well as more than thirty states in our own country. Eighty-seven percent of those who responded to the questionnaire had worked either full or part time while attending school. They had held jobs such as doorman, caddie master, clerk, horse trainer, telephone installer, undercover detective, radio reporter for "Shadow Traffic," meat cutter, bartender, and teacher at the Berlitz School of Languages. Hundreds of those receiving degrees were over the age of twenty-six, and many were in their forties, fifties, and sixties. There were more single parents in 1982 than there had been in previous graduating classes. One of the older students receiving a bachelor's degree in social welfare was a sixty-year-old widow who had raised three grandchildren while attending classes; at the same time, she had worked for the Philadelphia antipoverty agency and helped initiate a program to feed needy senior citizens.

A number of that year's graduates were policemen. One Philadelphia officer had spent seven and a half years working toward his B.A. in criminal justice. A New Jersey state policeman completed his B.A. in political science while working at his full-time job and caring for a sick wife who had been hospitalized three times. "Between tuition and medical expenses," he wrote, "I never thought I would see the day I would graduate from Temple. But with the encouragement of my wife, and the guidance and instruction I received from a most professional faculty, I was able to make my dream come true."[17]

For one mathematics major, earning a degree meant waking up at 3 A.M. every day to work the morning shift at United Parcel Service before attending classes. Another student persisted in her studies for nine years in order to earn a bachelor's degree, working eight hours every day during that time, and not sleeping at all on those nights when extra study was required. "I felt discouraged many times," she admitted, "but I never thought of quitting. My philosophy is: a quitter never wins, and a winner never quits."

A navy veteran of the Vietnam war who had worked as a cowboy, a bartender, a welder, and a taxi driver, and had entered Temple's School of Law under Sp.ACE, finally received his law degree at the 1982 commencement exercises, demonstrating not only his own determination, but also the value of Temple's flexible professional school admissions programs.

After commenting on some of these inspiring stories, I reminded the graduates and their families that Temple's first president had had an enormous love for people and a deep belief in their ability to achieve their dreams. "Russell Conwell founded Temple almost a hundred years ago," I said, because "he had an idea that higher education should be available to anyone with talent and the inclination to work hard." In his famous "Acres of Diamonds" lecture, Conwell remarked that true greatness often goes unrecognized and frequently resides in the person "sitting next to you or in yourself." Temple's class of 1982 undoubtedly boasted an ample supply of this kind of true greatness.

---

[17] Temple University Commencement Address, May 27, 1982, in the author's files.

A month after the commencement exercises, as I was leaving office, the *Temple University Alumni Review* asked whether I thought Temple would be able to continue to fulfill Russell Conwell's original mission or would have to change its course to accommodate changing times. My response was: "No. It will not change its course. The historic mission of educating the newcomers to higher education – the immigrants from Europe in the past, and the so-called 'new minorities' today – is still a mission of the institution."[18]

Russell Conwell's objectives, I added, would have to be redefined for every generation, and adjustments would have to be made for students' changing needs. Moreover, I expressed the certainty that, when new fields developed, Temple would adjust to those changes without abandoning the notion of broad liberal learning.

As this is written, very early in the twenty-first century and more than twenty years after I retired from the presidency, Temple University continues to follow its founder's mission.

---

[18] *Temple University Alumni Review*, vol. 32, no. 4, Spring 1982.

Retirement

A S OF JULY 1, 1982, MY TITLE was changed from president to chancellor of Temple University. The "chancellor" title can mean many things in American higher education. It can mean the head of a state system of colleges and universities in which the individual unit heads are labeled president, as in the State University of New York, or it can mean the reverse, where the president is the head of the system and the unit heads are called chancellor, as in California. At Temple, as at the University of Indiana and elsewhere, the chancellor may be the retired president and carries this title instead of president emeritus. Millard Gladfelter, Temple's president from 1961 to 1967, was Temple's first retired president to be named chancellor; I was the second. (It now seems to be established procedure, with my successor as president, Peter Liacouras, following me as chancellor as well.) As chancellor, our only obligation was to serve the university in whatever manner was mutually agreeable to the president and the chairman of the Board of Trustees.

I liked my new title because it testified to my continuing relationship to the university, but it was unclear about what I actually did, especially to those outside the university. In some cases, a retired president who is designated chancellor may receive a salary; in my own case, I neither expected nor received any stipend other than an office and some secretarial help.

I knew I would miss the responsibilities, challenges, and exhilaration of leading a great and complex urban university. But I looked forward to a less strenuous life where, with fewer meetings on my daily calendar, I could do more reading and writing. I looked forward to keeping my own schedule rather than being a captive of mandatory appointments. Certainly, I thought I would have more leisure time to play tennis and get into better physical condition.

I still felt that two of the more difficult issues facing colleges and universities were those with which I had struggled over the previous two decades: race relations and the inadequacy of American elementary and secondary education. After the great progress made in the 1960s and early '70s, it seemed to me that this country was going backward. I was afraid that intolerance and racial hatred were spreading again, and I was convinced that people of good will had to do something about it. Before the Civil Rights Movement in the 1960s, when racial segregation and overt discrimination were the norm, college students had been among the first to try to change the system. College-age youths of both races marched together in Washington, D.C., in 1963, and from Selma to Montgomery, Alabama, in 1965; and they cooperated in organizations like CORE, the NAACP, and SNCC (Student Non-Violent Coordinating Committee). Yet in June 1982, I had witnessed a return of black–white polarization that was becoming "almost as bad as when it was dictated by law and by custom," as I told a reporter on my last day as president.

At the same time, colleges were not only enrolling many students who were deficient in mathematics, but even more who could not read and write properly. Increasingly, universities' energies as well as our funds were being consumed by remedial work. Somehow, this trend had to be reversed.

Temple University's TEAM program for U.S. Army troops in Europe had been established to overcome these deficiencies among recruits. When similar programs were launched in the 1960s, including the LIFT program at Lincoln University and the TOP (Temple Opportunity Program) at Temple, we educators predicted that in another five or ten years, as high schools improved and students became better prepared for college, colleges wouldn't have to be involved in remedial work. Yet in 1982, as I left Temple's presidency, I was worried because we still didn't have a handle on the problem. Sadly, as I write this shortly after the turn of the twenty-first century, it doesn't seem to me that we're as close as we should be to solving it. I am certain, however, that we must continue to seek answers to the deficiencies in our educational system.

My first assignment as chancellor, suggested by Liacouras, was to represent the university's (and his) interests in Temple projects in Europe and the Middle East and report to him with up-to-date information on our programs. I agreed that it was an excellent idea to touch base with our programs – especially, in one case, with the U.S. Army in Germany – as a way of indicating that the new president was committed to supporting them. At the same time, I appreciated the chance to go through some "decompression" after the difficult final year of my presidency and get some vacation with Addie. I also recognized that it would be helpful for me to be out of the new president's hair at the beginning of his administration. Thus, in July and August 1982, I visited our programs in London, Frankfurt, Rome, Athens, and Israel, and met with Temple staff, U.S. Army officers and enlisted men, and European and Israeli officials.

During my first retirement year, Dr. Philip Yanella and I decided to assemble and co-teach a course called "The College and American Society." Prior to my retirement, Dr. Yanella and I had taught an American studies course to honors students, and our collaboration had been quite successful. Earlier in my career, I had designed and taught courses on "The American Idea" and "American Ideals and Institutions" at Colgate, and I enjoyed working on a similar syllabus for this new course. Moreover, Phil and I agreed on many controversial issues, including the existence of a large gap between American rhetoric and American practices in economic and social matters. But on other issues, including the extent to which government could be effective in solving social problems, we disagreed. Both of us believed that government had a crucial role on the economic side of dealing with these issues, but Yanella would go much further than I in bringing government into the picture. Since both of us felt it was important for students to witness a thoughtful discussion of information, even between parties who disagree, we took turns leading and participating in classroom exchanges.

Our working relationship was excellent. Dr. Yanella assigned all literary works, while I handled historical, political, and constitutional readings. Despite the great advancements made during previous decades, race relations still played a leading role in many of our discussions. It was a very stimulating course, and I was sorry to have to give it up after 1983, when my responsibilities outside the university increased.

In addition to teaching and lecturing during that 1982–83 school year, I visited various Temple donors to help the president and the Development Office with their continuing fund-raising efforts. I met with the board of the Albert M. Greenfield Foundation in Philadelphia; flew out to Michigan with Vice President Lee Wenke to secure a gift from the Kresge Foundation; and accompanied Wenke and Joseph Morelli, associate vice president for development, on a trip to New York, where we visited foundations, companies, and individuals who had been past or potential donors. President Liacouras also encouraged me to visit Florida to meet with alumni and other Temple supporters, most notably alumna Esther Boyer Griswold, then in her eighties, and her husband, Earle. During my presidency, the Griswolds had pledged some $12 million to the university through an irrevocable unitrust. In 1985, that donation and additional Griswold support resulted in changing the name of Temple's School of Music to the Esther Boyer College of Music.

Another time-consuming activity was my involvement as the prime witness in a class-action arbitration case. This had been filed by the Temple chapter of the AAUP, which sought to reverse the retrenchment notices sent before my retirement to fifty-two faculty members. Settlement of the suit required four days of arbitration, preceded by at least six strategy sessions with Temple staff and Temple's general counsel, the law firm of Ballard, Spahr, Andrews, and Ingersoll.

There were many tense moments and emotional outbursts during the arbitration hearings. The union lawyer charged that "the administration acted in a cavalier manner without any concern at all for the rights of faculty members." I replied that I had been reluctant to use the retrenchment process as outlined in the union contract, and that my administration had taken every possible step to consult and work with the union in an attempt to avoid retrenchment. "As a long-time professor and member of the American Association of University Professors (AAUP) and a supporter of tenure for faculty," I added, "I thoroughly resent counsel's use of the word *cavalier* – knowing, as I do, that we anguished, and then delayed our action until the last possible moment while seeking an alternative solution."

On another occasion during the hearing, Temple's attorney, Ted Martineau, assumed an accusatory and hostile manner toward John Roberts, head of the faculty union. In the midst of his harangue, I called for a recess.

"Ted," I told him, "we are going to lose this case if you keep attacking John Roberts. He is the voice of reason within the AAUP; he has always been cooperative and tried to work things out as best he could, and this is obviously apparent to the arbitrator. Knock off the criticism." After the recess Ted did use a more conciliatory approach. Following four days of hearings, the arbitrator ruled that none of the union's charges were valid. Temple had won on all points of disagreement, confirming the fact that we had honored the union contract and acted in accordance with its terms.

Despite the arbitrator's rulings, the national AAUP censured Temple. Although censure in itself doesn't involve any legal sanctions against the university, for many faculty it is evidence that professors are not treated fairly.

This censure vote struck me as unreasonable, and I said so in two lengthy phone conversations with the AAUP's associate secretary, Jonathan Knight. The AAUP's policies precluded publishing the official response of Temple's Board of Trustees. However, the AAUP did print portions of my letter to the association, dated April 13, 1985, in the AAUP Bulletin's *Academe*. Two sentences from the letter will sum up one of my major points: "Evidently, AAUP wants to 'have it both ways'; it believes it can negotiate a contract, submit grievances to binding arbitration, and then circumvent the final decisions in some other way. Obviously, AAUP should never have gotten into the union business if abiding by fairly negotiated contracts can lead to censure by national AAUP."

In spite of the fact that censure may not have been as serious in university affairs as it had been before the AAUP opted for collective bargaining, it was still not helpful to the university, and I felt strongly that we should push the AAUP to examine its position and change its approach. Later, the Temple faculty union severed its formal relationship to the national AAUP. And much later, in 1995, the AAUP finally removed Temple from its list of censured institutions.

The AAUP arbitration wasn't the only case that occupied me during my early retirement. A number of court cases required my deposition or testimony as well. One case was related to personnel matters in our nursing school and concerned a teacher/administrator's contract that had not been renewed. Another case involved a suit by an assistant professor in the Pan-African Studies Department who had been denied tenure after being rejected by his department, his college, the dean, and the Board of Trustees. There was a federal court case concerning our U.S. Army TEAM project contract, in which a competing university disputed the award of the army contract to Temple. Still another dealt with Temple's status as a state-related university – specifically, the tax-exempt status of bonds Temple had issued. In addition, I was consulted by Temple's counsel in regard to resolving Title IX women's sports questions, since I had been a defendant in the original *Haffner* case and knew the entire history of the university's increasing its support for women's athletics.

I hoped that, with my personal knowledge about each of these matters, I was helping my successor in some small way and removing a few things from his busy schedule. Looking back, however, I can see the merit in a retiring president, for his own peace of mind, withdrawing himself entirely from the affairs of his university, unless there is some extraordinary situation in which the new president requires him to be involved.

Because I was very interested in Philadelphia's black-oriented Freedom Theater, I was asked to chair its fund drive for the construction of a new theater in its quarters on North Broad Street. Since the Freedom Theater co-produced a number of plays with Temple's Theater Department, I agreed to chair the drive, but only if the theater appointed a black co-chair. James Wade, who later operated a cable television company in Philadelphia and had previously been a member of Pennsylvania Governor Milton Shapp's cabinet, agreed to serve as co-chair with me.

These activities, as well as serving on three corporate boards plus the board and executive committee of the Pennsylvania Higher Education

Assistance Agency (PHEAA), which met in Harrisburg about twice a month, kept me very busy. My schedule was not as crowded as it had been while I was president, but I was amused when friends stopped me on the street to inquire about my health, followed by: "And what are you doing with all your free time?" Also, ironically, while president of Temple I had been asked to serve on several boards because I was the chief executive of a large and important university, but after I retired, organizations wanted me to join (or even chair) them because I would now have more time to assist them. Others suggested that by keeping active in community affairs, I would provide a good role model for retirees. Ultimately, I decided to resign from several boards in order to concentrate my energies on those to which I could make a significant contribution.

As a lifelong academic, I learned a great deal from my three business boards, and I in turn contributed to them a viewpoint different from those of the businessmen and lawyers who made up the bulk of their membership. I received honoraria of between $100 and $500 for attending meetings, and from one board a modest annual retainer, but financial considerations were certainly not my primary reason for continuing with them.

Early in my Temple career, I had become a director of Bell of Pennsylvania, then a wholly owned subsidiary of AT&T. Bell's CEO was William Cashel, whom I had known since I was president of Lincoln University. Serving on that board was fascinating, particularly during the time of its divestiture from AT&T under federal court order for antitrust reasons. AT&T was a safe and profitable company whose stock was held by thousands of ordinary citizens, most of whom considered it to be a benevolent monopoly. They, along with officers and employees of the company, feared its impending break-up. When AT&T was dismembered in the early 1980s, I was kept on the Bell of Pennsylvania board for two years beyond the regular retirement age of sixty-six in order to provide some continuity during the complications involved in reorganizing the companies.

In 1968, while still at Lincoln, I had been visited by R. Stewart Rauch, chairman of the Philadelphia Savings Fund Society (PSFS), who brought with him two members of his board, Morris Duane and Julius Rosenwald II (who was also a Lincoln trustee). At that time, this venerable savings bank was encountering difficulty recruiting black college graduates, and I was able to give Rauch some information about the sensitivities of these young students and the type of recruiter who would be able to convince them that jobs offered by the PSFS would provide for advancement. As a result of our conversation, Rauch and his colleagues asked me to serve on their board. I agreed and continued to serve on that board after I became Temple's chancellor, until I reached the PSFS mandatory retirement age of seventy.

When I joined the PSFS board in 1968, it was considered a great privilege to be selected. No honoraria or fees were provided for board members. During my board tenure, the assets of PSFS increased from less than $1 billion to about $20 billion. With that growth, however, came all kinds of growing pains and difficulties, many of them resulting from a federally managed PSFS acquisition of Philadelphia's very troubled Western Savings Bank in 1982.

While on the PSFS board, I helped recruit Frederick S. Hammer from Chase Manhattan Bank in New York as chairman and CEO. Fred had been a student of mine at Colgate and a member of the tennis team during the time I served as assistant coach. I knew him well and regarded him as a highly energized, hard-driving, bright young leader in his late forties. I met and talked with him several times, touting PSFS and life in Philadelphia, and probably had a good deal to do with his accepting the chairmanship. Later, he may have regretted this dubious favor.

When PSFS assumed responsibility for the debts of Western Savings, the Federal Deposit Insurance Corporation (FDIC) determined that Western's "good will" credit could be paid off over twenty years. I expressed substantial reservations about using "good will" to offset debt in the bank's takeover of Western, but along with other doubters I deferred to the businessmen and bankers on the board, who assured us that the FDIC commitment made the arrangement reasonable. Then, without warning, during the savings-and-loan crisis of 1989, the FDIC changed its mind and refused to honor its prior commitment. This led to the bank's demise in 1992, almost six years after I had retired from its board. Litigation by bank stockholders to recover some of the assets of Meritor (PSFS) continues at this writing. The apparent moral is: Outside directors can be helpful to a company or a bank but appear to be helpless when a federal agency changes its policies or regulations.

The third business board on which I served was the Philadelphia Contributionship, a unique property liability insurance company founded by Benjamin Franklin "and friends" in 1752, when the insurance industry was still in its infancy and actuarial science was virtually unknown. The Contributionship began as a "perpetual" insurance company in which insurees deposited a single premium and after a few years received dividends on those premiums. I served on the Contributionship Board for eighteen years, until I reached the retirement age of seventy-five. Over that time, the Contributionship acquired the Germantown Insurance Company, on whose board I also sat, and a security alarm system company, which related directly to insuring homes.

Like PSFS, the Contributionship was a prestigious company whose board had wonderful meetings where we debated the business issues confronting insurance companies and the company's historic mission. These meetings were followed by sumptuous dinners, with discussions of local and national public affairs, often including invited guests. Fees paid to board members were very modest – $100 per meeting when I joined – but the service to the community was substantial, resulting in reasonable insurance rates and in charitable contributions to local nonprofit organizations.

Serving on all three of those boards struck me as both an honor and a fine experience. I gained a good deal of knowledge about business and the changes occurring in banking, insurance, and the communications industry. I also reached the conclusion that managing a large company is no more complex or difficult than managing a large university. In fact, with the various constituencies that have to be satisfied within and outside the university, the latter job is probably more difficult. And if one has to deal with a medical school and hospital, as well as big-time athletics, that makes the managerial aspects of the job even more complex. A corporation has a clear mission, measured through profits and stock values and pursued by a clear chain of command through a clear system of incentives, all responding to a demanding group of investors as its primary stakeholders. A university is much more amorphous – more like a symphony orchestra that consists entirely of first violinists. Its power is diffused, and its success is more difficult to measure. The prime stakeholders – the students – exert no real, lasting power (except at moments of high student and national dissent about public policy issues affecting the university.) In any case, the students depart after four or five years.

Presiding over a large urban university is like being a government official – most likely, the mayor of a small city. The popular notion that universities have nothing to do with the real world has been proved erroneous over the past four decades. If anything, it now seems as if *all* "real world" issues are fought out on university campuses.

In any case, I hope I brought some perspective to the corporate boards on which I served. At the same time, I gained more perspective myself regarding the challenges in human relations and delegation of authority that confront anyone who runs any large organization, academic or commercial.

Another interesting business assignment concerned the Coca-Cola Company. Every year and a half or two, Coca-Cola and McDonald's Corporation sponsored executive seminars for eighty to one hundred of their top executives from around the world. McDonald's, known mainly for its hamburgers, was actually Coca-Cola's biggest customer, so the two companies worked together on several projects. The executive seminars brought high-level managers together in a comfortable setting for three days of intensive discussion of domestic and worldwide issues, whether or not they had any direct relationship to the two companies. The idea was to provide the business officers with a broad overview on national and international policy questions and an opportunity to discuss them in a relaxed manner. These seminars involved little in the way of formal corporate business, but a good deal of informal business give-and-take took place over cocktails and at meals.

C. Wadsworth Pratt Jr., my boyhood friend from Milwaukee, was responsible for my role in these Coca-Cola–McDonald's seminars. Waddy and I had played tennis, attended high school, and bought our first car (a Model-T Ford) together. In fact, I drove Waddy to his job-seeking appointment at Coca-Cola in Chicago after his graduation from the University of Wisconsin. Now, decades later, he was the Coca-Cola executive most responsible for servicing Coke's McDonald's account.

Waddy and two other Coca-Cola senior vice presidents visited me in the spring of 1982 to solicit my suggestions for programs and speakers for the Coca-Cola–McDonald's seminar that fall. I gave them a number of ideas, and we met again in Atlanta. At the close of our Atlanta meeting, they asked me to take over the fall 1982 seminar, complete the organization of it, and serve as chairman – inviting the speakers, delivering opening remarks and introductions, and summarizing the conference at its close. In January 1986, I was selected to help organize and chair a second conference and later, in 1993, to provide program suggestions and procure several speakers for another seminar. Coca-Cola generously paid all my expenses connected with these conferences. And Coke's honoraria, while not as large as those for nationally recognized speakers, were more than I had ever received for academic assignments.

Working with the Coca-Cola people was sheer joy, not least because of the financial resources at my disposal. For many years, I had arranged conferences and procured speakers for universities where I taught or served as president. There was always a strict financial limit – usually quite low – on what one could pay them. But for the Coca-Cola–McDonald's seminars, money was no problem. If the standard lecture fee for a prominent speaker was $35,000, no one blinked. Consequently, speakers I introduced as chairman, many of whom I had recruited personally, included the economists Milton Friedman and Lester Thurow; Edward Heath and Malcolm Fraser, former prime ministers of Great Britain and Australia, respectively; Robert McNamara, former secretary of defense and president of the World Bank; former Secretary of State Henry Kissinger; America's United Nations Ambassador Jeanne Kirkpatrick; and the syndicated columnist George Will.

As chairman, I felt it was my responsibility to make certain that the executives received more than one viewpoint. For instance, when I found that Coke's leaders wanted the conservative Milton Friedman to speak on "The Changing Worldwide Economic Outlook," I suggested balancing his appearance with the liberal Lester Thurow of the Massachusetts Institute of Technology.

By and large, these sessions were some of the most absorbing of my career. Of course, there were a few disappointments. An after-dinner "Inspirational Talk on Human Relations" by Tony Alessandra, a professional sales and communications speaker chosen by Waddy Pratt (who had heard Alessandra speak at another dinner meeting), was supposed to be entertaining. But it turned out to be a series of off-color ethnic stories that were so raunchy that several of the top executives walked out. For another session, I had personally invited Warren Bennis, a professor at the University of Southern California's School of Business. He had published a great deal on the traits of successful business and professional leaders. I had known Bennis for years and had read much of his very well-written work. Also, we had been together socially when he was president of the University of Cincinnati, especially when Temple played football against Cincinnati. His speech at the seminar was well organized and researched, and it would have gone over very well in a collegiate business school setting. But it was too academic and bookish for his audience of practical business executives. Perhaps I should have anticipated this negative reception. On the other hand, as I tell myself when things go wrong, "You can't win 'em all."

In the late summer and fall of 1982, I was offered executive positions by several nonprofit organizations and one company, but I turned them down. I felt I was not in a position to accept a full-time post, and in one case I did not want to move to Harrisburg, Pennsylvania (or anywhere else, for that matter), until some of my responsibilities at Temple University had been completed and until Addie and I had had a chance to unwind a bit. Then, early in 1983, I was contacted by board members of the Foreign Policy Research Institute (FPRI) in Philadelphia to see whether or not I would be willing to serve as their president.

The FPRI had been established by Professor Robert Strausz-Hupé in the mid-1950s as a foreign policy think tank within the University of

Pennsylvania's Political Science Department. Strausz-Hupé was a conservative visionary who was one of those credited with inventing the term *geopolitics*. He left Penn to become an effective U.S. ambassador to countries as varied as Sri Lanka and Turkey. In 1983, the FPRI still maintained a tenuous connection with Penn but was entirely independent insofar as finances, staffing, and programs were concerned. Because it had recently lost the support of the Sarah Mellon Scaife Foundation in Pittsburgh, which had provided substantial grants to the institute over the years, its financial position was precarious. (Scaife had shifted its funds to a conservative group in Boston, headed by a former officer of the FPRI.)

The FPRI had a reputation for being conservative and hawkish in the views expressed in its publications. My question to board members was whether they would want a known liberal like me to head their organization. As a Jeffersonian liberal who had given a great deal of thought to the liberal–conservative debate, I was greatly influenced by Americans' delayed reaction to the horrendous happenings in Germany and Europe before World War II, and by my personal experience as a combat infantryman. Although I had reservations about blaming everything negative that was going on in the world after World War II on the communists and the Soviet Union, I was extremely critical of the Soviet system and the communist ideology.

The FPRI recruiters answered that as long as I was interested in American foreign affairs – from a policy rather than a theoretical point of view – my bringing a different approach to the institute would be helpful. After considerable soul searching concerning my ideological fit in the organization and how much administrative responsibility I wanted to take on so soon after retiring as president of Temple, I decided to accept the presidency of the FPRI as a part-time position.

My job was to work with the young scholars at the institute to strengthen its programs and finances. Since I had studied and taught the history of U.S. foreign policy – or "diplomatic history" – in my younger days, getting back to the substantive nature of the FPRI's work appealed to me. My responsibilities turned out to consume more than the two to three days a week I had planned to devote to the institute, but I was still able to accomplish a good deal of work at Temple as well. Because I knew about the FPRI's precarious financial condition, I agreed to accept the rather modest annual salary of $25,000.

I worked at the institute from spring 1983 through fall 1989. Even though my own position on some foreign policy issues differed from that of the FPRI staff, I came to respect their scholarly approach and the manner in which they reached their conclusions. I believe they also respected my approach.

One of the contexts in which it was possible to express my own views on foreign policy and ideology came in the regular conferences between FPRI representatives and the Soviet Institute of the USA and Canada, an agency of the Soviet Academy of Sciences. During my tenure at the FPRI, we met twice in Moscow and twice in Philadelphia, at Temple University's Sugar Loaf Conference Center, the former home of Albert M. Greenfield that his foundation had donated to Temple. At these conferences, arms control, "Star Wars" (the Strategic Defense Initiative), U.S. relations with the Soviet Union in general, and other pertinent subjects were debated at great length over a period of three to five days.

During visits to the United States, the Soviet representatives were always anxious to see the sights of Philadelphia, including Independence Hall and the Liberty Bell. On their final trip to Philadelphia in 1988, they expressed a desire to see the Barnes Foundation and its holdings of Impressionist and pre- and post-Impressionist paintings, as well as Philadelphia's Rodin Museum. Some of the Russians had seen Rodin's sculpture in Paris and had heard about the Rodin Museum; others wished to compare Impressionist paintings in the Barnes collection with those in the Hermitage Museum in Leningrad. The group was incredulous when they were told that both of these museums had been established and were supported by private funds.

Addie and I were as interested in the Impressionist art in the Hermitage in Leningrad as the Russians were in the Barnes and Rodin collections. In November 1986, we visited the Hermitage for the third time (our second trip under the auspices of the FPRI) and saw a large special Impressionist exhibition. On that occasion, we looked out the museum's windows and watched detachments of Soviet soldiers marching in preparation for a celebration of the seventieth anniversary of the Russian Revolution. Side trips like those to Leningrad sometimes made us all feel like tourists, even though the major effort of the official FPRI representatives, and most of our time, was involved in the structured conferences with the Soviet Institute in Moscow.

The last trip, in October–November 1986, was rockier than any of our previous visits. We got off to a slow start because the Soviet Union would not issue us visas. The Soviets claimed that the United States was at fault for tensions between the United States and USSR, but after much uncertainty we finally departed, two days late, visas in hand. We reached Moscow soon after an imprisoned American journalist, Nicholas Daniloff, who had been accused of spying, was released by the Soviets.

Because of the visa mix-up, everything had been canceled by the Russians. Reviving the conference, locating hotel rooms, and arranging rail reservations to Leningrad were monumental tasks. Arriving at the Moscow airport, we had difficulty locating a Soviet Institute bus to take us into the city. Then our hosts had to make numerous phone calls before we were finally driven to the Academy of Sciences Hotel, where we sat for several hours on our suitcases in the entrance lounge with dozens of Russians, who were also waiting for rooms, before our FPRI delegation was given keys to rooms scattered throughout the hotel. The hotel was a run-down facility where the plumbing worked like some Rube Goldberg contraption: The faucets in the bathroom sink were connected to a hose attached to the bathtub and shower. If one faucet was turned on, the other was inoperative; if I brushed my teeth, my wife could not run water in the bathtub. In addition, half of the light fixtures were broken.

Government and Academy of Science officials appeared less cordial than on previous visits. There were no banquets or toasts like those given in our honor during earlier Soviet conferences. Vodka flowed much less freely, and no drinks were served before 2 P.M. (This was also partly due to Mikhail Gorbachev's attempt to combat widespread Soviet alcoholism.) One could, however, get the Russian version of champagne with evening meals, and when wine was served, it was generously filled to the brim of eight-ounce water glasses. Since meals at the Academy of Sciences Hotel were miserable, some of us in the FPRI group decided to venture out to a restaurant where only foreign currency was accepted, having found that dollar bills (although technically illegal) waved before taxi drivers and maitre d's worked wonders.

In this 1986 visit, we had an hour-and-a-half briefing, which U.S. Ambassador Arthur Hartman conducted in a soundproof and espionage-proof glass bubble on the top floor of the U.S. Embassy. At our briefing several years earlier, we had enjoyed an elegant breakfast at the ambassador's home, where he had spoken freely, although he often pointed at and spoke to the chandelier on the ceiling, indicating that somebody was obviously listening and taping his remarks.

In April 1988, when I chaired the last FPRI exchange with the Institute of the USA and Canada, six Soviet officials came to Philadelphia to discuss U.S. and Soviet foreign policy with us. At our previous session in Moscow, the Russians' positions had been almost totally inflexible. They hadn't accepted any of the American suggestions on arms control in any form, and we were subjected to dissertations on the superiority of Soviet approaches to everything from missile regulation to policies toward African nations. But in 1988, for the first time, a semblance of freedom of thought and expression – the *glasnost* promoted by Soviet chief Mikhail Gorbachev – seemed to have penetrated the Soviet academy. As we debated in our formal meetings and took long walks along Sugar Loaf's tree-lined paths, there was much more open give-and-take than in previous meetings.

In one informal evening session at the nearby home of the investment banker Keen Butcher, an FPRI trustee, the discussion became exceedingly warm and friendly. Subjects like banking and religion – which had little to do with our formal sessions – were examined over wine, vodka, and other refreshments. The Russians, having known only a communist system, asked many embarrassingly naive (to some Americans) questions about American banking, like who could borrow money from the banks and how interest rates were determined. Fortunately, Butcher was able to answer them all, just as a professor might in a basic economics course. Perhaps because of the setting (a comfortable study in a private home with a pleasant, soft fire in the fireplace), not to mention the wine and vodka, several of the Soviet Institute representatives let their hair down about their respect for religion and their support for restoring religious observance in communist Russia. These discussions, formal and informal, foreshadowed the opening up of the Soviet Union, despite the fact that Gorbachev's *perestroika* (restructuring) had not yet taken place.

While our FPRI delegation was conducting meetings with the Soviet Institute during the 1980s, the FPRI was also conducting a research program on "The Future of the Soviet Union." That study, presented at a weekend conference in New York in late 1988, perceptively concluded that the Soviet Union was in decay and that communism had lost its grip on the population. Within a year, the Berlin Wall was opened, and the communist bloc had fallen. The Soviet Union itself died two years later.

The FPRI also undertook a study called "Friendly Tyrants," the idea of Daniel Pipes, who became director of the institute in 1986. This work proved to be of interest to both liberals and conservatives. Like "The Future of the Soviet Union," it culminated in a rousing conference, a book, and a number of other publications. These conferences and publications were closely followed by policymaking agencies in the U.S. government.

While working at the FPRI, I was invited twice to deliver papers in Taipei, Taiwan. Both were delivered at meetings of the Graduate Institute for American Studies of Tamkang University, held every four years. These were opportunities to renew acquaintances and become familiar with developments on the island since our last visit there in 1976, when I was president of Temple. In 1984, I delivered two papers, one on "The United States and the Republic of

China on Taiwan," and the second on "Soviet–American Relations." Indeed, there had been many changes on Taiwan by 1984, and there were still more changes by our subsequent visit in 1988. On both occasions, our small group of foreign scholars was invited to attend magnificent Chinese banquets; we were flown (as in 1976) to the southern tip of the island at Kaohsiung to view Taiwan's huge ship-building facilities and steel mills, and then on to Taroko Gorge – "a photographer's paradise," in Addie's words.

Also fascinating on each trip was a flight to Quemoy Island, which was almost completely occupied and fortified by the Taiwan military, since it was only one-and-a-half miles from the Chinese mainland. Somehow, in its obsolescence, it reminded us of France's Maginot Line of World War II; how simple it would be for communist China to attack around and beyond Quemoy, just as it had been for the Germans to skirt the Maginot Line in 1940. However, we all understood the symbolic value of the island to the Taiwanese.

On the 1984 trip, Addie and I took a side journey to Thailand and had a wonderful experience enjoying its enchanting culture; ornate gold temples; orange-robed, barefooted Buddhist priests; foot-long papayas; floating markets; and overwhelming hospitality. Arriving at the Bangkok airport, we were surprised to hear our names announced over the loudspeaker. A junior bank officer and a chauffeur-driven limousine awaited us, ready to deliver us to the beautiful old Oriental Hotel. This hospitality came about as the result of a casual remark about our coming trip to Morris Dorrance, chairman of the Philadelphia National Bank, which did a good deal of business with Thai banks. To our embarrassment, we later learned that several Thai alumni of Temple University had borrowed a car and come to the airport to meet us. Fortunately, we were able to get together with them at our hotel soon after we checked in.

Several days later, Addie and I organized (as we had in Taipei) a Temple alumni chapter at a dinner given for us by twenty enthusiastic graduates. We also spent a full day visiting historical remains of ancient Thailand with a Thai alumnus of Temple's dental school. The following day, Addie and I met with faculty and officers of the University of Chulalongkorn in Bangkok. A final highlight was celebrating the king's birthday by watching the elaborate fireworks display from the roof of a Buddhist Seminary residence hall.

At the Tamkang University conference in 1988 in Taipei I presented a paper on "A Reassessment of U.S. Policy Toward the Republic of China," in which I argued that Taiwan's democratic movement and its establishment of representative government boded well for the Republic of China's relations with the United States. Four years earlier, I had frankly stated that relations were not as satisfactory as they might have been because of the lack of democracy in Taiwan. I was flattered that my two papers on U.S.–Republic of China relations, despite their critical assessment, were published in English and Chinese in three different books in Taipei.

Although the conferences in Moscow and Taipei were important, and the oopportunity to engage in some foreign policy research and to write several papers on the subject was enjoyable, any lasting contribution I might have rendered to the FPRI was in another area. On taking over the leadership of the institute, I found that it was not at all well known in the Philadelphia area. Those who did know it thought its activities were focused exclusively on Soviet–American relations. Few people seemed to realize that the institute had done a great deal of other work and that its major publication, the quarterly journal *Orbis*, was highly respected in academic and government circles in the United States and abroad. This lack of knowledge about the institute was one reason its financial support was so narrow.

It soon became apparent to me that some kind of public education program was needed and that the FPRI should pursue projects that appealed to both liberals and conservatives. Our first effort was to mount a project called "Inter-University Seminars on Foreign Affairs." This was a public forum series aimed at capturing the attention of informed citizens around Philadelphia, and bringing together representatives of the region's many universities, for stimulating presentations and discussions of American foreign policy. These were held late in the afternoon at sites donated by several banks and the Bell of Pennsylvania telephone company. At first I was able to get the Ford Foundation to fund the project; after that, the Exxon Educational Foundation and other organizations and individuals pitched in. Faculty from the University of Pennsylvania, Temple University, Villanova, LaSalle, Rutgers, the University of Delaware, St. Joseph's, and many other nearby colleges participated, and we were able to form an advisory council from the universities.

In securing speakers for this series, we emphasized the working scholar or retired government official rather than incumbent government officials who were sponsored by the local World Affairs Council and whose remarks would be prescribed by government policy. The series attracted audiences consisting of teachers, professors, lawyers, businessmen, and others, many of whom had strong opinions about foreign policy issues and were quick to ask challenging questions and argue with speakers when they disagreed. The discussion periods following the lectures almost always brought out the variety of positions held by the articulate audience. The series raised the FPRI's visibility in Philadelphia and led to increased memberships and subscriptions, plus a greatly broadened base of public support, intellectually and financially.

In addition to the Inter-University Seminars, we established a luncheon series held in Center City restaurants entitled, "Where Business and Politics Meet." As a result of these programs and a heightened fund-raising effort, we managed to eliminate the quarter-of-a-million-dollar accumulated deficit and actually placed the institute on stable financial footing. The seminars and various types of noontime meetings, plus an annual gala, continue to support the institute both substantively and financially.

Our success at the university level led me to believe that the FPRI could be equally productive with secondary school teachers. Consequently, aided by the exceptional work of Alan Luxenberg, the FPRI's assistant director (and later vice president) and several high school teachers and administrators, we launched an educational program for teachers in foreign policy (including weekend academies). Funding was secured from those individuals and agencies who recognized deficiency in the training of teachers in this field. When great changes occurred in the Soviet Union in the late 1980s and early 1990s, this educational program became exceedingly important in broadening the FPRI's outreach and service, and consequently its fund raising. The educational program accomplished so much that, after I retired as president of the FPRI, the institute brought all of its educational activities under a new entity called the Marvin Wachman Fund for International Education.

I worked at the FPRI for six years and subsequently remained on its board and later became vice chairman and then chairman of its executive committee. No doubt I would have stayed longer at the FPRI but for an unexpected crisis that commanded my attention.

In April 1989, Kenneth Reeher, executive director of the Pennsylvania Higher Education Assistance Agency, was indicted for allegedly taking a kickback from a company with which the PHEAA had negotiated a contract. The agency had been established by the Pennsylvania General Assembly in 1963 to issue grants and loans to Pennsylvania college students; I had been one of its board members since its inception. By 1989, over the quarter century in which the PHEAA had operated, undergraduate enrollment in Pennsylvania institutions had increased by more than 350,000. This was due in good part to the post–World War II baby boom, but it was greatly assisted by the agency's work. I had seen the positive impact of the PHEAA's program at Lincoln, at Temple, and throughout the state in both private and public institutions and was convinced that the agency had to continue and be further developed in order to aid needy students in a society and an economy that demanded higher education for success.

The agency, I felt, represented government at its best, both in the manner in which it served students and families of Pennsylvania and the manner in which it was administered. In my twenty-five years on the board, I could not recall a single issue that was decided on a partisan basis. By legislative action, the board had always comprised an equal balance of Democrats and Republicans from the General Assembly. Although the board was dominated by the dozen members who were legislators, it also included the Pennsylvania secretary of education and three public members (nominated by the governor and confirmed by the Senate), of whom I was one.

Because of the formal charges levied against Ken Reeher, who had been the agency's chief executive almost since its creation, he was forced to take a leave of absence. This created an administrative crisis for the PHEAA. Since I had been a board member of the agency from its very beginning, the board members believed I knew enough about the agency's operations to run it, and they asked me to take over as executive director for the duration of Ken's trial. I believed strongly in the mission and the work of the PHEAA, so it was an easy decision for me. I accepted the appointment. I had spoken with Ken, with members of the board, and with a number of staff members and was satisfied that Ken was innocent of all charges made against him.

As I took over the agency's reins, there was a good deal for me to learn, but I did not find the task too difficult. After all, I had spent twenty-five years driving the two-hundred-mile round trip to Harrisburg from Philadelphia for board and committee meetings. Consequently, I was quite familiar with the staff, with the agency's development, and with its problems. I received a full-time salary but without the incentive payments that were added to Ken Reeher's salary.

I found plenty to occupy an interim chief executive officer. My most serious challenge at first was to deal with very low staff morale. Many of the agency's top executives and some others had been questioned by the Federal Bureau of Investigation about the alleged kick-back scheme and felt insecure about their jobs; several had hired lawyers of their own. Also, they were unsure about the position of Ken Reeher, the man who had hired them and to whom they felt very close. I spent many hours counseling and reassuring these staff members.

In addition, there were serious glitches in the mainframe computer system that served the multibillion-dollar state and national loan programs. On top of all this, some of the "credit enhancers" (usually very large banks that backed bonds issued by the agency) were downgrading the PHEAA's credit standing. Finally, the agency needed to rent additional office space and plan for a new building to consolidate its operations.

Despite the cloud these problems had cast over the organization, there was no question in my mind that Ken Reeher and his staff had developed an exceptional government agency. They were always looking for ways to better serve the state, the students, and the academic institutions of Pennsylvania. When student loan servicing was a state and national concern, they developed an efficient Student Loan Servicing Center, which managed loans for students not only in Pennsylvania but in many other states as well. Fee income from this center ingeniously paid for most of the PHEAA's administrative costs. When Pennsylvania schools needed to train more teachers in science and mathematics, the PHEAA staff came up with a program that encouraged college students to enter those fields. When computer education became absolutely necessary, the agency's staff cooperated with the General Assembly as well as with schools and colleges to develop an effective program. When federal programs for assistance to the middle class proved inadequate, Ken's staff came up with a plan whereby the PHEAA could issue tax-exempt bonds and provide loans to those students and their families at moderate interest rates so that they could afford to attend college.

It was my responsibility to make certain that these creative juices were not turned off by the PHEAA's crisis and to keep the agency moving forward on its mission.

I quickly realized that in order run the PHEAA effectively, I would have to move to the state capital, Harrisburg. Addie and I were fortunate to find an apartment next door to the agency, where we lived (except for weekends) from April until November 1989. At the same time, I continued to fulfill my obligations, in Philadelphia and elsewhere, to the FPRI and Temple University. Although many Philadelphians, legislators, and other Pennsylvanians consigned to work in Harrisburg think of that city as the end of the world, we had found throughout our lives that you can always find interesting things to do in any community. Harrisburg was no exception.

In keeping with a well-known bit of marital humor ("For richer and for poorer, but never for lunch"), I had promised Addie not to come home for lunch after retirement. But our Harrisburg apartment was so close to my work that, except for infrequent business luncheons, I was there for lunch on most days. It was also nice to have a convenient, informal place to which I could invite a staff member for a private conversation over a sandwich at noon or a drink after work.

Addie and I managed to work out a pleasant routine, and life moved along smoothly until one very windy day. As Addie later told it, "I was engrossed at the computer in our tiny spare bedroom beside the open window in our sixteenth-floor apartment when a sudden gust of wind slammed the door shut. I was too focused to notice. Sometime later, when I decided to get a drink of water, I discovered that the door was shut tight and would not budge. Unconcerned, I continued working at the computer, but as time passed, it dawned on me that I was locked in, with no telephone. I began to try anything sharp in sight, to loosen the door handle, unscrew the doorknob, or the door hinges. With a small knife, I actually pulled off the door hinges. But all in vain. The door was effectively glued shut from fresh paint and humidity; I only succeeded in cutting my finger. Another hour passed, and lunchtime approached. A little panicky, I looked out the window and down to the sidewalk, sixteen floors below. Two or three people were walking by. Emboldened by the distance, I raised the window wider, waved both arms wildly to get attention and shrieked, 'Help! Help!'

"First, a couple of people looked up. Then, a crowd gathered. Someone screamed at me, 'Don't jump! Someone's coming!' It had worked. It was not long before I heard voices, the unlocking of the apartment door, soothing tones from the manager, and grunts from the forceful heaving of a body against the bedroom door.

"Finally, the door moved an inch. After another shove, the burly maintenance man and the door fell in together, rescuing me. This, of course, happened on one of the few days Marv did *not* come home for lunch!"

Early in July, I had a personal crisis of my own – an operation on my two big toes, both of which had been badly damaged in my younger days by excessive tennis playing on cement and asphalt courts. The toes eventually became so painful that I experienced difficulty walking, let alone playing tennis. For about five weeks I hobbled around on crutches in huge, ugly sandals, and Addie did all the driving. This annoyance served as a useful reminder that I could no longer function at quite the top speed that I liked to think I was capable of.

Throughout the spring, summer, and early fall months of 1989, the combined efforts of the talented top staff and I led to improved staff morale, in spite of the continuing investigation and trial. I often stayed late after regular working hours with members of the staff in order to meet deadlines. With the help of a consulting firm, we were able to develop the basis for an effective new computer system for servicing loans. We also rented adequate space for the agency's operations and developed plans for an outstanding new facility near the state capitol where the great bulk of the PHEAA's work could be done.

When September came, I joined several legislators and friends who testified in federal court on Ken Reeher's behalf. While we awaited the verdict – and since my feet had healed sufficiently – Addie and I took off on the sort of jaunt for which my retirement was intended: a reunion of my 66th Infantry Division. This began in England, where we had trained, and continued to our World War II combat areas in Normandy and Brittany. Thirty Panther Division veterans and their wives enjoyed extraordinary receptions given us by the mayors of St. Nazaire and Lorient as well as other small towns along the Normandy coast. Many people came out to welcome and honor us as though we had singlehandedly saved the French people. We division members held private ceremonies, dropped wreaths at sea off the port of Cherbourg (where our comrades had died in December 1944), and spent hours at the cemeteries near Omaha and Utah beaches. We viewed row upon row of small crosses (as well as occasional Jewish stars) that stretched out almost as far as the eye could see. We prayed in the tiny army chapel nearby for those who had not survived, and thanked God that we had.

Just before the end of our trip, I received a transatlantic phone call giving us the welcome news that the jury had cleared Ken Reeher of all charges. After our return from France, I arranged to transfer the PHEAA's leadership back to Ken, and on November 1, 1989, Addie and I were able to leave Harrisburg.

I remained very active on the PHEAA's board until September 1994. I almost left the board at one point when my previous term expired, but several Republican leaders went to Governor Richard Thornburgh, a Republican, to plead directly with him to appoint me to another four-year term, even though I was a Democrat. They said that they valued my experience as an educator and knew me as someone they could work with. I mention this here as an example of the bipartisan, nonpolitical nature of the PHEAA – a condition that was soon destroyed.

When Ken Reeher decided to retire in 1992, I was deeply involved in selecting a new chief executive. After a national search, Jay Evans, who had served as Reeher's deputy, was chosen to succeed him. Jay was eminently well qualified: He had been the PHEAA's chief government relations contact in Washington and Harrisburg, and for many years he had directed the agency's Federal Loan Program.

But in 1994, Pennsylvania's outgoing budget secretary, Michael Hershock – who had not sought the PHEAA director's job in 1992 – decided he would like that position. It would enable him to remain in Harrisburg and earn a salary considerably higher than the amount he earned in the governor's cabinet. Hershock was a Harrisburg veteran who had persuaded Governor Robert Casey to appoint him to the PHEAA board several years earlier, and he had played his political cards astutely: While budget secretary, he had worked with the governor and legislative leaders on a budget satisfactory to both parties. Now it was payback time, and Hershock persuaded the governor and a number of key Republican and Democratic legislators to back him for the PHEAA post. When Hershock tried to get me to support his selection as CEO of the PHEAA, I suggested to him that he would make a great number two man, one who could take over in several years, when Jay Evans retired. It would be unfair to oust Jay, who was doing an excellent job, I told Hershock.

Hershock made no direct reply to my comment, and I had no way of knowing how much he had already done behind the scenes to gather votes to remove Evans. However, as soon as I called several legislators on the board to reaffirm their support for Jay, I realized how much damage had been done.

The board's discussions regarding the ouster of Evans and his replacement by Hershock were disgraceful. Despite my heated, and repeated, objections by reference to previous board practices and Robert's Rules of Order, the chairman, State Representative David R. Wright, permitted Hershock not only to participate in the discussion but even to argue for himself and to vote on his own appointment in executive session. I can only speculate that Wright took this position because it was that of the Democratic members of the board who were more senior in the state legislature than he was. Since Jay was not a voting board member, he was not present and was given no opportunity to defend his stewardship.

I argued: "This is a paid staff appointment, which should be handled in executive session without the candidate's (that is, Hershock's) presence." But Wright, the chairman, and others who initially supported my position simply caved in to the pressure of board member Vincent Fumo, a powerful Democratic senator from Philadelphia.

"Hershock has the right to vote because he's a member of the board," Fumo insisted. Fumo was supported by several Republicans who were eager to reward Hershock for his work as budget secretary.

At the last moment, I called an official very close to Governor Casey to see if Hershock's appointment could be postponed. He contacted a number of people in the governor's office and even spoke to the governor himself before

calling me back a couple of days later to say, "Sorry Marv. It's a done deal."
I had been around long enough so that I should have realized earlier what
was happening. This was one of a number of occasions in my life when my
approach of dealing with a difficult situation by appealing to the good will
and fairness of individuals failed me. I was very disappointed and angry with
my colleagues and friends on the board.

In the final analysis, I felt it was my duty to make sure that Jay Evans's
faithful service was recognized and that he was not totally mishandled. After
many long meetings, and hours of legal and political wrangling, Jay was given
another position and guaranteed that position for his final three years before
retirement. That was the only positive aspect of this episode.

Given my opposition to Hershock's appointment, my service on the
PHEAA board became quite dispensable to the new CEO and some of his
supporters. My term, which had expired nine months earlier, was not renewed
by Governor Casey – who was, after all, a prime mover in securing the PHEAA
position for his budget secretary.

Despite my thirty years' tenure, I certainly was not going to fight to remain on a board that was in danger of becoming a political patronage haven.
The biweekly or weekly trip up the Pennsylvania Turnpike for PHEAA meetings was something I could do without, and I did not fight to serve another
term. It had been a privilege to serve the PHEAA for all those years, and I
continue to believe it is a most important agency for Pennsylvania students
and their families. But I was eager to move on to other, stimulating activities.

My next job was serving as consultant to the Annenberg Research Institute,
an independent scholarly organization in Philadelphia engaged in the study
of Judaism and the Middle East. The institute's chairman, Albert Woods, had
asked me to help find a new chief executive. At the same time, I had been asked
by the Philadelphia City Board of Trusts to help find a new president for Girard
College, a city-owned elementary and secondary school for orphans endowed
in 1831 under the will of the banker Stephen Girard. I also had assignments
with the New Jersey Higher Education Agency and the Middle States Association of Colleges and Schools to examine curriculum and accreditation issues
at several colleges.

The 1990s had begun, for Addie and me, with a three-week tour of South
Africa in February. It was our fourth trip to that country. In 1981, we traveled
for almost a full month in the Republic of South Africa, sponsored by the
United States–South Africa Leader Exchange Program (USSALEP), a private,

Quaker-influenced organization. Apartheid in all its virulence was still in full bloom then, but the program's leaders wanted to maintain communication between the United States and South Africa. Addie and I were members of a group of eight educators who had been asked to visit the major universities and technical institutes throughout South Africa in order to study its higher education system.

When we visited in 1981, South Africa's apartheid regime operated five separate categories of colleges and universities: for black Africans, for Afrikaans-speaking whites, for English-speaking whites, for colored (that is, mixed race) students, and for Asians. Our group had met with the heads, key faculty, and students from each category. We had also interviewed the minister of education, Dr. Gerrit Viljoen, as well as the Zulu chief Mangosuthu Buthelezi, the head of South Africa's largest black tribe, and about a half dozen black and colored leaders, including Bishop Desmond Tutu. All these meetings convinced us that, although South Africa had made some progress in providing education for blacks, it had a very long way to go before it would be able to provide equal educational opportunities for them.

On our return in 1990 – underwritten by the Southern African Forum, an interracial South African business and labor group – we found a sea change in attitudes and outlook since 1981. President F. W. deKlerk had already announced prospective changes in legal and constitutional matters relating to racial separation. The ban on the African National Congress had been lifted, and hotels, restaurants, and beaches were finally open to all races. We saw blacks dining and staying at the same hotels as whites, and swimming in the same pools. There was also noticeable growth in the black middle class, and blacks were no longer required to carry passes. In addition, two flagship institutions – the University of Cape Town and the University of Witswatersrand in Johannesburg – enrolled many more black students. However, the precarious political and economic position of the technically "independent" homelands (Bantustans), the overpopulated black townships typified by Soweto, and illegal settlements like Crossroads, along with the poor educational system for blacks, showed us the hurdles yet to be overcome in order to end apartheid completely. Further complicating the situation was the struggle for power between the Xosa-led African National Congress and the Zulu-led Inkatha, a feud that produced much bloodshed in the Province of Natal.

We were there at a historic moment. President F. W. deKlerk not only had announced great changes in the country but had freed the greatest black antiapartheid leader in South Africa. We were in Cape Town the weekend that Nelson Mandela was released from prison there. In the home of South African friends, we were able to watch the stirring event on television. Very much impressed by the transformation which had already taken place, we were convinced that, with Mandela's release and deKlerk's reforms, South Africa was destined to have an entirely new government structure.

These changes led to an openness of discussion and a critical analysis of possibilities for the country's future that we had not heard before. Once again, we enjoyed a lengthy conversation with Gerrit Viljoen, then the minister of constitutional development and national education, who had become President deKlerk's chief adviser on ending apartheid. His entire approach had changed in nine years. He spent a good deal of time with us outlining the difficulties he had had in attempting to upgrade black elementary and secondary education – still segregated and inferior – while simultaneously integrating the education system.

A few days after our session with Dr. Viljoen, Addie and I had a long dinner meeting with Peter deLange, former rector of Rand Afrikaans University and previously chairman of the national commission that had been recommending reform of South Africa's entire education system during our 1981 visit. By 1990, deLange had become head of the Broederbund, a formerly secret, and still powerful, organization of Afrikaner leaders. His conclusions as to why South Africa's white leadership was now embracing radical change were among the most cogent we heard.

Advocating change, deLange indicated, was a matter of self-interest for the Nationalist Party's leadership. It was either that or preparing for revolution. This position represented a major shift in the Afrikaner leadership's thinking, which had previously stonewalled all objections to apartheid. He candidly expressed his opinion that it was absolutely necessary to improve the quality of life for black Africans and to mainstream them. One got the feeling from deLange that the Afrikaner leaders knew they were sitting on a time bomb. Given the vastly high fertility rates of blacks and coloreds, the whites' choice amounted to getting out of the country or resigning themselves to a lower standard of living. The only solution, he felt, was to incorporate South Africa's entire population, including all races, into full participation in the country's economy and government.

In the black Bantustan of Bophuthatswana, the wealthiest of the South African homelands, we met with the government ministers, who were very cordial but painted a far too rosy picture of how they benefited from the formal political separation from South Africa. They did not recognize that Bophuthatswana could not survive without substantial subsidies from the South African government.

Since relatively few Americans had spent time in South Africa or had the opportunity to meet as many South African educators, politicians, and professionals as we had, I was asked to give a number of talks about that country and our experience of it after our return. In an op-ed article for the *Philadelphia Inquirer*, I stressed the difficulties South Africa would encounter in attempting to obliterate apartheid, especially in reducing unemployment and the 50 percent illiteracy rate in many parts of the country. Programs dealing with education, jobs, and housing for millions of oppressed blacks would have to be developed. It was also necessary, in my opinion, for South Africans to develop a different constitution to support their new and radically changed society. In a few years, this was indeed done; as I write, South Africa has a new constitution and a new, black-dominated African National Congress government. But the residue of apartheid's long presence there has not receded so easily.

Near the end of 1990, I was asked to take over as acting president of Philadelphia College of Textiles and Science while its capable president, James P. Gallagher, visited Italy on a six-month sabbatical. "Textile," as it used to be called locally (until it changed its name to Philadelphia University in 1999), is a vocationally oriented college of about 3,400 students, only ten minutes from our home. It's a school that represents the rich variety of educational options available to American students: Textile built upon its strong niche in the textile field by adding a school of architecture, expanding its business school and health services programs, and broadening its general education curriculum. Eight years after I stepped down as Temple's president, I was pleased to be active once again in administration, curriculum development, student activities, and fund raising – especially on a much smaller and more manageable campus. Although Textile is a unique college, many of its challenges were similar to those I had encountered as president of Lincoln and Temple, such as budget balancing, fund raising, and student disciplinary matters.

Then in late May 1991, while still at Textile, I gave the commencement address at Albright College, a small liberal arts school of about 1,400 students in Reading, Pennsylvania, approximately fifty-five miles from Philadelphia. David Ruffer, Albright's president, had announced only a few days earlier that he was leaving, but I was unaware of that surprising news until I arrived on campus. I was even more surprised in August, when Albright's trustees asked me to serve as interim president for a year while the college sought a permanent president. Since I would soon turn seventy-five, I was flattered by the offer. I also presumed this would be the last such offer I would receive.

I accepted, and Addie and I moved to Reading for the 1991–92 academic year.

We first had to decide whether to rent a furnished apartment or live in the vacant president's home, a few blocks from campus. Ultimately we decided to use the president's house, rent furniture, and bring some of our own items from Philadelphia. Even with rented furniture, the president's house was a comfortable place in which to live and entertain. Student recruiting functions, alumni receptions, faculty meetings, and parties for trustees were all held there.

The warmth and hospitality of people in Reading and at Albright helped smooth our adjustment. For example, I had a number of monthly meetings to attend in Philadelphia on Wednesday afternoons and evenings. When Albright's faculty members learned that it would be difficult for me to attend some of their Wednesday meetings, they unanimously agreed to change their meetings to another day so that I could participate. That was typical of the kind of cooperation I received.

The president's office was located on the first floor of Albright's Administration and Library Building. Students and faculty were free to walk into the office without an appointment, although they normally checked first with the president's secretary. Because the admissions office was in an adjoining suite, and the reception desk was outside my door, I was able to chat informally with potential students and their parents on Saturday mornings when student recruitment took place on campus. There were also programs held in the chapel on Saturday mornings for potential students and their families, and I was usually asked to speak at them.

At a small college like Albright, the president gets personally involved in all types of student matters every day. He may be called on in disciplinary cases at an early stage. He certainly attends as many athletic events as possible. My wife and I were invited to faculty homes for dinner and other social events in which students were sometimes included. I was interviewed on the student radio station several times and even enjoyed answering critical questions from student leaders, since they had a softer edge to them than those posed to me by students at Lincoln and Temple.

When word eventually got out on campus that I had been a tennis player, and still played from time to time, Dale Yoder, Albright's tennis coach and chairman of the History Department, invited me to play. After learning that I had beaten the coach, Gene Shirk, the ninety-year-old cross-country coach and former mayor of Reading, quickly spread the word around campus. In some quarters, particularly among faculty, that may have been more significant than anything else I accomplished during my year there. In fact, at a surprise seventy-fifth birthday party given me by the faculty, I was presented with a cartoon-like poster with an ancient wooden tennis racket and a can of tennis balls attached over a statement indicating that I had humbled the likeable tennis coach/history professor.

After I left Albright there were probably some who remembered only that tennis match – and my having changed a long tradition of holding commencement exercises in the football stadium by ordering a large tent erected in the middle of the campus for the event. I did this because Albright had a history of extreme heat (with no shade) or rain at graduation events in its stadium, including the one at which I received an honorary degree. Since there was rain on graduation day, we were fortunate to have the tent, but the year after I left, graduation ceremonies returned to the football stadium. Several years later, I felt vindicated when, after more inclement graduation day weather, the event was changed back to the site I had selected.

My transitional administration had to deal with some serious problems facing the college. Albright had suffered an enrollment decline and an operating deficit in each of the three years prior to my arrival, and its freshman class was getting smaller each year. The college, in aiming to become more selective, had been rejecting candidates who were quite competent to perform college work but were not at the highest level in their high school graduating classes. Some faculty quipped that Albright was trying to become "Swarthmore on the Schuylkill River."

In addition, Albright's nursing program was being closed down, further exacerbating the decline in total enrollment. What's more, the college appeared to be giving less emphasis to the sciences and business – key programs at the college in previous decades – in favor of the humanities and the arts, a development related to the construction of a new and modern Fine Arts Building. Finally, Albright wasn't sufficiently following up with its applicants; its financial aid office wasn't closely tied into the PHEAA, which handled loans and state grants for students. As a board member and former CEO of the PHEAA, I contacted the agency's staff, and they generously agreed to help Albright in its student financial aid efforts. Had it been asked, the agency would certainly have done so much earlier.

Since Albright, like many small colleges, is a tuition-dependent school, the decline in enrollment was the main cause of its financial difficulties. Albright had a modest endowment of between $17 million and $18 million (market value), of which $9 million to $10 million was unrestricted. But annual operating deficits had been whittling away the unrestricted portion. Market forces and investment decisions were positive, so the total endowment (restricted and unrestricted combined) actually grew a bit during the operating deficit period. But that situation could not continue indefinitely.

All of this may have had something to do with David Ruffer's resignation as president and his acceptance of another presidency, at a private college in Florida. As he left office, Ruffer made a number of long-deferred personnel decisions and terminated five top administrators. Unfortunately, for the college and for me, the individuals dismissed were under contract and had to be compensated for at least another full year, whether they worked or not. As a result, I was forced to rapidly approve some appointments in order to keep important college departments functioning. For example, Elizabeth Van Velsor, who had rather limited experience as a student recruiter, was named acting director of admissions by the vice president of academic affairs, Dr. Eugene Lubot. Fortunately, she did an excellent job. Elizabeth was a resident of Reading, an alumna, and had some firsthand knowledge of alumni affairs and admissions. She responded to our suggestions and used her creative instincts to weather a difficult year.

Because of the declining number of student admissions, one of my top priorities was to get personally involved in the activities of the Admissions Office. I arranged to have reports presented every week at the president's cabinet meetings and frequently invited the acting director of admissions to be present. Officers of the college made many productive suggestions for boosting enrollment, including finding new geographical sources of potential students and soliciting more recommendations from United Methodist Churches (since the college was related to that denomination). At the same time, the admissions staff increased its efforts, visiting more high schools than ever. By the end of April 1992, Dr. Lubot was able to report that freshman enrollment projections were up by 54 percent over that same time the previous year. He credited much of the upturn "to the new financial aid procedures which are 'user friendly.'"[1] The consequence of all these activities was a substantial increase in the number of new students entering Albright in the fall of 1992.

Some people may wonder about the role of an interim president. The job is not, as many think, simply that of caretaker, making certain that the college does not slide backward. In uncertain economic times, no college can afford to coast for a year; it must keep moving forward on all fronts. In addition to concerns about Albright's admissions, enrollment, and financial condition, it was also my obligation to make certain that Albright's excellent curriculum continued to serve the students' needs. Moreover, it was important to

---

[1] *Reading Eagle/Times*, April 25, 1992.

strengthen Albright's reputation and its relationships with community leaders in the Reading area and beyond. Finally, since I was brought in at almost the last moment – immediately after the resignation of the former president – it became my responsibility to assist the trustees in their quest for a permanent new president.

During my year at Albright I undertook a review of the college's entire administrative structure. This was performed with the assistance of other Albright officers as well as Jesse Cantrill, a professional management consultant with Hay Associates in Washington, D.C., and a personal friend. That review culminated, at the close of my tenure, in a complete report that was then presented to the new president. I also asked Dr. Lubot to chair the Faculty Planning Committee and coordinate its review of all Albright academic programs and schedules as well as the staffing necessary to carry out these programs.

Both of these reviews outlined how the college could streamline its curriculum and administration to its advantage. Nevertheless, many of Albright's faculty members – so cooperative on most matters – felt threatened by this kind of review and resisted it. Implementation of these recommendations had to wait several years until the new president was ready to accept them and act to change direction. Faculty members are generally perceived as liberal and interested in change, at least concerning the nation and the world. But they often instinctively resist change when it comes to academic and curricular matters.

I spent a great deal of time on Albright's search for a new president, beginning with a written outline of the pros and cons of hiring an executive search firm. Using such a firm had become common practice for colleges seeking a new president, but since I had already been involved in a number of searches, the board decided to forgo an executive search firm and ask me to serve in that capacity instead, thereby saving the college somewhere between $50,000 and $60,000. Although I voluntarily accepted this additional responsibility, I would not recommend taking on such assignments to other interim presidents.

Presidential searches can be quite perfunctory, particularly if a popular inside candidate is already available. This college's search was anything but perfunctory. Because of Albright's fine reputation as a traditional liberal arts college with a good future, and in spite of its shaky financial picture at that time, there were more than a hundred applicants for the presidency. So I was drawn into much more activity – including visits to the campuses of the final three candidates – than I had anticipated.

The final three candidates were the cause of lengthy debate within the search committee, but it all ended with very positive support for Dr. Ellen Hurwitz, the vice president for academic affairs at Illinois Wesleyan

University. For Albright, her selection was a remarkable first in both gender and religion. Albright is historically related to and modestly supported by
the United Methodist Church. It was not surprising, therefore, when an objection to the appointment of a Jewish woman came from a clergyman who was
an alumnus of the college. He was the single dissenter on the forty-member
Board of Trustees but became, after her election, a staunch supporter. In recent
years, what were once church-affiliated colleges have increasingly tended to
select presidents without regard for their religious background. In any case,
at Albright the matter of gender was more important than religion, and it
took the strong arguments of some women faculty members to push through
the appointment of Albright's first female president. That, too, has developed
into something of a trend at institutions that previously chose male presidents
exclusively.

My year at Albright ended on a positive note, much as it had begun.
Officially, it closed with an outdoor, do-it-yourself ice-cream-sundae party at
the end of June 1992, sponsored by students and faculty. The organizers hung
thank-you notes from the entire community on a tree – a creative way to say
goodbye.

The milestone of 1992 was the celebration of our fiftieth wedding anniversary
in June at Temple University's Conference Center, the Albert M. Greenfield
Sugar Loaf facility, near our home in Chestnut Hill. Guests included old tennis
buddies, college classmates of Addie's, friends and relatives from across the
country, and colleagues from Colgate, Lincoln, Temple, Textile, Albright, and
the FPRI.

Addie and I have frequently reflected on our good fortune and on the
manner in which our marriage filled out our personalities and brought us so
much happiness. Despite her commitment to assist me in every way over the
years, from typing my doctoral dissertation in 1942 to serving as manager of
our household and first lady of colleges and universities, Addie retained her
own individual and professional interests by teaching, serving as a judge for
theater productions, and joining theater and ballet boards of directors.

Although we have had disagreements over the years – mainly concerned
with bringing up our children and being on time for events – we learned
early to compromise when necessary and to respect each other's views and
individuality, so that each year brought us closer together.

As things turned out, Albright was not my last assignment, after all. While still
at Albright I had received a telephone call from Richard Breslin, president of

Drexel University, requesting that I serve as consultant to one of Drexel's major planning committees in the fall and winter of 1992. I accepted the assignment and found myself quite busy while Addie and I again readjusted to living in Philadelphia full time.

Then, in the early spring of 1993, I was again asked to help out in Harrisburg. The Pennsylvania Association of Colleges and Universities (PACU) wanted me to serve as its interim president while the organization searched for a new permanent president. PACU had its beginnings in 1896 when a group of private college presidents organized "to foster the interests of higher education in the commonwealth." It eventually developed into the most ecumenical and inclusive of all state organizations of higher education institutions in the country and was a model of cooperation between public and private sectors. Through its staff in Harrisburg and its committees, publications, and annual meetings, PACU managed to hold the leaders of its various member colleges and universities together and present a positive and reasonably united front to the public, the Pennsylvania state legislature, and the executive branch of the government. The organization had certainly carried out its founders' intent and furthered the interests of higher education in the state.

However, tensions had developed among its member institutions due to several factors: the development of a community college system, the conversion of the state's teacher's colleges into broader universities, and the increased blurring of borders between independent and public institutions in the competition for private and state funds. Demographic changes and financial difficulties exacerbated this stress. The independent or private sector felt put upon and unappreciated. It selected strong leaders and became more combative. At the same time, some college presidents in the public sector felt that the state funds being directed to private institutions were draining financial support that rightly belonged to them.

It was in this climate that PACU's president, Gary Young, resigned. Since I had taught at and presided over both public and private institutions, presidents in both camps felt that I could be a moderating force capable of bringing them together.

This time, Addie and I did not move to Harrisburg. Instead, we spent two or three days a week there, staying in a hotel. Thanks to the telephone and fax machine, I was able to conduct much of PACU's business from my desk in the chancellor's office at Temple University.

My job with PACU was to get the private and public colleges to work together on issues affecting higher education in the state – a daunting task, since the private sector, represented by the Commission for Independent

Colleges and Universities (CICU), was rumbling with hints of seceding altogether from PACU. But I felt it was possible to convince the public and private
college presidents to work cooperatively again, as they had in earlier years. It
was important that our higher education community present a common voice
to the state legislature and the executive branch in order to win support for all
institutions. Every legislator had some type of institution in his district, and if
the institutions appeared to be squabbling over funds, this could have a serious negative effect on all of them. I met with the executive committee of CICU,
composed of key private college presidents, so that I could understand their
position and explain it to presidents in the other sectors, represented by the
Commission of Commonwealth Universities (state-related institutions), State
University System (former teachers' colleges), and Community Colleges. Since
our offices were in neighboring suites, it was convenient for me to meet weekly
with the staff heads of each of the commissions representing the four sectors.
These meetings led to broad agreement on educational issues satisfactory to
all of the sectors.

The upshot was that the separatist movement cooled off, and a measure
of cooperation between private and public institutions was re-established.
However, by 1996, three years after my six-month role ended and a new PACU
president had taken over, the CICU had become stronger than ever and appeared to be assuming functions (like educational research and lobbying the
legislative and executive branches of the state government) previously performed by PACU for all sectors. Naturally, this development raised questions
in some quarters regarding PACU's future. In some states, especially New
York, umbrella associations like PACU were phased out of existence by divi-
sions between the private and public colleges and universities, and it appeared
that the same thing might happen in Pennsylvania, which I believe would be
unfortunate. Time will tell.

In 1992, when I left Albright College, Fred Gross, founder and principal stock-
holder of Technology Specialists, Inc. (TSI), had asked me to serve as an
academic consultant with his company, which operated computer facilities
for colleges. Fred's previous company, Systems and Computer Technology,
Inc. (SCT), had solved a big technological problem for Temple University in
the mid-'70s when faculty and administrators were complaining that they
couldn't get the timely information and services they required from our large
computer system. Gross was a hard-driving, technology-trained businessman
from New York who had built SCT into the foremost computer facilities management firm serving colleges and universities. He regularly reported to me

between 1976 and 1982 on Temple's computer progress and problems, so I came to know him well. Later in the '80s, Fred took SCT public, left its leadership, and launched TSI.

Since I had a good idea of what colleges and universities looked for when they sought assistance outside of their own staff for their computer operations, my responsibilities at TSI constantly expanded. From being an intermittent consultant to the company, I eventually became a member of its corporate board, and in February 1995 I was elected chairman of that board. During my activities with the company, Fred Gross had no official management role or title at TSI, but as founder and chief investor his influence was indirectly felt. As a representative of TSI, I visited colleges and universities to speak with presidents and other high-level administrators about their computer needs and the option of employing outside managers to fill them. Those activities kept me close to developments in higher education and led to my reconnecting with some university executives with whom I had lost touch during the previous decade. I was happy to be involved in this commercial venture, since so many of the small and medium-size institutions lacked the personnel or know-how to deal with the ever expanding importance of computer and related technology, and it was important that they secure effective outside help.

I quickly found myself on the cutting edge of a technological revolution every bit as profound as the civil rights revolution I had participated in at Lincoln University. Whereas several valiant attempts in the 1970s and '80s to introduce computer technology into college teaching had received only minimal acceptance, by the 1990s instructional technology had become exceedingly important, and the use of computers in classroom instruction was quite common. For example, when Temple University contracted with SCT in the mid-'70s to manage its computer facilities, its primary goal was to organize its financial, administrative, and research programs more efficiently. By the turn of the century, however, like most other institutions, Temple was encouraging its faculty to use the new technology wherever applicable and using computer technology to link its campuses for teaching as well as administration. On-line teaching, e-mail exchanges between professors and students, and academic chat-room discussions were not unusual. Also, Internet-based "virtual universities" had been especially set up in several states to serve an older, working student clientele who wished to take courses at times and places of their own choosing through use of personal computers.

In the '90s, TSI installed technology like PictureTel so that some of its clients, like the New York Institute of Technology, could offer courses to students at various campuses. With PictureTel, a professor at one location could communicate, by computer and television screen, to groups of students at other sites as though they were all in the same room. But with the increasing use of the Internet later in the 1990s, a revolution in distance learning took place. And with the addition of voice and video to laptop personal computers, the technology became even more convenient for learners. Universities were able to give courses at remote sites, even overseas. Institutions like for-profit Phoenix University offered courses without any physical campus or required on-site instruction. Universities scheduled instruction for small groups of students, or individuals, at various locations, something that previously would have been financially infeasible.

In the midst of this explosive growth, Fred Gross was charged with securities fraud on allegations that he had inflated the assets of SCT – his original company – at the time of its public stock offering. Fred contended that he had left the technical matters of accounting to certified public accountants and his lawyers. A number of college presidents who had dealt with Fred and SCT, including me, agreed to appear as character witnesses on his behalf in the Federal Courthouse in Philadelphia, where he was tried. Despite our testimony, he was convicted of fraud and spent about sixteen months in a minimum security facility in the early 1990s.

Notwithstanding this setback, by 1995 TSI had become very attractive to medium-size colleges that were unable to hire the specialists required to set up and manage twenty-first–century, cyber-age technologies. Its rapid growth and profitability also made it appealing to investors. Fred Gross, having completed his jail term, decided to sell TSI and did so in the first quarter of 1996. I anticipated that the new owners, a group of venture capital investors from Chicago led by Robert E. King, would select a new board, and I would move on to other things. Instead, the new owners asked me to remain on a larger and more diverse board of directors and continue to serve as chairman.

TSI was renamed Collegis and soon moved its headquarters from suburban Philadelphia to suburban Orlando, Florida, where its new owners had had favorable experience with other companies. For me, this meant commuting by airplane to board meetings.

Collegis added new, well-staffed technical, strategic, and other services and quickly expanded its client base. The company found a special niche in the community college sector and won technology management contracts with six of New Jersey's community colleges, as well as with similar institutions in Florida, New York, Massachusetts, New Mexico, and California. It also had many contracts with larger universities, four-year liberal arts colleges, law schools, and Howard Hughes Medical Institute in Maryland. In 1997, Collegis acquired the Institute for Academic Technology (IAT) of the University of North Carolina, an outstanding center for course development.

For several years, Collegis grew at a rate of about 50 percent per year. At the end of 2003, despite a national recession and much lower growth rates, the company had continued to increase in size and employed 1,000 individuals. That number included those at its headquarters in Maitland, Florida, and at one hundred campus sites around the country. In addition to fifty-three long-term contracts, the company had forty-five limited engagements and partnerships.

Technology is now flourishing in academia. There is no doubt in my mind that on-line teaching and learning will continue to expand. All fields will be affected in some way by the new technology and its software. But the undergraduate college campus will remain strong, because no technology can replace face-to-face education, oral discussion, and debate. Co-curricular activities, including student government, dramatics, debate clubs, and sports and social events, will also continue to be important for the growth and development of young people.

For a number of years, Addie and I had spent the month of February in Florida, and we thought we might some day want to extend our Florida stay to three or four months a year. So we purchased a condominium on Longboat Key, Florida, off-shore from Sarasota. Longboat Key is fairly close to Maitland, the headquarters of Collegis, so our Florida apartment proved quite convenient. Although I turned eighty-three in 2000, I served as acting chief executive of Collegis for much of the year after the regular CEO resigned in January. Other officers of the company remained, including the executive vice president and chief financial officer. Because the major investors, especially Bob King, were "hands-on" people, my job wasn't as difficult as it might seem. My academic persona probably helped the company get through this administrative transition. Traveling to institutions in order to put out fires and solicit new business did increase, but I still had ample time for my own personal affairs. Being able to use the Florida residence as my office for two months while also reading, writing, and playing tennis proved to be a good arrangement. Keeping in touch with leaders in the college and university community who are dealing with the impact of technology on higher education (as I did in the course of my work with Collegis until April 2004, when the company was sold) kept me looking toward the future.

In this presumed twilight of my life, I find myself recalling the old adage of athletes: "The older you get, the better you were." I have written this memoir with considerable reluctance. As we grow older, too many of us seniors dwell excessively on the past and the supposed good old days of our youth. The blessing of all my retirement jobs, including my involvement with Collegis, is that they have kept me focused on the present and the future and, consequently, have given me reason to endure. At this writing, I continue to be in my office at Temple University regularly, assisting this progressive institution in whatever way I can.

As I look back, I realize that the connecting thread throughout my life has been my desire to make a contribution to higher education. That desire burns as brightly today as it ever did in the past, and whatever contributions I have made have been repaid many times in the rich experiences that academia has bestowed upon me. Perhaps it is foolish for someone my age to focus on the future when my future is so uncertain. But, then, my future was always uncertain, and things always took care of themselves.

ACKNOWLEDGMENTS

WHEN I RETIRED AS PRESIDENT of Temple University in 1982, I had no intention of writing the story of my life. I was still too busy even to think about such an effort. However, some years later I was asked to write an article about my experiences in the 1960s as the white, Jewish president of the oldest black college in the United States, Lincoln University in Pennsylvania. Colleagues suggested that I had been at Temple University as vice president, president, and chancellor for a longer time and should include my life and work at Temple. Others suggested that I should at least summarize my early life and education and my World War II military service. Still others felt that I should include highlights of my retirement years. The result is this book.

I'm grateful to a number of people who assisted me with suggestions and comments. Richard Severo read the entire manuscript and made helpful suggestions, as did Marshall Fishwick. The Lincoln University chapter was strengthened by Richard Winchester and by helpful comments from Emery Wimbish and Grace Frankowsky.

I'm indebted to George Ingram for his gracious permission to make use of his unpublished piece about my presidency of Temple. He had consulted with me on that article and then made some excellent suggestions on an early version of my own chapter. Previously, George had worked with me on many of my speeches and my annual presidential reports. Consequently, his draft and my Temple chapter contain some of the same factual material gleaned from those speeches and reports and also from news releases. David D. Randall made valuable suggestions about the Temple chapter. Herbert Bass, James Hilty, Stanton Felzer, and James Shea were also helpful.

I am especially beholden to Dan Rottenberg, without whose editing I could not have shortened a much longer version of this memoir for publication. Lorraine Gardner also assisted me very much on that task, and in clarifying and editing the material. I appreciate very much the patient assistance of the staff of Temple University Press, including the editor-in-chief, Janet Francendese; the director, Alex Holzman; and the senior production editor, Jennifer French; as well as the assistance of the copyeditor, Susan Deeks.

Finally, I must express my deepest love and appreciation to my wife, Addie, for encouraging me to complete this memoir and for preserving many of my letters to her, as well as her year-end letters to family and friends. These helped in assuring that the chronology and substance of the story – particularly the early years – were factually correct.

INDEX

DR. MARVIN WACHMAN is a former President of Temple University as well as of Lincoln University.